Cultural Contextualization
of Apologetics

Cultural Contextualization *of* Apologetics

Exploration and Application of Apostle Paul's Model

MATT W. LEE

WIPF & STOCK · Eugene, Oregon

CULTURAL CONTEXTUALIZATION OF APOLOGETICS
Exploration and Application of the Apostle Paul's Model

Copyright © 2022 Matthew W. Lee. All rights reserved. Except for brief quotations in critical publications or reviews, no part of this book may be reproduced in any manner without prior written permission from the publisher. Write: Permissions, Wipf and Stock Publishers, 199 W. 8th Ave., Suite 3, Eugene, OR 97401.

Resource Publications
An Imprint of Wipf and Stock Publishers
199 W. 8th Ave., Suite 3
Eugene, OR 97401

www.wipfandstock.com

PAPERBACK ISBN: 978-1-6667-3198-9
HARDCOVER ISBN: 978-1-6667-2516-2
EBOOK ISBN: 978-1-6667-2517-9

JANUARY 24, 2022 8:45 AM

Contents

List of Tables | vi

Preface | vii

List of Abbreviations | ix

CHAPTER 1   INTRODUCTION | 1

CHAPTER 2   PAUL'S CULTURAL CONNECTION | 13

CHAPTER 3   PAUL'S CULTURAL CONNECTION THROUGH
            CULTURAL SOLIDARITY AS THE WISDOM FIGURE | 49

CHAPTER 4   CULTURAL CONTEXTUALIZATION
            OF PAUL'S APOLOGETICS SPEECHES | 84

CHAPTER 5   CULTURAL CONTEXTUALIZATION
            OF SECOND-CENTURY APOLOGISTS | 122

CHAPTER 6   CULTURAL CONTEXTUALIZATION
            OF APOLOGETICS PREACHING | 162

Bibliography | 177

List of Tables

1. Simple List | *66*
2. Antithetical List | *69*
3. List of Paul's Speeches in Acts | *86*
4. Scheme of Paul's Culturally Contextualized Apologetics Speeches | *106*

Preface

OVER THE CENTURIES, the field of Christian apologetics has arguably been an area for specialists. However, with ever-present oppositions and evolving objections to the Christian faith permeating the daily lives of average Christians, it is becoming increasingly clear that apologetics prowess must be cultivated in everyone who follows Jesus. The joy, confidence, and conviction produced by apologetics should readily be available to a larger audience than before.

To make apologetics a part of a general curriculum for all Christians, it must first overcome cultural barriers. I experienced this assessment turning into a firm conviction through various apologetics engagements. In real-life situations, I found myself pushing against invisible walls when cultural issues were neglected in apologetics. With mere rational arguments presented as a defense of Christianity, my answers did not seem to track with many of the non-believers nor resolve their skepticism. People simply had different obstacles in coming to the Christian faith, particularly their own cultural presuppositions.

Hence, I needed to discover what the relevant questions were before preparing persuasive answers. What was truly keeping them from opening their minds to the Christian faith? How do we present, defend, and commend Christianity to people whose culture gives them a frame of mind—the one that cares very little about how rational the arguments are? How do we best communicate the truth for such people? I then asked whether the world of the New Testament and the ministry of Apostle Paul could be used as a helpful model for apologetics with cultural engagement. What insights can we extract from his apologetics engagements?

With the helpful supervision of Dr. Timothy Paul Jones, I delved into the exploration and application of Paul's apologetics to search for the answers. Crafting my findings as a Ph.D. dissertation and seeing its completion was

Preface

made possible due to outstanding direction from Dr. Jones, to whom I am thankful. Then came along the transformation of that project into a book through earnest encouragements from Dr. Sung Wook Chung. It is with sincere gratitude that I acknowledge his guidance, wisdom, and care. I had always prayed that my work would somehow, someday be able to contribute to advancing new discussions about how we best engage in apologetics communication in contemporary settings. I wish to thank the editorial team at Wipf & Stock for making that prayer a reality through this book.

I must additionally acknowledge the love and support I received from my mentor, Dr. Jung-Hyun Oh, during the process of writing. Apart from his backing to help me pursue a scholarship, this book would not see the light of day. I must also confess that I am grateful to be part of the Sa-Rang Church community. More specifically, Shekinah Worship Team members, my Discipleship Training members, and members of the Young Adults Singles Ministry have sustained me through their love and prayers. Dr. Jung-Hyun Oh and the members of SaRang Church have a special place in my heart.

Likewise, I owe a debt of gratitude to Dr. Doug Birdsall, whose mentorship and gentle encouragement have sustained me through the difficult times. God used Dr. Frank James, III in his divine moment to remind me of the importance of this writing, and I would like to express my gratitude. Dr. Constance Cherry's friendship and comradery enriched me tremendously, and I am thankful to share this Kingdom partnership. My parents-in-law, Insoon Jane and Keun-sik Park, surrounded me with support and prayers, and I am forever grateful to them.

Lastly, I would like to express my love and appreciation for the sacrifice that my family have made over the years of my academic journey and ministry. Olivia Heun and Matthew Ghunhoo have endured reduced accessibility and attention of their daddy, yet were so patient and understanding through the process. I am so thankful that God has granted me such wonderful children. Most importantly, invaluable and enduring support has come from the love of my life, my partner in life and ministry, Lindsey. My lovely wife has consistently offered sincere encouragement, loving affirmation, and prayerful intercession. I would not be who I am without her being my suitable helper. It is to them I am dedicating this book.

Matthew Wonjoon Lee
Seoul, Korea
August 2021

List of Abbreviations

Apo.	Artistides' *Apology*
Leg.	Athenagoras' *Legatio*
DeR.	Athenagoras' *De Resurrectione*
1 *Apo.*	Justin Martyr's *First Apology*
2 *Apo.*	Justin Martyr's *Second Apology*
Dia.	Justin Martyr's *Dialogue with Trypho the Jew*
Add.	Tatian's *Address to the Greek*
Ecc.	Eusebius's *Ecclesiastical History*
Epi.	*Epistle to Diognetus*

Chapter 1

Introduction

In 2016, the *Oxford English Dictionary* selected "post-truth" as its word of the year. The dictionary defines post-truth as "relating to or denoting circumstances in which objective facts are less influential in shaping public opinion than appeals to emotion and personal belief."[1] The selection of the word suggests how the shaping of public opinion now takes place less with facts and more with an emotional appeal or personal belief.[2]

Numbers of scholars articulate such a trend. In *Moral, Believing Animals*, Christian Smith argues that rational choice theory that sees human beings as actively using rational information to arrive at both personal and social formation does not adequately account for human culture and practices. Smith contends that human beings "build up their lives from pre-suppositional starting points in which place our trust and that are not derived from other (rational) justifying grounds."[3] This assessment explains why "a convincing narrative appealing to a pre-possessed set of beliefs and emotions holds more sway than any fact-laden argument that poses a threat to those sincerely held beliefs."[4]

James K. A. Smith equally recognizes a need to re-assess the traditional understanding of the role rational justification plays in a belief formation. For this reason, he disputes the idea that education and worldview

1. Oxford Dictionaries, "Word of the Year 2016 Is...".
2. Colson, "Post-Truth Society," 112–13.
3. Smith, *Moral, Believing Animals*, 150.
4. Adam McDuffie, "Searching for Truth in a Post-Truth World," 75–76.

formation mainly involves ideas and information—a form of rationality.[5] Instead, Smith contends that the ultimate factor critical to one's beliefs and worldview formation is one's desires.[6] He further argues that human desires are shaped by "cultural practices as secular liturgies" along with habits of the physical body instead of mere rationality.[7]

If cultural practices function as liturgies that shape one's desire and worldview, unprecedented cultural practices stemming from an "image-based digital world" reduces not only an appeal for rational justification but also an ability to process it.[8] Andrew Root, leaning into Jean Baudrillard's insights, warns that an image-saturated world "liquefy and thin out the ability to construct meaning that connects to experiences and relationships outside the image-based mediated machines themselves."[9] Root takes notice of the cultural change that disables one from making meaningful connections between language and symbols to reality, advocating that now this post-secular society requires a new perspective on faith formation.[10]

One must not overlook the implications of these cultural changes and renewed theoretical assessments of belief formation have on apologetics. Challenges arising from different cultures have generated a variety of apologetic responses throughout history; therefore, changes are needed in the way apologetics engages the audiences of today's world.[11] The world now requires a renewed approach that supplements apologetics that heavily depends on rational appeal.

Many voice the same need. James Sire, in *Apologetics Beyond Reason: Why Seeing is Really Believing*, argues that while apologetics that appeals to reason has been effective to the general audience in the past, "others in our postmodern world have come to distrust reason, and the arguments of the modern Christian rationalists now seem irrelevant, doubtful, and lifeless."[12] Furthermore, Sire detects a "growing failure of arguments to move students and others toward Christian faith and the rising possibility of doing apologetics with attention to why people today actually do become

---

5. Smith, *Desiring the Kingdom*.
6. Smith, *You Are What You Love*.
7. Smith, *Desiring the Kingdom*, 121–22.
8. Root, "A Screen-Based World," 237–44.
9. Root, "A Screen-Based World," 239–41.
10. Root, "Faith Formation in a Secular Age," 128–41.
11. Dulles, *A History of Apologetics*.
12. Sire, *Apologetics beyond Reason*, 16.

Introduction

Christians."[13] In the book *The End of Apologetics: Christian Witness in a Postmodern Context*, Myron Bradley Penner stresses the need for "a shift from an epistemological focus on the rational justification of Christian beliefs to a hermeneutics concerned with explicating and understanding the life of faith."[14]

In an apt summary, Alister McGrath too offers a critical assessment of the current state of apologetic communication while echoing the opinion of other apologists. He writes,

> We must realize we are free to develop apologetic approaches that are faithful to the Christian gospel on the one hand and are adapted to our own cultural situation on the other. By doing this, we are repeating the method of "traditional apologetics" while responding to the changes in the cultural context toward which it is directed. We simply cannot use an apologetic approach developed to engage eighteenth-century rationalism to defend the faith to twenty-first-century people who regard rationalism as outdated and constricting! For example, postmodernity finds appeals to rational argument problematic. But it is deeply attracted to stories and images. Furthermore, postmodernity is more interested in a truth that proves itself capable of being lived out than being demonstrated by rational argument. This helps us understand why "incarnational apologetics," which emphasizes the apologetic importance of faithful living, has become so influential in recent years . . . we can easily rise to this new challenge, usually not by inventing new approaches to apologetics, but by recovering older approaches that the rise of rationalism seemed to make obsolete.[15]

Bernand Van Den Toren in *Christian Apologetics as Cross-Cultural Dialogue* reaffirms the common sentiment amongst these apologists:

> Apologists have, at the same time, become aware that they need to address a multiplicity of audiences. In our 'global village,' modernism and postmodernism are just two cultural options among many—often vibrant—alternatives such as Islam and Buddhism. In this new environment, many of the older apologetic models have become obsolete, because they are answering questions that many are no longer asking and which have never been the most important questions outside the Western world. Rather than an

---

13. Sire, *Apologetics beyond Reason*, 9.
14. Penner, *The End of Apologetics*, 35.
15. McGrath, *Mere Apologetics*, 26.

apologetic witness that addresses a reportedly universal rationality, we need 'local' or 'audience-sensitive apologetics' that take the particular culturally embedded outlooks of the changing audiences into account.[16]

While these cultural changes indeed pose a challenge to the rationalistic approaches to apologetics, they can also open up "an opportunity for a different approach to apologetics—particularly one based on Christian beliefs and confidence to display in words and deeds the certainty of those beliefs."[17] In order to tackle the current challenge and navigate a way forward, Christian apologetics must thus explore what apologetics approach or strategy adequately addresses cultural concerns. How does one effectively carry out apologetics ministries to those who are enculturated differently? Where do we look for such a model?

A MODEL FOR CULTURALLY CONTEXTUALIZED APOLOGETICS

I argue that Paul carried out culturally contextualized apologetics, presenting a model for culturally effective apologetics. I argue that Paul's cultural contextualization in his apologetics takes place through the establishment of cultural connections with his audience and through the defense of the Christian faith against cultural objections using the Christian life as an appeal. I further argue that the first generation of apologists immediately following Paul also reprised his cultural contextualized apologetics and thus this apologetics model has merit for an apologetics ministry for today.

I aim to substantiate my argument by showing that Paul's culturally contextualized apologetics takes place through the establishment of cultural connection. The first way Paul forges the cultural connection is by the use of cultural point of contact and culturally contextualized communication that includes the use of specific language and forms that generate greater cultural receptivity from the audience. The second way Paul forms the cultural connection is by building up cultural solidarity with the hearers, which gains him admission into the hearers' culture, allowing him to speak as a cultural insider.

Furthermore, Paul's apologetics speeches not only feature cultural connections and cultural solidarity, but they also work to address cultural

---

16. Toren, *Christian Apologetics as Cross-Cultural Dialogue*, 11.
17. Jameson, "God, Post-Truth," 187.

INTRODUCTION

objections against the Christian faith. Paul's culturally contextualized apologetics defends and vindicates the gospel through his apologetics speeches that highlight both the life of Christ and the Christian life. Moreover, Paul's apologetics speeches are culturally contextualized for they consistently pattern a cultural connection and cultural solidarity, along with a virtuous Christian life, all the while presenting the life of Christ, particularly the exposition of the resurrection, to respond to cultural objections.

Apologetics of the first-generation apologists immediately after Paul exhibits features of culturally contextualized apologetics that Paul models. In other words, the Greek apologists in the second century, namely Aristides, Athenagoras, Justin Martyr, Tatian, Melito of Sardis, and the Epistle of Diognetus incorporate the cultural connection and cultural solidarity. Their apologetics equally responds to cultural objections through the presentation of a virtue of the Christian life and the resurrection of Christ, solidifying the fact Paul provided a model for culturally contextualized apologetics.

A VARIETY OF APPROACHES IN APOLOGETICS

Despite the need to consider an apologetics strategy that engages cultural issues, the literature and research on this subject have been limited to the following areas. Many apologetics publications discuss the rationale and logic of apologetics.[18] Another strand of literature treats the historical development of apologetics.[19] Some deal with specific topics in philosophy, science, and archaeology.[20] Other works focus on the religio-cultural aspect such as postmodernism, particularly addressing a need to engage the millenials.[21] Various dissertations and projects aim to put forth the best strategy

---

18. Boa and Bowman, *Faith Has Its Reasons*; Groothuis, *Christian Apologetics*; Van Til, *The Defense of the Faith*; Craig, *Reasonable Faith*; Campbell-Jack et al., *New Dictionary of Christian Apologetics*; Craig, *Apologetics: An Introduction*; Frame, *Apologetics to the Glory of God*; Sire, *Apologetics beyond Reason*; Geisler, *Christian Apologetics*; Chatraw and Allen, *Apologetics at the Cross*.

19. Dulles, *A History of Apologetics*; Edgar and Oliphint, *Christian Apologetics Past and Present*; Edwards et al., *Apologetics in the Roman Empire*; Geisler and Zukeran, *The Apologetics of Jesus*.

20. For Philosophy: Plantinga, *Warranted Christian Belief*; Plantinga and Wolterstorff, *Faith and Rationality*; Helm, *Faith and Understanding*; Sennett and Groothuis, *In Defense of Natural Theology*. For Science: Dembski, *Intelligent Design*; Dembski and Ruse, *Debating Design*; Johnson, *Darwin on Trial*. For Archaeology: Price, *The Stones Cry Out*.

21. McDowell, *Apologetics for a New Generation*; Clark and Geisler, *Apologetics in the New Age*; Penner, *The End of Apologetics*; Markos, *Apologetics for the Twenty-First*

in reaching certain target groups including particular congregations or age brackets, such as youth or college students.[22] Other dissertations and unpublished writings have also dealt with the religio-cultural aspects, particularly in different religious contexts such as Hinduism, Buddhism, and Islam.[23] They all offer insight for using concepts beyond sound rationality or how to best defend the truth to a niche audience, yet without considering what factors constitute cultural engagement in apologetics.

Moreover, even fewer research projects and publications are found on Paul's apologetics or even New Testament apologetics. Most of these works are published as articles and thus do not extensively cover Pauline apologetics. Among them, the predominant number of articles restrict their research to Paul's Areopagus speech only.[24] To note, Norman Geisler published a book entitled *Apologetics of Jesus: A Caring Approach to Dealing with Doubters*, asserting that Christ's miracles, parables, reasoning, and prophecy serve as means of apologetics, but the work does not discuss Paul's apologetics at all.[25]

Century.

22. Francis, "Training Church Members to Integrate Apologetics with Evangelism at First Baptist Church of Walton, Kentucky"; Todd, "Teaching Worldview Apologetics to Increase Evangelistic Confidence at Piperton Baptist Church, Collierville, Tennessee"; Buck, "Apologetics Preaching Today in the Context of a Local Church"; Lau, "Intentional Instruction in Christian Basics and Apologetics: Giving Christian Students More Confidence in Their Faith"; Joo, "The Use of Apologetics in Evangelism: A Model for University Teaching Ministry"; Miller, "Preaching in a Postmodern Setting: An Analysis of the Apologetic Preaching of Mark Driscoll"; Kretzschmar, "Effective Apologetics Education for Lutheran Youth in a Postmodern Age".

23. Forbes, "A Christian Apologetic to a Buddhist Christ"; Roseman, "A Christian Apologetic to the Doctrine of Grace in Shin Buddhism"; Rahbar, "Christian Apologetic to Muslims," 353–59; Schirrmacher, "Muslim Apologetics and the Agra Debates of 1854: A Nineteenth Century Turning Point," 74–84; Tilak, "A Christian Worldview Apologetic Engagement with Advaita Vedanta Hinduism".

24. Bailey, "Acts 17:16–34," 481–85; Charles, "Engaging the (Neo) Pagan Mind: Paul's Encounter with Athenian Culture as a Model for Cultural Apologetics (Acts 17:16–34)," 47–62; Colaclides, "Acts 17:28a and Bacchae 506," 161–64; Dahle, "Acts 17:16–34: An Apologetic Model Then and Now?" 313–16; Croy, "Hellenistic Philosophies and the Preaching of the Resurrection (Acts 17:18, 32)," 21–39; Gray, "Athenian Curiosity (Acts 17:21)," 109–16; Jipp, "Paul in Athens: The Popular Religious Context of Acts 17," 524–26; Jipp, "Paul's Areopagus Speech of Acts 17:16–34 as Both Critique and Propaganda," 567–88; Keown, "Congregational Evangelism in Paul: The Paul of Acts," 231–51.

25. See Geisler and Zukeran, *The Apologetics of Jesus*.

INTRODUCTION

Perhaps this is due to the popular notion, as some argue, that there was "no formal genre of apologetic in the ancient world."[26] However, Mark Edwards, Martin Goodman, Simon Price, and Christopher Rowland conclude that

> a commonsense view of genres like 'epic' or 'tragedy' is indeed that they exist unchanging over time and across cultures, and that individual works of literature instantiate the relevant genre more or less successfully . . . However, this view of genre (as that of pigeonhole works such as in New Testament studies) that they serve as a means of classification, has come to seem deeply unsatisfactory to literary critics. Genre should not be seen as a mechanical recipe-book for the production of texts, but rather as a discursive form capable of constructing a coherent model of the world in its image. Genre is thus best seen as a way of talking about the strategies of writers (and readers) in different cultural traditions and particular contemporary situations . . . Within the New Testament there are already signs that apologetic elements are beginning to intrude, as writers of texts intended for insiders inevitably have to wrestle with doubts and uncertainties felt by members, simply because they too reflect the values and assumptions of society at large.[27]

Along this line, Loveday Alexander suggests categorizing the book of Acts as an apologetics text.[28] She contours numbers of ways the book of Acts can be classified: Type 1–internal apologetic, functioning as inner-church polemic; Type 2–sectarian apologetic, functioning as self-defense in relation to Judaism; Type 3–apologetic work addressed to Greeks, functioning as propaganda or evangelism; Type 4–a political apologetic, functioning as self-defense in relation to Rome; or Type 5–apologetic addressed to insiders, functioning as legitimation or self-definition.[29] After reviewing various difficulties in categorizing the book of Acts in all of those types mentioned above, as well as refusing to label the book as apologetical historiography, Alexander contends that the book is an "apologetics scenario" that intertwines speeches and narratives together.[30] However, she does not treat apologetical merits of Paul's speeches in her discussion.

---

26. Edwards et al., *Apologetics in the Roman Empire*.
27. Edwards et al., *Apologetics in the Roman Empire*, 2–5.
28. Alexander, "The Acts of the Apostles as an Apologetic Text," 15–44.
29. Alexander, "The Acts of the Apostles as an Apologetic Text," 16–19.
30. Alexander, "The Acts of the Apostles as an Apologetic Text," 20–32.

On the other hand, more interesting and viable projects have been published in recent years concerning the cultural aspect of apologetics. Among the more recent and closer to the direction of this book is Paul Gould's *Cultural Apologetics: Renewing the Christian Voice, Conscience, and Imagination in a Disenchanted World*.[31] Gould defines cultural apologetics as "the work of establishing the Christian voice, conscience, and imagination within a culture so that Christianity is seen as true and satisfying."[32] Using "voice, conscience, and imagination," Gould argues that apologetics must broaden its approach.[33] He too sees Paul's Mars Hills speech as presenting a model for cultural apologetics in that he claims that Paul "outflanked" and "confronted" the Athenians.[34] He emphasizes that the longing of human beings for truth, goodness, and beauty is satisfied in Christ and the gospel, and the work of cultural apologetics is to use reason, conscience, and imagination to present the Christian faith as the most satisfying and desirable.[35] Yet, Gould's alternative to traditional apologetics is to work to remove the cultural barrier. Such removal takes place through the recognition of the Christian faith as a public faith, seeing Jesus as a person of wisdom and tacking on "culture-shaping institutions such as universities, arts, and media."[36] However, Gould does not address the specific elements involved in bridging the audience to the gospel message through cultural connections, as this book seeks to accomplish.

Along this line, *Christian Apologetics as Cross-Cultural Dialogue* by Benno Van den Toren is a welcome contribution to the subject matter at hand.[37] Van den Toren begins by identifying the complexity of interaction between the modern and the postmodern, as well as the nature of the multicultural world.[38] He asserts that increasing realizations of the great diversity of cultures at a local context creates both challenges and possibilities in apologetics today, asserting that "decisive divide between the gospel of the enlightenment and the gospel of Jesus is not epistemological but anthropological," demystifying the modern quest for human autonomy

---

31. Gould, *Cultural Apologetics*.
32. Gould, *Cultural Apologetics*, 21.
33. Gould, *Cultural Apologetics*, 22.
34. Gould, *Cultural Apologetics*, 23–25.
35. Gould, *Cultural Apologetics*, 27–34.
36. Gould, *Cultural Apologetics*, 34.
37. See Toren, *Christian Apologetics as Cross-Cultural Dialogue*.
38. Toren, *Christian Apologetics as Cross-Cultural Dialogue*, 11.

INTRODUCTION

and espousing strong biblical anthropology that leads to a need for culturally minded apologetics.[39] Van den Toren raises the idea that culturally minded apologetics involves cultural communication that subjects itself to thinking and attitudes that are deeply embedded in particular traditions of the audience.[40] He asserts that cross-cultural persuasion becomes possible when one "encounters radically different structures of understanding and reflection that have the integrity of their own."[41] However, his conceptualization and arguments do not demonstrate specific factors involved in such cross-cultural persuasion as I aim to exhibit in this book.

SIGNIFICANT MOVE FORWARD

Even though the history of research and published works reviewed here offers valuable insight into the current cultural challenge, work still is needed that offers both theoretical and practical models for apologetics communication at a scholarly level. Many previous studies provide a helpful springboard for discussion, as well as awareness of the need to strategize a new approach to apologetics communications in this changing culture. Yet, a model of culturally contextualized apologetics in this book will be proven to be significant in the following ways.

First, this book will contribute to both Pauline scholarship and studies in apologetics by carrying out a cultural exegesis of the world surrounding Paul. By analyzing how Paul contextualized his communication and consequently established a cultural connection with his audience, I hope to provide insights on how Greco-Roman culture and Paul's interaction with it affected his apologetics communications. Since I specifically focus on the significance of Greco-Roman rhetoric as a cultural context in Paul's speeches, the book will offer a different perspective than the discussions that deal with Paul's rhetoric in his epistles.

Second, this book aims to further Pauline and apologetics scholarship by offering biblical exegesis on Paul's apologetics speeches in connection with cultural contextualization. I will zero in on Paul's apologetics speeches and distinguish key factors that consistently appear in Paul's apologetics speeches to expand the academic discussion of speeches of Acts. Successful works have been carried out in Paul's kerygmatic speeches,

---

39. Toren, *Christian Apologetics as Cross-Cultural Dialogue*, 30.
40. Toren, *Christian Apologetics as Cross-Cultural Dialogue*, 33.
41. Toren, *Christian Apologetics as Cross-Cultural Dialogue*, 33.

but no substantial work has been published on Paul's apologetics speeches.[42] Findings in this book will fill that void. Analysis of Paul's apologetics speeches will also provide valuable insights on factors involved in culturally relevant apologetics preaching.

Third, I trust that the book will further illumine historical exegesis of the second-century Greek apologists in their cultural context. I identify and analyzes the cultural connections and cultural solidarity in the works of the Greek apologists in the second century. The book will help illuminate the rationale behind various approaches that major apologetics figures undertook in the second century to engage the culture that had not yet understood Christianity.

Finally, I desire to offer a practical resource through the book as well. Since the book discusses real persons in real history beyond mere conceptual reflections, it will present Paul and the first generation of apologists as a potential model for culturally contextualized apologetics. Moreover, it traces the model used by Paul and his immediate successors into contemporary apologetical preaching. The book thus seeks to advance the discussion on how faithful and culturally viable apologetics takes place in the post-truth culture by articulating a model of culturally contextualized apologetics from Paul.

OUTLINE

To make the case for Paul's culturally contextualized apologetics, I will pursue the following outline. This chapter introduced the need for a new apologetics mindset due to the limits of apologetics that heavily relies on rational justification. It also introduced a number of apologists that voice the same concern. This chapter presents the argument that Paul offers a model for culturally engaging apologetics through his culturally contextualized apologetics. As mentioned above, the elements of culturally contextualized apologetics are Paul's establishment of cultural connection and his persuasion from the Christian life that counters cultural objections. The chapter also surveyed the history of research and concludes that there is a void that needs to be filled in the studies in both Paul's apologetics and what entails culturally relevant apologetics. The significance of the book lies in the fact that the study contains cultural, biblical, and historical exegesis.

42. See Dibelius, *From Tradition to Gospel*; Dodd, *The Apostolic Preaching and Its Developments*; Alexander, "The Acts of the Apostles as an Apologetic Text."

Introduction

Chapter 2 shows how Paul engages in culturally contextualized apologetics through the establishment of cultural connections. It begins by briefly delineating the concept of cultural point of contact as that which establishes a common ground with the audience.[43] Analysis of Paul's non-canonical quotes recorded in the New Testament reveals Paul's familiarity with contemporaneous philosophies, and the chapter draws implications on such familiarity has on the establishment of the cultural point of contact. Moreover, the chapter discusses how Paul builds yet another cultural connection, this time through Paul's communication that uses features of Greco-Roman rhetoric. It is a cultural aspect Paul cannot overlook since excellence in rhetorical skills is tied to the degree of receptivity from his hearers. The chapter thus shows the cultural status of rhetorical skills enjoyed in the world of Paul. The chapter further examines the oratory genre in Greco-Roman rhetoric and illumines Paul's speeches in light of such genre. It argues that rhetoric in itself was Paul's enculturated communication method, a way to establish a cultural point of contact.

Chapter 3 demonstrates Paul's engagement in establishing cultural solidarity as a wisdom figure. It surveys the role the sages played in philosophical discourses in the Greco-Roman culture, as well as the significance of the role of sages in Hellenistic royal courts. Paul's engagement with those in Hellenistic royal courts demonstrates that Paul functioned as a wisdom figure and thus again forms a cultural connection that gains his admission to the hearer's culture. Furthermore, the chapter argues that Paul further fortifies his cultural solidarity as he presents himself as the wisdom figure through his suffering narrative. Analysis of Paul's *peristasenkataloge*—the suffering list—and the cultural background in Paul's world show that Paul's contemporaneous audience would have perceived his tribulation as verification of Paul's status as a sage.

Chapter 4 analyzes all of Paul's apologetics speeches in light of culturally contextualized apologetics. The chapter first identifies all of Paul's apologetics speeches in Acts that merit analysis. Paul's apologetics speeches are recorded in Acts 14:15–18, 17:22–31, 24:10b-21, and 26:2–23, 25–27, 29. Then, it is argued that all of Paul's apologetics speeches reveal a pattern, akin to that of kerygmatic speeches. The patterned elements in the scheme are cultural connection, cultural solidarity, presentation of a virtue of

43. Cornelius Van Til first coined the term "point of contact" to denote that knowledge which a believer and a non-believer hold in common. Here I use the term similarly except that common ground arises from cultural considerations. I discuss my use of the term in greater detail in the subsequent chapter.

the Christian life, and the exposition of the resurrection. In other words, analysis of Paul's apologetics speeches evidences Paul repeatedly incorporating cultural connection by the use of cultural point of contact and enculturated communication method, as well as cultural solidarity with the audience in his speeches. The chapter continues by further identifying factors involved in Paul's apologetics speeches: they present the virtue of life of the Christian life, as well as the life of Christ in exposition of the resurrection, as the responses to cultural objections to the Christian faith. Paul presents the Christian life as a defense and vindication against cultural objections that exist in both Jews and pagans. Paul also includes the exposition of the resurrection, the life of Christ, to play a role in setting forth a Christian message. The chapter concludes that Paul models culturally contextualized apologetics by addressing the cultural issues that stand against the Christian faith. Taken all together, it is argued that the scheme common to these speeches consists dual elements: cultural connection (via cultural point of contact, enculturated communication, and cultural solidarity) and assertion of the Christian message against cultural objections through the Christian life.

Chapter 5 exhibits how the first generations apologists after Paul follow Paul's model of culturally contextualized apologetics. Particularly focusing on Aristides, Athenagoras, Justin Martyr, Tatian, Melito of Sardis, and the Epistle of Diognetus, each apologist display cultural connection, cultural solidarity, and the use of the Christian morality to answer cultural objections. The chapter summarizes how interactions with various parts of Greco-Roman culture and ancient philosophy functioned as a cultural point of contact and help solidify Christian identity despite popular perception. It also sums up how the Christian life of morality and sexual ethics vindicated the faith against the Greco-Roman culture.

Chapter 6 summarizes the findings, analyze them, and present a way forward for Christian apologetics in light of apologetics preaching. It first surveys and delineates modern approaches to apologetics preaching. Traditionally, apologetics preaching has followed the four systems of apologetics, namely classical, evidentialistic, presuppositional, and fideistic. Paul, on the other hand, not only is the apologetics preaching *exemplar*, his culturally contextualized apologetics speeches shows a way forward in apologetics preaching. With that in view, I now turn to discuss Paul's cultural connection.

Chapter 2

Paul's Cultural Connection

Reconstructing Paul in light of his cultural context has been garnering increased interest in recent years.[1] N. T. Wright, among many, voice a need to investigate further the subtle relationship Paul has with his cultural context.[2] Likewise, Adolf Deissmann articulates the importance of this scholarship, asserting that "It must not be supposed that St. Paul and his fellow-believers went through the world blindfolded, unaffected by what was then moving the minds of men in great cities."[3] He says apostles were "familiar with the institutions and customs that the Empire had brought with it."[4] Johan Thom echoes this judgment when he writes,

> Reconstructing the cultural and conceptual contexts in Paul's letters and other New Testament texts originated and in which they were intended to be understood is one of the biggest hermeneutical challenges facing New Testament scholars. These contexts the author could have expected his ideal audience to know and to have in common with himself. They formed a cultural repertoire of linguistic, historical, social, or religious knowledge which author and audience shared and which had to be applied in reading and understanding a text.[5]

1. Dodson and Briones, *Paul and the Giants of Philosophy*, 1.
2. Wright, *Paul and the Faithfulness of God*.
3. Deissmann, *Light from the Ancient East*, 340.
4. Deissmann, *Light from the Ancient East*, 341.
5. Thom, "Paul and Popular Philosophy", 47.

If one wants to investigate how Paul engaged in apologetics, Thom's suggestion must be taken seriously. C. Kavin Rowe also advocates for "a historicized discussion" of the New Testament text.[6] The goal of this chapter is to apply the same principle in formulating a model that is culturally contextualized apologetics.

In this light, I make the case that the modeling of Paul's cultural connection becomes perceptible by analyzing Paul's employment of cultural elements found in the contemporaneous culture, namely the use of non-canonical quotes and enculturated communication via Greco-Roman rhetoric. Analysis of non-canonical quotes reveals not only Paul's familiarity with the contemporaneous culture but also its function as a cultural point of contact. Equally, analysis of Greco-Roman rhetoric and its narrative function in speeches attributed to Paul demonstrates the purposes in portraying Paul as an enculturated figure. Cultural point of contact combined together with enculturated communication forges a cultural connection, and Paul models it. Before turning to the analysis of Paul's use of non-canonical quotes, some preliminary thoughts are in order.

PRELIMINARY THOUGHTS

The Importance of Contextual Background

An analysis of Paul's use of non-canonical quotes and the use of Greco-Roman rhetoric found in Paul's speeches can greatly benefit from three preliminary concepts. The first is Leon Morris's seminal work that seeks to understand apostolic preaching by way of investigating keywords according to the background of the Greek Old Testament, the papyri, and the rabbinic writing. Morris exemplifies the strategy that this book takes in analyzing Paul's use of non-canonical quotes in light of the culture when he writes, "The importance of all this is that much of the New Testament was written to people living in a Gentile environment . . . we cannot overlook the extent and the significance of this usage."[7] Thus, background research on the quotes is the focal point of the investigation, which will shed greater light on its function in context.

6. Christopher Kavin Rowe judges that the "one New Testament text that best encompasses the difficulties and promises of thinking through the particularity of Christian theological knowledge and its embeddedness in a comprehensive pattern of life is the Acts of the Apostles." Rowe, *World Upside Down*, 3.

7. Morris, *The Apostolic Preaching of the Cross*, 15.

Point of Contact

The second is the concept of point of contact. The term is mostly associated with Cornelius Van Til's presuppositional apologetics. However, the term has developed and thus carries multiple connotations. For Van Til, point of contact is the innate sense of God in all human beings although non-believers would suppress the sense of God.[8] Since everyone bears the image of God without exception, suppressed knowledge of God establishes a point of contact by which truth concerning God's existence can be generated.[9]

Correspondingly, reformed epistemological apologetics slightly modifies this concept of point of contact to signify the establishment of epistemological common ground with a non-believer. This variation, specifically attributed to Gordon Clark, suggests that one will have the same approach to knowledge regardless of their faith in God.[10] For Clark, ability to reason, although impossible apart from presupposing the Word of God as the only source of truth, provides a common ground—a point of contact.[11] Another adaptation of the term appears in Edward Carnell's apologetics approach. Carnell points out that "Jesus satisfies the convictions of the heart as well as the demands of a critically disciplined intellect" and argues that apologists must "consistently build a useful point of contact between the gospel and culture."[12] As shown, the point of contact can denote innate knowledge of God, rationality, and connections made between the gospel message and

---

8. Van Til, *The Defense of the Faith*.

9. Bahnsen, *Van Til's Apologetic*. Van Til's writing is notorious for its difficulty, but Bahnsen helps one grasp what Van Tilean presuppositional apologetics entails by explaining that Van Til's presuppositional apologetics is essentially an argument from the 'impossibility of the contrary.' It is an assertion that challenges non-believers to try to come up with a satisfactory answer as to how to account for their knowledge and convictions given their worldview. Van Til's apologetics demonstrates that only a Christian worldview can offer convictions about meaningfulness and cogency of logic, science, and morality, which is the only premise capable of providing preconditions necessary to reason at all.

10. Clark, *Religion, Reason, and Revelation*.

11. Boa and Bowman help clarify Clark by writing, "By 'a common epistemological ground' Clark means the idea of non-Christians and Christians sharing the same approach to knowledge. For Clark the only sound approach to knowledge is to accept the Word of God in Scripture as absolute truth. The 'common psychological or ontological ground' is the image of God that exists in both Christian and non-Christian. The mind and being of the unregenerate is still created in God's image. As a result, non-Christians still know and think some truth." Boa and Bowman, *Faith Has Its Reasons*, 465.

12. Carnell, *The Kingdom of Love and the Pride of Life*, 7.

Cultural Point of Contact

Hence, third, I will draw from all of the previously discussed connotations of the term and add a necessary qualifier. I will qualify the term, point of contact, by adding a cultural dimension. In this book, cultural point of contact will denote both a common ground shared through an innate knowledge of God generated by cultural cues, as well as that ground formed by a uniform conviction or experience from a culture.

CULTURAL CONNECTION THROUGH CULTURAL POINT OF CONTACT: PAUL'S USE OF NON-CANONICAL QUOTES

There are places within Scripture where Paul introduces statements that have origins foreign to Scripture. These statements are referred to as non-canonical quotes. Even though the scholars have noted the occurrence of non-canonical quotes used by Paul, a literature that contains a serious treatment of these quotes as a set is very rare.[13] Despite the fact that these quotes appear to be Paul's engagement with the contemporaneous culture, no work has extensively covered its implications on apologetics.[14] Thus, an analysis of how Paul uses the non-canonical quotes grant clues to determine how or whether these quotes function as a cultural point of contact.

Since the aim of this book is to investigate matters pertaining to Paul, I will identify passages that contain non-canonical material within the

---

13. Joachim Jeremiah's *Unknown Sayings of Jesus* may be a publication that comes closest to a research on this type of subject. There is one article that deals specifically with Paul's use of non-canonical quotes as a set, not as an individual verses on which commentators have exposited. See Jeremias, *Unknown Sayings of Jesus*.

14. One rare exception to this is Vadim Wittkowsky's "'Pagane' Zitate Im Neuen Testament" (Pagan Quotes of the New Testament). Wittkowsky surveys the set of 'pagan quotes,' and traces the use of pagan quotes to other Jewish literature that employs the same technique. The work is profitable in that it also demonstrates how the second century apologists both Greek and Latin uses the identical strategy of using the quotes of pagans to make an agreeable case. However, the work does not discuss the origin of the quotes or cultural context in depth, nor does it give attention to apologetics implications as this chapter aims to do. See Wittkowsky, "'Pagane' Zitate Im Neuen Testament," 107–26.

Pauline corpus and the book of Acts only.[15] I will then assess these quotes by tracing their origin, giving a contextual background, followed by a survey of biblical interpretations of all of those passages. The analysis then will discuss how they function as the cultural point of contacts. John Polhill, along with numbers of others, identifies several key passages that contain non-canonical material.[16] The three verses are Acts 17:28, 1 Corinthians 15:33, and Titus 1:12. Next is an analysis of each of them to observe how Paul establishes connection with the culture.

Acts 17:28

In Acts 17:28, Paul delivers his apologetic sermon to those gathered in the Areopagus. Paul challenges the men of Athens to turn away from useless idols and believe in the resurrection of Jesus Christ. Paul's speech in Acts 17 contains these words:

Ἐν αὐτῷ γὰρ ζῶμεν καὶ κινούμεθα καὶ ἐσμέν, ὡς καί τινες τῶν καθ' ὑμᾶς ποιητῶν εἰρήκασιν, Τοῦ γὰρ καὶ γένος ἐσμέν.

---

15. It must also be noted that Paul's use of 'traditional material' is recorded in Acts 20:35, 1 Cor 7:10, 1 Cor 9:14, and 1 Thess 4:15. In each of these instances, Paul states that he was conveying the words of the Lord. In my evaluation it is clear that Paul's use of the tradition—the use of those quotes that are un-recorded in the gospel material, highlights several features. First, there are significant indications the source of Paul's quotations comes from the Jesus tradition. Any contention to challenge this notion proves to be unsuccessful and weak. Second, Paul demonstrates confidence and familiarity with the Jesus tradition in the quotes he uses. Paul's usage of traditional material as summary that hearers are aware that Paul is transmitting the words of the Lord. Third, Paul makes a sharp distinction between his own apostolic authoritative inspired utterances and the words of the Lord. This distinction adds even greater credibility that Paul is using the quotations without alteration or interpolation. Fourth and finally, Paul reveals a clear purpose in using Jesus quotations: he uses them when an appeal to the highest authority is necessary and beneficial. These sources deal with the traditional material more in depth: Richard Bauckham, *Jesus and the Eyewitnesses: The Gospels as Eyewitness Testimony* (Grand Rapids: William B. Eerdmans Pub. Co., 2006); Traugott Holtz, "Paul and the Oral Gospel Tradition," in *Jesus and the Oral Gospel Tradition*, ed. Henry Wansbrough (Sheffield: JSOT Press, 1991), 380–92; Eric Eve, *Behind the Gospels: Understanding the Oral Tradition* (Minneapolis: Fortress Press, 2013); Paul R. Eddy and Gregory A. Boyd, *The Jesus Legend: A Case for the Historical Reliability of the Synoptic Jesus Tradition* (Grand Rapids: Baker Academic, 2007); Jeremias, *Unknown Sayings of Jesus*.

16. Polhill, *Paul and His Letters*.

For "In him we live and move and have our being"; as even some of your own poets have said, "For we are indeed his offspring."[17]

Original Source of Acts 17:28

Scholars almost all agree that quotes found in Acts 17:28 are actually two quotes from two different sources.[18] The first one, "Ἐν αὐτῷ γὰρ ζῶμεν—In him we live," is distinguished from the second, "Τοῦ γὰρ καὶ γένος ἐσμέν—Indeed we are His offspring." Therefore, each component should be considered separately.

There are differing views as to the original attribution for the first quote. The most common attribution for "In Him we live" is the sixth-century B.C. Cretan poet Epimenides.[19] F. F. Bruce is among those who take this view, arguing that this quotation appears from the fourth line of a quatrain that has been preserved from a poem attributed to Epimenides.[20] Rendel Harris believes this quote is from an extended quote of this section of *Epimenides* in the Syriac father Isho'dad of Merv, about AD 850. Harris further notes how Clement of Alexandria in *Miscellanies* i.14.59.1 f., has claimed the line "The Cretans, always liars, evil beasts, idle bellies" to come from Epimenides as well.[21] Bruce also suggests that this may be a poem by Diogenes Laertius (*Lives of Philosophers* i.112), which is ascribed to a poem by Epimenides on Minos and Rhadamanthys.

Others, however, pose an alternate possibility for origin. Craig S. Keener introduces evidence for an alternate original source. He, along with few others, concludes that the sayings have been so generalized in the world of antiquity that Epimenides should not be attributed as the original source.[22] Keener believes that it may be a Lukan summary of a popular quote in circulation through generations. He draws attention to the fact that the

---

17. All Scripture references come from the English Standard Version unless stated otherwise.

18. Keener, *Acts*, 2653.

19. Keener, *Acts*, 2657

20. Bruce, *Commentary on the Book of the Acts*, 359.

21. Bruce finds that the original text would have read this way: "They fashioned a tomb for thee, O holy and high one—The Cretans, always liars, evil beasts, idle bellies! But thou art not dead; thou livest and abidest forever; For in thee we live and move and have our being."

22. Bock, *Acts*, 568.

quote lacks the Greek meter necessary for a poem, and that the language in the verse is more philosophical than poetic; and since Epimenides predates philosophy as a pre-philosophic poet, Keener concludes against the attribution of the quote to Epimenides.[23]

As a compromise between these two views, David Williams stresses that the first quotation does not have the diction or meter of poetry, indicating that Paul is not using the quote as a direct quotation but rather as an allusion. In other words, Paul is simply making a general reference to a popularly circulated idea.[24] Horatio B. Hackett also argues that Paul is using the quote as an allusion, not a direct quotation. Hackett takes Paul's introduction of the quotes in verse 28—"certain or some have said" —as Paul's way of generalizing the idea that appears subsequent to the introduction. He believes that Paul wants to convey the truth contained in the quotes. According to Hackett, the evidence is so plain and obvious that even secular poets recognize it by expressing it in their work. When Paul refers to "your poets" in the plural, he does so precisely because, Hackett argues, Paul knows of "other passages where the thought is found, with an inference that so obvious a remark must be a common one."[25] In this light, John Polhill equally deduces that the first part of verse 28 is a "more or less traditional Greek triadic formula."[26]

The second quote, "We are his offspring," features a better agreement: though some find the quote's origin in Cleanthes, it is generally accepted that Paul is quoting a Stoic poet Aratus of Soli, who lived in the first half of the third century BC[27] Aratus's fifth line of the *Phainomena* opens with the following words:

> Let us begin with Zeus. Never, O men, let us leave him unmentioned. All the ways are full of Zeus, and all the market-places of

---

23. Keener, *Acts*, 2658.
24. Williams, *Acts*, 307–308.
25. Hackett, *Commentary on Acts*, 209.
26. Polhill, *Acts*, 397.
27. Baum, "Paulinismen in Den Missionsreden Des Lukanischen Paulus: Zur Inhaltlichen Authentizität Der Oratio Recta in Der Apostelgeschichte," 405–36; Winter, "Introducing the Athenians to God: Paul's Failed Apologetic in Acts 17?," 38–59; Gendy, "Style, Content and Culture: Distinctive Characteristics in the Missionary Speeches in Acts," 247–65; Strandenaes, "The Missionary Speeches in the Acts of the Apostles and Their Missiological Implications," 341–54; Strait, "The Wisdom of Solomon, Ruler Cults, and Paul's Polemic against Idols in the Areopagus Speech," 609–32; Di Mauro, "Witnessing Lessons from the Areopagus," 186–95.

human beings. The sea is full of him; so are the harbors. In every way we have all to do with Zeus, for we are truly his offspring.[28]

The last set of words of this quotation is also found in Cleanthes's *Hymn to Zeus*, but without the parts that precede the quoted words. Because of this overlap, many commentators point out that Aratus may also be borrowing from Cleanthes, which is a widely accepted verdict.[29]

Interpretation of Acts 17:28

Paul proclaims that human beings are completely dependent upon God, particularly the Christian God, as the source of life and power for activities. By quoting a pagan source, "In him we live and move and have our being," Paul is challenging the pantheistic conviction of the people at Areopagus, as confirmed by their own poem. Paul certainly does not endorse this pantheistic idea about God—that god is everywhere and thus in him we live and move and have our being. Instead, Paul turns the perspective around to highlight utter dependence human beings have in the one true God by using the very quotation.

Witherington offers two arguments to support Paul's turning the table with this quote. First, the word *"Eν"* in the verse would mean not "in," but "by."[30] This notion certainly is possible and could have been interpreted that way by the original readers. Second, Witherington notes that even if the quote is attributed to Epimenides's *Hymn to Zeus*, everyone would have been aware of the fact that "Epimenides was no Stoic, being earlier than Zeno, and in any case an address to Zeus would not be seen as an address to the pantheistic deity of Stoicism."[31] Thus, it is clear that Paul did not intend to endorse a pantheistic notion with these quotes.

Furthermore, the quotation from Aratus does not convey Paul's affirmation of pantheistic kinship between God and humanity. Instead, Paul is proclaiming that God is the Creator and that human beings are God's offspring rather than little gods who are his offspring. Paul's idea here is not to emphasize existential identification with a deity, but instead to highlight human being's complete dependence on God. The opinion that Stoics

---

28. Bruce, *Commentary on the Book of the Acts*, 339.
29. I did not come across any opposing view to this opinion.
30. Witherington, *The Acts of the Apostles*, 529.
31. Witherington, *The Acts of the Apostles*, 530.

would have heard this quotation as a way for Paul to acknowledge humanity sharing in divine nature is erroneous. It is unlikely that such a pantheistic notion is what either Luke or historical Paul desired to communicate. On the contrary, Paul declares that God is the Creator and that human beings are subject to God as his offspring."[32]

Paul's Use of Acts 17:28 and Its Implication for Cultural Connection

Paul's use of quotations produces several outcomes. I suggest that first, he gains an audience's hearing by employing a Greco-Roman rhetorical methodology; second, he employs natural theology to support his case; and third, Paul establishes his case by launching a polemic against the listener's faith. Before discussing these matters in turn, a brief note on usage of the quote in ancient culture is helpful. Craig Keener explains:

> That the speech may give these quotations a sense foreign to their earliest usage may not have troubled Luke. Quotations were often given out of context; certainly they were reapplied for new purposes, as Jewish and Christian tradition regularly re-appropriates Scripture for new settings. Cicero uses Homeric characters to demonstrate principles of law; Seneca notes that writers often recycle Virgil's language in very different circumstances to depict something simply similar to what Virgil described.[33]

Keener, drawing from impressively wide sources from antiquity, explains the rhetorical effect achieved by quoting poets during this time. He states that writing and memorizing quotations from poets were included in a Greek's primary education; and as a result, reciting quotations from poets became part of the shared intellectual culture, naturally resulting in prolific proverbial quotations.[34]

Thus, considering this type of quotation usage was customary practice, Paul's use of these quotes functions to connect with the audience. Mikeal C. Parsons observes that appealing to and quoting authorities were acceptable rhetorical strategies of this time.[35] Parsons provides support by introducing Quintilian's quote, clarifying what is considered an authority:

32. Chance, *Acts*, 311.
33. Keener, *Acts*, 2664.
34. Keener, *Acts*, 2653.
35. Parsons, *Acts*, 247.

(Authorities are) opinions which can be attributed to nations, peoples, wise men, distinguished citizens, or famous poets. Even common sayings and popular beliefs may be useful. All these are in a sense testimonies, but they are actually all the more effective because they are not given to suit particular causes, but spoken or given by minds free of prejudice and favor for the simple reason that they seemed either very honorable or very true. [36]

Based on this, Paul is attempting to gain intellectual consent among the listeners using the rhetorical method familiar to them. There is a cultural connection taking place.

Next, Paul, by using a pagan poem, builds up his apologetics message through natural theology, establishing a sense of cultural point of contact. J. B. Lightfoot believes that Paul gives a nod to the element of truth in Greek poetry, despite the fact that their pantheistic worldview is in error. He argues that Paul brings out a conviction that is "deeply seated consciousness of men,"[37] and using it as a starting point of a conversation with pagans. Lightfoot also notes that if Paul were speaking to Jews he would have "turned to the other pole of natural theology—the oneness and distinct personality of God. That was an idea that had no distinct place in the Hellenistic mind, and therefore he could not make it the basis of any argument."[38]

William H. Willimon also notices Paul's appeal to natural theology. Willimon notes that this is not the only time Paul makes an appeal to natural theology. In Romans 1:18–23, Paul again employs natural theology to build his argument. He seeks to illumine the truth and condemn the status of pagan lives by the way of what is generally observed in the natural world.[39] In short, Paul does not communicate with those gathered in Areopagus with allusions to the Old Testament; rather, "Paul appeals to the natural revelation in order to present God as the Creator as well as the beginning point of his argument."[40]

Finally, in using non-canonical material, Paul launches a polemic against the Athenians' faith. Parsons believes that Paul's usage of non-canonical quotations functions as a "*probatio* (proofs) given to the

36. Parsons, *Acts*, 247.
37. Lightfoot and Witherington, *The Acts of the Apostles*, 233.
38. Lightfoot and Witherington, *The Acts of the Apostles*, 233.
39. Willimon, *Acts*, 143.
40. Thomas, *Acts*, 502–503.

Athenian audience."[41] Keener also emphasizes that Paul offers this common quotation from a Greek poem since the presentation of classical quotations were expected to be supplied as proofs to those hearing them.[42] Marshall further warrants this point:

> Paul thus takes over pagan Greek poems, expressive of Stoic philosophy, and applies them to God. A process of 'demythologization' was already underway in that for the Stoics 'Zeus' meant not the supreme god in Greek polytheism but the Logos. Paul was prepared to take over the glimmerings of truth in pagan philosophy about the nature of God. But whereas the Greeks thought of the divine nature of man, Paul would have thought of the way in which man is the image of God.[43]

1 Corinthians 15:33

In this section of the letter to the Corinthians, Paul discusses the resurrection of Christ, the resurrection of the dead, and the resurrection of the body, along with the mystery and victory associated with the resurrection.[44] Though this is not written to pagans, apologetical merit found in Paul's resurrection discussion warrants a need to consider this part of his letter. In particular, the section that deals with the resurrection of the dead is another place where Paul introduces non-canonical material. The verse is as follows:

> μὴ πλανᾶσθε· Φθείρουσιν ἤθη χρηστὰ ὁμιλίαι κακαί.
>
> Do not be deceived: "Bad company ruins good morals."

Original Source of 1 Corinthians 15:33

The quote appears in a fragment 218 of Menander's comedy *Thais*, the work that comes from third or fourth century BC[45] However, others also argue

- 41. Parsons, *Acts*, 247.
- 42. Keener, *Acts*, 2653.
- 43. Marshall, *The Acts of the Apostles*, 289.
- 44. I have taken these headings from ESV Study Bible.
- 45. Edmonds, *The Fragments of Attic Comedy*, 627. Thiselton also suggests that Jerome seems to be the first one to attribute the quote to come from Meander's comedy,

that the concept of securing morally edifying companions is generic and "nothing new (Proverbs 13:20; 14:7; 28:7; Sir 13:1)."[46] Moreover, Keener notes that Menander himself may have borrowed it from earlier usage.[47]

Hence, there is little question or discussion about the source of the quotation. Most commentators conclude that the source of the quote, would not carry much significance as the saying is commonly recognized as a proverbial statement.[48] Although one cannot conclusively decide whether Paul was familiar with Greek literature, yet it is not too difficult to acknowledge that the quotation was readily available to all. In short, it is likely that the quotation simply was a common saying that happened to appear in Menander's comedy.

Interpretation of 1 Corinthians 15:33

Three imperatives are found in 1 Corinthians 15:33, "Do not be misled, come back to your senses, and stop sinning." Given the context, "do not be misled" is supported by the proverb that provides the reasoning—for bad company corrupts good character. Those who deny the resurrection are those who are misleading the Corinthians. They simply possess "fundamental ignorance of God since resurrection is the climax of God's redemption of the world and the key event that culminates in his being 'all in all.'"[49] This is especially a sharp punch to those who claim to have special spiritual knowledge (as Paul discusses in earlier chapters of 1 Corinthians), yet they do not understand that ignorance of God results in immorality.[50] This immorality then can eventually corrupt the entire community.

Michael Cover argues that the quote "is part of a broader rhetorical strategy and signifies *in nuce* the literary and theo-dramatic mode of 1 Corinthians."[51] He denies that the quote is "a piece of unreflective rhetorical adornment," while proposing that Paul "knows the aphorism from a popular collection, akin to the famed Menander's *Maxims*, which would

---

but he does not provide the source. Thiselton, *The First Epistle to the Corinthians*, 1254.

46. Keener, *1—2 Corinthians*, 129.
47. Keener, *1—2 Corinthians*, 129.
48. Fee, *The First Epistle to the Corinthians*, 856.
49. Naylor, *A Study Commentary on 1 Corinthians*, 400.
50. Garland, *1 Corinthians*, 722.
51. Cover, "The Divine Comedy at Corinth," 533.

become a common text in Hellenistic Greek education."[52] Cover believes Paul's coordination between this quote and the text from Isaiah 22:13 carries significance.[53] He believes that Paul's choice to place greater weight on the quote, and use Isaiah to provide footing is noteworthy.[54] Citing scholars such as Müller, Stowers, Engberg-Petersen and others who point to the existence of intertextuality between classical tragedy and the Pauline letters, Cover assesses the quote to function as a tool "far from being a mere throw-away line."[55]

Additionally, Thiselton takes note of the concept of "ὁμιλίαι" or "company" used in this quotation. He informs that while the term can denote "association," "company," or a "clique, a group, or a gang" that has a notion of membership. "ὁμιλίαι" would be a group or clique that regularly meets together, is able to exercise peer pressure, the "in-group" to which one's life is closely bound.[56] Thus, Paul wants to convey: first, that God's victory over corruption is effective over all forms of corruption—corruption of creation, the corruption of body, and the corruption of morality; and second, the resurrection account, which announces the gospel, brings with it the freedom to be released from the "corruption influences in the forms of various vices, especially idolatry, sexual immorality, and greed that flow from that false wisdom."[57] In other words, God's victory in resurrection completely un-does all the moral corruption produced by bad company.

---

52. Cover, "The Divine Comedy at Corinth," 532.

53. Cover, "The Divine Comedy at Corinth," 532.

54. Cover, "The Divine Comedy at Corinth," 533.

55. Cover argues, "Looking at a range of passages from 1 Corinthians 5–15, Paul's quotation of Menander provides a key to understanding the 'new comedic' shape of Paul's rhetoric and theology. To argue that comedy rather than tragedy is the dominant theo-dramatic mode of 1 Corinthians does not mean that the perceived presence of the tragic in the letter misses the mark. To the contrary, implicit in the claim that Paul's framing of 1 Corinthians echoes elements of New Comedy is the understanding that one finds in both Paul and Menander a conflation of the high and the low, of the divine and the everyday, of the tragic and the comic. Previous work on Philippians suggests that just such a nuanced dramatic modality was at play in Paul's construction of Christ as a comic hero." Cover, "The Divine Comedy at Corinth," 533.

56. Thiselton, *The First Epistle to the Corinthians*, 1254.

57. Ciampa and Rosner, *The First Letter to the Corinthians*, 793.

Paul's Use of 1 Corinthians 15:33 and its Implication for Cultural Connection

Roy E. Ciampa and Brian S. Rosner state, "Paul's use of the quotation, rather than being a clue to the sources of his own thought, indicates Paul's sense of where the ideas he is countering comes from."[58] To those who are under the influence of people who deny the resurrection, living as if there is no Parousia or reality to come, Paul "appeals to a worldly proverb to show that the Corinthians lack common sense as well as spiritual insight (cf. Mark 4:24)."[59] By using a common epigram or proverb that Corinthians may well have been familiar with, Paul critically appeals to the natural ground to make his point clear. Paul is using the quotation as an "epigram" (according to Rosner), a "proverb" (according to Naylor, Keener, Witherington), and a popular "maxim" (according to Thiselton). "The rhetorical force of Paul's use of this proverb is powerful: These Gentiles Corinthians are condemned out of the mouth of their own cultural heritage even apart from Scripture and apostolic tradition."[60] In *Homilies on Luke* 31.3, Origen writes, "But even if Paul takes an illustration from Gentile literature, he takes words even from what is foreign to us to sanctify them."[61]

Based on this, Paul is again shown to employ cultural connection through a form of cultural point of contact to advance his argument. His commendation of Christian faith through the discussion of resurrection in this section of his writing gains greater strength via cultural point of contact. Such a cultural point of contact is made through the usage of this non-canonical quote found in 1 Corinthians 15 and widely accessible to his original hearers. Paul employs a cultural point of contact to bolster his case.

Titus 1:12

In Titus, Paul lays out the qualifications of leadership in the church. In the midst of this discussion, Paul turns on a sharp criticism against those who are acting out of line with the gospel. In this criticism, Paul borrows from a non-canonical material once more.

---

58. Ciampa and Rosner, *The First Letter to the Corinthians*, 792.
59. Naylor, *A Study Commentary on 1 Corinthians*, 447.
60. Witherington, *Conflict and Community in Corinth*, 292.
61. Origen and Lienhard, *Homilies on Luke: Fragments on Luke*, 127.

εἰπέν τις ἐξ αὐτῶν, ἴδιος αὐτῶν προφήτης, Κρῆτες ἀεὶ ψεῦσται, κακὰ θηρία, γαστέρες ἀργαί.

One of the Cretans, a prophet of their own, said, "Cretans are always liars, evil beasts, lazy gluttons."

Original Source of Titus 1:12

Paul introduces this quotation in a rather direct manner. Donald Guthrie asserts that the source of the quotation is Epimenides, a sixth-century philosopher who had received elevated status to mythical honors by his own countrymen.[62] Epimenides is not only taken as a philosopher, but is recognized also as a prophet. Clement of Alexandria, in *Stromata* chapter 14, recognizes that Paul grants a measure of truth to the words of the "prophets" like Epimenides and is not ashamed to quote Greek poems to "build them up and direct them to self-examination."[63] This explains why Paul begins the quote by stating "a prophet of their own."[64]

Marshall and Towner understand this quotation to have come from an *Ode Concerning Oracles*.[65] Yet, since this quotation occurs in Callimachus's *Hymn to Zeus* (270 BC) as well, others attribute the statement to him though it is generally affirmed that the hymn comes before Callimachus.

Interpretation of Titus 1:12

William Mounce pays attention to the Greek in this text. A verb form of "Κρῆτες" (Cretan)—"play the Cretan"—translates to, "to lie."[66] Cretans were notorious enough to form a verb out of their name to mean "lie."[67] Moreover, "κακὰs—evil" coupled with, "θηρία—animal," comes to mean "vicious"—figuratively here to denote a person with a "bestial nature."[68]

---

62. Guthrie, *The Pastoral Epistles*, 200.
63. Alexandria and Ferguson, *Stromateis, Books 1–3*, 66.
64. Guthrie, *The Pastoral Epistles*, 200.
65. Marshall and Towner, *A Critical and Exegetical Commentary on the Pastoral Epistles*, 200.
66. Mounce, *Pastoral Epistles*, 399.
67. Mounce, *Pastoral Epistles*, 399.
68. Knight, *The Pastoral Epistles*, 299.

The recurring occurrence of "αὐτῶν" and "ἴδιος" forms "their own," and "makes the prophet's identification with the Cretans very specific."[69]

Supplementing the findings from investigating the technicality of words, George Wieland says I. F. Sanders offers a cultural background in the formation of public perception. He notes that it was "specifically the Cretan claim to possess the tomb of Zeus that provoked the accusation "Cretans are always liars" in Callimachus's *Hymn to Zeus*.[70] He further explicates that such characterization is deeply embedded in the culture since "the currency of such terms as κρητίζειν, to lie, κρητισμός, falsehood, and the expression, πρὸς Κρῆτα κρητίζειν, "to meet craft with craft," suggests a widespread perception.[71] Cretans' breaking of a treaty and subsequent massacre is well known as a prime example of the Cretans' "habitual ferocity" and their well-admired ability to "prevaricate their ways out of danger."[72]

This background hints the reason why Paul, following up on verse 13, says, "This testimony is true."[73] Paul identifies those misleading false teachers as possessing infamous Cretan character. "The apostle is about to urge Titus to take a strong hand with the unruly element in the church, and is priming him on the well-known characteristics of the people with whom he is dealing."[74]

Riemer Faber identifies Paul's agenda in advancing a major theme centered around the quote.[75] He first observes that this is the first time the entire hexameter is employed in a literature though the quote in its entire hexameter does appear later on in history.[76] Faber believes that Paul "quotes the entire verse because each phrase in it is relevant to the argument that is developed in the immediate and general context."[77] Furthermore, Faber says,

> The entire verse is cited to illustrate Paul's argument in 1:10–16, and its function in its immediate context reveals that a major

---

69. Knight, *The Pastoral Epistles*, 298.
70. Wieland, "Roman Crete and the Letter to Titus,"345.
71. Wieland, "Roman Crete and the Letter to Titus," 345.
72. Wieland, "Roman Crete and the Letter to Titus," 346.
73. Mounce, *Pastoral Epistles*, 398.
74. Marshall and Towner, *A Critical and Exegetical Commentary on the Pastoral Epistles*, 202.
75. Faber, "'Evil Beasts, Lazy Gluttons,'" 135–45.
76. Faber, "'Evil Beasts, Lazy Gluttons,'" 137.
77. Faber, "'Evil Beasts, Lazy Gluttons,'" 137.

theme, broached at the outset and permeating the entire letter, is encapsulated in it. The citation of Epimenides in 1:12 is not intended as racist slur, polemic invective, or philosophical dilemma; rather, its purpose is to show that doctrinal error is accompanied by moral corruption. This theme, which courses throughout the letter, is employed to exhort Titus and the Christians on Crete to see the basis, nature, and effect of joining sound teaching with good practice.[78]

Paul's Use of Titus 1:12 and its Implications for Cultural Connection

Paul uses the quotation to criticize false teachers who are teaching things they ought not to teach, proving themselves to be liars. Paul uses the quote "in an almost parenthetical manner," yet voices a strong criticism against those living in sin.[79] Thiselton renders that Paul cannot be applying this to every single member of Cretan demography; if taken literally, the Cretan prophet's evaluation of his people would also be self-contradictory and fall apart because the Cretan prophet's verdict itself would be a lie too.[80] Thus, Paul uses the quotation to establish a general point that will have wider appeal and acceptability, providing further support for his argument.

For this reason, Thiselton suggests that this phrase may be functioning as the "liar's paradox."[81] If one takes the quotation literally, it creates a logical conundrum—whether Cretans accusing Cretans as being always a liar, in itself can be logically established or not. Thus, Paul is employing this logical conundrum to parallel the Christian's behavior with that of Cretans.[82] However, Marshall and Towner deny this possibility, arguing that there is no indication or acknowledgment of Paul raising this type of a logical issue by this quote. In other words, the quotation is not used here as a paradox.[83]

---

78. Faber, "'Evil Beasts, Lazy Gluttons,'" 145.

79. Thomas D. Lea and Hayne P. Griffin, *1, 2 Timothy, Titus*, The New American Commentary (Nashville: Broadman Press, 1992), 289.

80. Thiselton, "The Logical Role," 207–23.

81. Thiselton, "The Logical Role," 207.

82. Thiselton, "The Logical Role," 207–23.

83. Marshall and Towner, *A Critical and Exegetical Commentary on the Pastoral Epistles*, 203.

Again, "the character of the Cretans displayed itself so clearly that confirmation of the severe judgment comes from every direction and is not limited to a single century."[84] Polybius, a Greek historian writes, "So much, in fact, do love of shameful profit and greed prevail among them that among all men Cretans are the only ones in whose estimation no profit is ever disgraceful," in *The Histories* VI. 46.[85] Cicero, in *Republic* III. ix.15 writes, "Indeed (men's) moral principles are so divergent that the Cretans ... consider highway robbery to be honorable."[86] Livy, a Roman historian, Plutarch, a Greek essayist and biographer, and other historical evidence voice the same opinion of Cretans.[87] Hence, Paul is merely introducing a general statement, a popularized perspective.

Paul's usage of the term prophet demonstrates that what he conveys as a true statement in verse 13 is genuinely an affirmative assessment of Cretans themselves.[88] The quote reflects the usage of a common title, though perhaps prejudicial, assigned to them.[89] Mounce introduces Chrysostom's verdict as to why Paul uses quotations from a secular writer: "It is because we put them most to confusion when we bring our testimonies and accusations from their town writers when we make those their accusers, who are admired among themselves."[90] Similar to the other non-canonical quotes, Paul is again shown to appeal to general cultural understanding to reinforce his argument. This is another demonstrative case of cultural point of contact adopted to fortify his reasoning.

ANALYSIS OF PAUL'S USE OF NON-CANONICAL QUOTES AS CULTURAL POINT OF CONTACT

Observations

What does Paul's use of non-canonical quotes reveal? Upon survey of Paul's use of non-canonical material, several features become prominent. First, the question of the quotations' original sources is relatively insignificant as

---

84. Hendriksen, *New Testament Commentary*, 353.
85. Polybus, *The Histories*, 413.
86. Cicero, *The Republic*, 197.
87. Hendriksen, *New Testament Commentary*, 353–54.
88. Knight, *The Pastoral Epistles*, 298.
89. Mounce, *Pastoral Epistles*, 399.
90. Mounce, *Pastoral Epistles*, 399.

they all are popularized ideas. All of the sayings Paul employs in his speech are either proverbial or general in nature. They do not seem to offer theologically revolutionary perspectives; instead, they merely reaffirm what the hearers perhaps already know.[91]

Second, all of the quotations that come from non-canonical sources are used with a purpose to gain mutual agreement and understanding. Paul's main aim in using these quotations is again not to steer their thinking in any new direction; but rather to bring their mind in conformity to what the apostle wishes to communicate. Abraham J. Malherbe points out how this strategy was popular among philosophers of Paul's time as he writes,

> What was important was the wisdom contained in the poems, not their authorship, and they could be quoted without any attribution of authorship. Moral philosophers, who attempted to reform the masses, used these sayings because they believed the poets were the authorities of the masses and representatives of the common wisdom. By quoting proverbial statements from poets, a teacher could assume that they expressed the thought and feeling of men generally, just what many think about wealth and the other objects of their admiration, and what they consider would be the greatest good derived from each of them.[92]

This use of popular quotes by moral philosophers in the Greco-Roman world parallels that of Paul in both the intent and functions of the quotes.

Third, it demonstrates Paul's ability to use a quote as a rhetorical tool.[93] Quotes have specific functions in the context.[94] At Areopagus, it is used to refute the very worldview that produced the quote. Paul uses the pagan quote to refute pagan; in the discussion of the resurrection, plurality found in bad company, is dominated by the all-encompassing power of the resurrection. Cretans' lies are to be substituted by moral characters of the Christian leaders. While it may be improbable to decipher the precise degree of familiarity Paul had with the Greco-Roman literature and culture, at least one can confirm his connection to the culture at large. Considering the fact that those non-canonical quotes find their sources in a variety of

---

91. At the same time I would stress that Paul recognizes that the quotes do not carry the same authority as the Scripture.

92. Malherbe, *Light from the Gentiles*, 94–95.

93. Wittkowsky argues that the quotes are also used as an intertextual reference to Jewish polemics against paganism. See Wittkowsky, "'Pagane' Zitate Im Neuen Testament."

94. I will treat this subject in greater detail in chap. 4 of this book.

popular cultural expressions such as a poetry, a comedy, and a hymn to a pagan god, one can also potentially also find reasons to support Paul's resourcefulness in the culture.

Fourth, Paul's use of quotes functions as cultural point of contact. To recall the discussion on the topic introduced earlier, cultural point of contact is an appeal to innate knowledge of God (whether recognized or suppressed in human beings) or a shared common ground that establishes a point of connection, through expressions in culture. Dibelius has argued that Paul's Areopagus speech largely consists of a Hellenistic monotheistic sermon that has no Christian content before the last two verses, based on the theology as well as the appearance of the pagan quote.[95] However, Colin Hemer argues for a different function of the quote: "that a speaker with an urgent message to communicate to hearers of an alien mind must find a point of contact and will not hit them mechanically with a starkly unsympathetic barrage of alien thought in alien terminology."[96] "The interconnection of faith and ethics is therefore not presented as specific to the Christian offer, but rather as a possible point of contact with other (not only religious) worldviews."[97] Paul communicates his message but with that in which has a cultural context and familiarity. Through the use of non-canonical quotes, Paul is able to draw connection from those cultures in his communication.

Beyond the Quotes: Implications of Paul's Cultural Point of Contact

But is there any indication that this meaningful connection with the culture takes place not just in his use of quotes but in other aspects of the culture? While a full treatment of Paul's relationship with contemporaneous philosophy would require a book of its own, I will briefly survey various ways Paul is perceived under the lens of philosophy, extracting how it relates to Paul's cultural connection.

Modern scholars have repeatedly dialogued concerning Paul's connection to Greek culture via philosophy; they are not the first to take

---

95. Dibelius, *Studies in the Acts of the Apostles*, 43.

96. Hemer, "The Speeches of Acts: Pt 1: The Ephesian Elders at Miletus; Pt 2: The Areopagus Address," 248–49.

97. Červenková's work deals with Tertullian, but the same principle applies here. Later on in this book, I make the argument that apologists in the second century in fact model Paul. Červenková, "De Religione: How Christianity Became a Religion," 107.

note of this.[98] Attempts to place Paul in his cultural circumstances through philosophy date back to the Early Church.[99] Malherbe cites Tertullian and Jerome for this idea: Paul's words were taken to have "so many affinities with the popular philosophy of his day, especially as it was represented by Stoicism and Cynicism."[100]

Yet, such categorization requires discretion. One, it is unhelpful to frame Paul in the mold of a philosophical school such Stoicism or Middle Platonism, or to essentially interpret him as operating as one of the representative figures of such schools. Troels Engberg-Pedersen,[101] in *Paul and the Stoics*, makes an ill-advised step as he takes the two-step interpretative pattern: He initially and briefly attends to differences between Paul and ancient philosophy, then disproportionately ties superficial similarities between Paul and Stoicism to demonstrate Paul's indebtedness to the Stoic model.[102]

Two, as much as analyzing Paul in light of his cultural context is profitable and necessary, one must also recognize the complexity of thoughts, ritualistic practices, and philosophies that constituted the Greco-Roman world of Paul.[103] Agreeing with this view that Paul's world is complex, Johan Thom suggests that zooming into Paul's world exhibits the traces of "popular philosophy," hinting at his rhetorical training, as well as Paul's cultural connection to the intellectual world of his audience.[104]

Thom defines the term "popular philosophy" as those philosophical thoughts prevalent and available in the first-century in various cultural expressions.[105] A survey of the literature, including Cynic and Stoic philosophy, characterizes the popular philosophy. "Bion of Borysthenes, Teles, C. Musonius Rufus, Seneca, Epictetus, Dion Chrysostom, Plutarchus, Maximus of Tyre, Libanius, Socrates and even Tertullianus" are some possible figures of the popular philosophy, but Thom proposes the Pythagorean work *Golden Verses*, the *Hymn to Zeus* by Cleanthes, and

---

98. Malherbe, *Light from the Gentiles*, 197.
99. Malherbe, *Light from the Gentiles*, 197.
100. Malherbe, *Light from the Gentiles*, 197–98.
101. Engberg-Pedersen, *Paul and the Stoics*.
102. Engberg-Pedersen, *Paul and the Stoics*, 103.
103. Wright, *Paul and the Faithfulness of God*, 246–58.
104. See Thom, "Paul and Popular Philosophy."
105. Thom, "Paul and Popular Philosophy," 49–56.

the Pseudo-Aristotelian treatise *On the Cosmos* as the better sample that presents Paul's interaction with the popular philosophy.[106]

In fact, N. T. Wright argues for this idea:

> Paul did not, then, derive his key ideas from his non-Jewish environment, but nor can his relationship with that environment be labeled simply 'confrontation.' It is far more subtle. He did not, indeed, take over his main themes from the worlds of non-Jewish politics, religions or philosophy, but nor did he march through those worlds resolutely looking the other way and regarding them as irrelevant. Nor did he say they were all completely wrong from top to bottom. When he says that all the treasures of wisdom and knowledge are hidden in the Messiah, he does not mean, as did some who believed that all truth was contained in the Bible, that one could throw all other books away . . . Paul began as a Jew and went out from there into the world of non-Jewish ideas, religions and political systems. He firmly believed that he was called to be the Apostle to the Gentiles; and, with that historical starting-point in mind, (Paul) in fact engaged with those aspects such as systems, practices, and ideas (in a variety of ways.)[107]

---

106. Thom, while denying the suggestion that Paul borrows from these philosophies, investigates which concepts and motifs of popular philosophies form the conceptual background of Paul. In short, Thom notices a cultural connection that exists between Paul and popular philosophies in the areas of cosmological and theological topoi. Cosmological topoi paralleled between Paul and popular philosophy appears in Paul quoting Cleanthes, but also in the resemblance of Pseudo-Aristotle features with Rom 1:18–32. Pseudo-Aristotle in On the Cosmos stresses that the knowledge of God is "possible in principle for those who have been trained mentally to deduce from his actions in the cosmos who and what God is." This discussion of topoi illustrates how Paul's discussion of cosmological topoi could have functioned as a cultural point of contact, too. Furthermore, Thom continues by noting that "prepositional metaphysics" are visible not just in Stoicism but also in Cleanthes and Philo. Paul and popular philosophy both share God as the agent of creation, evidenced by similar language such as 'in' and 'through' and much more. He explains that "such formulations are also found in Peripatetic texts like On the Cosmos rather suggests that such formations formed part of the popular-philosophical cultural repertoire, and were thus available to be used by (Paul) as would suit his purpose." Certainly, determining the degree to which Paul was exposed to popular philosophy may be untenable. However, the possibility and the forging of cultural connection that Paul is able to establish becomes more justifiable as one considers how cultural points of contact concepts are readily accessible to Paul in the culture. Thom, "Paul and Popular Philosophy," 49.

107. Wright, *Paul and the Faithfulness of God*, 1407.

Paul's Use of Non-Canonical Quotes and Implications for Cultural Connection

Paul's use of non-canonical and traditional material demonstrates Paul's flexible and competent use of all types of resources, ranging from popularized and culturally accepted statements to the elements of natural theology. These appear as spots of cultural point of contact in Paul, and purposes in making cultural connections. As shown above, non-canonical quotes that Paul uses are popularized sayings that were familiarized in the world of that time. He employs the quotes to connect with his hearers, gain greater appeal, and ultimately to prove the truthfulness of his message.

Moreover, Paul's acquaintance with contemporaneous philosophy established a cultural point of contact with the audience as conversion in Greco-Roman culture was "usually defined in terms of reorientation of beliefs and behavior within the context of a supportive community— would be the often dramatic stories of conversion to philosophy."[108] The writings of Dio Chrysostom, Epictetus, and Musonius Rufus are a few of the "numerous examples of Stoic-Cynic preaching that aimed at producing deep conversion."[109] "Paul's context was first-century Greco-Roman society, a world filled with religious and philosophical ideas disseminated by philosophical giants . . . Paul's life and ministry were contextualized."[110]

Given this, it would be erroneous to dismiss Paul's use of non-canonical quotes as having no meaning or intentions. Clarence Glad reaffirms how this cultural connection can take place by introducing the concept of adaptation: "The idea of adaptability in the Greco-Roman world was common during Paul's time among different segments of society [and was] a concern of politicians, public speakers, philosophers, religious leaders, and even stage actors."[111] "Regardless of how we classify Paul, throughout his career, he was a leader who needed to be attentive to different aptitudes among his converts so that he could adapt his methods in a manner appropriate to their condition."[112]

---

108. Hubbard, *Christianity in the Greco-Roman World*, 92.
109. Hubbard, *Christianity in the Greco-Roman World*, 74.
110. Dodson and Briones, *Paul and the Giants of Philosophy*, 2.
111. Glad, "Paul and Adaptability," 17–36.
112. Glad, "Paul and Adaptability," 26.

CULTURAL CONNECTION THROUGH THE USE OF GRECO-ROMAN RHETORIC

Having investigated Paul's cultural connection through the cultural point of contact, I now turn to assess Paul's model of cultural connection via enculturated communication. Expressed differently, it is an inquiry into how else Paul engaged with the culture. I suggest that Paul established connection with the culture not only through the use of non-canonical quotes, but also through what I will call enculturated communication.

Enculturated communication is not simply a use of translation. Rather, it is a process that aims to speak in a way that relates to the cultural and social setting in which communication is carried out. Cross-culturally, it connotes that those engaged in culturally effective communication would discover "symbols and cultural forms that people being ministered to would understand and appreciate to express their new faith."[113] This also means that communication takes place in a way that hearers are able to process on their terms; ensuring that communication establishes both connections and clarity.[114]

Thus, I now aim to decode the heart of Paul's method of communication. As stated above, cultural connection through culturally appropriate communication is not concerned with the use of correct translation or language. In fact, it is needless to discuss what language Paul and his hearers spoke because such a question does not generate disagreements among scholars.[115] The greater issue at hand is not one of linguistic nature; instead, it is a matter of cultural relevance.

When one wishes to investigate how Paul communicated in his cultural context, two routes are available. The first is to approach it through his epistles.[116] This approach allows one to delve into Paul's letters with an

---

113. Hiebert and Meneses, *Incarnational Ministry*.

114. Jones, "Moving from Cross-Cultural to Intercultural Collaboration in Missions," 57–61.

115. Stanley Porter argues that the opinion is universal, but cites one exceptional episode. He notes that even though Greek was the *lingua franca* of the Roman Empire in the first century, there is an incident in Lystra that seems to have confronted Paul with communication issues during his missionary trips. He proposes that Paul and Barnabas "came in contact with those who spoke one of the local languages, probably one of the new Anatolian languages." Porter, "The Language That Paul Did Not Speak," 131–49.

116. Despite the unanimity of opinions on the issue of Paul's language, countless debates have been waged concerning how much rhetoric should be attributed to Paul. Scholars also have widely ranging opinions concerning rhetoric found in Paul's epistles.

aim to detect signs and hints of rhetorical features.[117] The second way is to reconstruct Paul through Lukan narrative.[118] This approach identifies Luke's portrayal of Paul as illumined by the literary unity and socio-cultural setting.

The route I will take on this book is the latter. Since the central thrust of my exploration aligns with apologetics, such a course better suits the purpose. In fact, speeches attributed to Paul in Acts stand out as the best specimen in reconstructing Paul and his cultural context in association with his apologetics.[119] Thus, in the following, I will inspect Paul's apologetics speeches in Acts, rather than his letters, to deduce ideas concerning the kinds of culturally contextualized communication the speeches reveal. Through it, I argue that speeches attributed to Paul model enculturated communication. This is demonstrated by first dealing with the significance of Greco-Roman rhetoric in the culture as one considers the effect it has on audience reception. I will also highlight the status of the oratory genre and speeches in the Greco-Roman culture and suggest that Paul's speeches are constructed to demonstrate faithfulness to this genre. Through these discussions, I will conclude that Paul employed enculturated communication via Greco-Roman rhetoric, thus producing cultural connection. First, I turn to the significance of Greco-Roman rhetoric in culture.

Some argue that his letters are imbued with Greco-Roman rhetoric, while others simply label Paul not as a rhetorician but as an epistolographer. To be exact, a judgment regarding the degree in which Paul was either a rhetorician or an epistolographer is beyond the scope of this book. Hence, the focus of this book will be on the use of Greco-Roman rhetoric in speeches attributed to Paul in Acts.

117. Porter's analysis of Pauline epistles as it relates to ancient rhetoric is comprehensive and engaging. See Porter, *Paul and Ancient Rhetoric: Theory and Practice in the Hellenistic Context*.

118. Neyrey, *The Social World of Luke-Acts*; Tannehill, *The Narrative Unity of Luke-Acts*; Talbert, *Perspectives on Luke-Acts*; Meeks, *The First Urban Christians*; Kuhn, *The Kingdom According to Luke and Acts*.

119. Though it is true that Luke is the author of the book of Acts, there is not a significant reason to cast doubts on the accuracy and authenticity of Paul's speeches. For instance, in the treatment of Paul's Areopagus speech, Eckhard J. Schnabel explains, "Orators who were invited by the magistrates of a city to demonstrate their rhetorical abilities and their philosophical orientation usually gave a day's notice to prepare their declamation on a predetermined topic. They would compose the declamation, write it down, memorize it, and present it without reliance on notes to the audience. Since such declamations were often copied and circulated in the city in the early imperial period, it is not impossible that the speech of 17:22–31 is the summary of a written source." Schnabel, *Acts*, 720.

The Significance of Greco-Roman Rhetoric in Culture

Through his seminal work, *Light from the Ancient East: The New Testament Illustrated by Recently Discovered Texts of the Greco-Roman World*, Adolf Deissmann has drawn attention to the close correlation between social class and literary culture.[120] As he discusses the historical, social, and cultural background of "primitive Christianity," he points out that literary sources "fairly well acquaint" the reader with the ancient city-life, while the ancient villages and small countries are "seldom touched upon in the literature."[121] Yet, the discovery of new texts from the Greco-Roman world through papyri shows that "for the most part, the pages of our sacred Book are so many records of popular Greek, in its various grades; taken as a whole the New Testament is a Book of the people."[122]

Modifying Deissmann's assessment, Malherbe notes that scholars have not only recognized that Deissmann's samples are limited, but also that New Testament writings carry a variety of connections with the Greco-Roman literature, demonstrating varying levels of social status as revealed through the literature of this time.[123] That includes allusions to the classics such as those found in Paul's use of the non-canonical quotes, providing a bigger sample than Deissmann's.[124] Malherbe argues that an array of literary forms points to the presence of those who both "express high appreciation of the art of persuasion, rhetorical ability, and interest in the art."[125] Literary forms and types suggest interactive relationship the New Testament world shared with the culture.

In addition, Stanley Porter observes that the Greco-Roman world of the first century was one of the first cultures that enjoyed a multilingual setting with an increasing abundance of written literacy.[126] What relationship does ancient literate culture and its cultural environment have with Paul? Porter introduces three different views regarding this issue.[127] The

---

120. See Deissmann, *Light from the Ancient East*.
121. Deissmann, *Light from the Ancient East*, 264–65.
122. Deissmann, *Light from the Ancient East*, 143.
123. Malherbe, *Light from the Gentiles*, 92–95.
124. Malherbe, *Light from the Gentiles*, 92–94.
125. Malherbe, *Light from the Gentiles*, 104.
126. Porter, "Ancient Literate Culture and Popular Rhetorical Knowledge."
127. Porter's classification is helpful in sorting through various approaches taken by scholars concerning Paul's association with philosophy. I agree that general approaches to assessing Paul in this regard fall into one of these categories.

first view sees rhetoric being so prevalent within the ancient culture that Paul was highly versed in it; the second view reasons that Paul was formally trained as a rhetor, similar to the Second Sophists; and the third view perceives Paul having no rhetorical training, but accompanied by a letter-writer who received grammatical education.[128]

Among these perspectives, Porter admits that it is impossible to construct an air-tight proof of one or another.[129] However, he concludes that since it is reasonable to find Paul as an "active member of this literature culture," it is also sensible to conclude that "Paul was rhetorically sophisticated in the sense that he seems to have grasped the persuasive possibilities of his language and its letters."[130]

Porter adds that this verdict is substantiated further when Paul's two certain sources for his communication are considered.[131] Firstly, it is the "apparent recognition that the Greek language has certain resources that are part of its structure that enable the author to structure his communication in such a way as to maximize its persuasive force." Secondly,

> [Paul] formulated his means of address of his audience in such a way as to ensure that he positioned himself in relation to them so that he could communicate his rhetorical intent, and he did not hesitate to provide various means of evaluative language that indicated not just his thoughts but feelings about the actions and words that he was conveying and to which he was responding.[132]

Hence, as revealed in the above discussion, Greco-Roman rhetoric possessed a unique place in the culture. Even though rhetoric, "defined in the strictest sense, is the art of persuasion as practiced by orators and described by theorists and teachers of speech," as George Kennedy explains, the Greco-Roman world understood rhetoric to be "extended to include the art of all who aim at some kind of attitude change on the part of their audience or readers."[133] While one of the "concrete manifestations" of rhetoric is oratory, other literary forms and speeches that were re-worded before or after the actual speaking event share techniques of oratory and are

---

128. Porter and Dyer, "Ancient Literate Culture and Popular Rhetorical Knowledge," 105.
129. Porter and Dyer, "Ancient Literate Culture and Popular Rhetorical Knowledge," 107.
130. Porter and Dyer, "Ancient Literate Culture and Popular Rhetorical Knowledge," 108.
131. Porter and Dyer, "Ancient Literate Culture and Popular Rhetorical Knowledge," 108.
132. Porter and Dyer, "Ancient Literate Culture and Popular Rhetorical Knowledge," 108.
133. Kennedy, *The Art of Rhetoric in the Roman World*, 3.

categorized as rhetoric in the cultural setting of the Greco-Roman world, in so far as they aim at persuasion or attitude change.[134]

Consequently, Greco-Roman rhetoric functioned as one of the most important modes of communication. There was a growing appreciation for eloquence, making way for growing desire for formal training for rhetoric.[135] Greco-Roman rhetoric's underlying art involved moving the audience to a "predetermined purpose," considering a successful persuasion a victory.[136] Thus, ancient Greeks were heavily drawn to the power of the spoken word. Duane Litfin writes,

> Oratory carried a strong dramatic appeal to the ancient Greeks. For a people who had been nursed on heroic figures single-handedly facing fearsome challenges, the drama of oratory was immensely attractive. The earlier Greeks would have had little stomach for the gore of the later Roman gladiators, but they would surely have understood their dramatic appeal. For the Greeks this appeal was embodied in oratory: the challenge laid down and not to be escaped, the lone figure rises to the occasion, a hush falls over the audience. The suspense, the anticipation, the delight of watching the speaker succeed through the astonishing brilliance of his words and ideas—it was a drama more or less reenacted on each new occasion. Moreover, it was not a drama of long ago and far away in which the audience participated vicariously; it was here and now, and they were directly playing their crucial part. It was only to be expected that they thrived on eloquence and submitted themselves willingly to the sway of orators.[137]

Thus, Greco-Roman rhetoric was one of the most important modes of mutual communication between the speaker and the hearers. Litfin writes, "Rhetoric, then, played both a powerful and pervasive role in first-century Greco-Roman society" a commodity both "produced and consumed" by all.[138] Rhetoric also was believed to play an integral role in people's judgment and decision-making during this time.[139] In other words, Greco-Roman rhetoric was not only a main form of communication but also was the very

---

134. Kennedy, *The Art of Rhetoric in the Roman World*, 3–5.
135. Litfin, *Paul's Theology of Preaching*, 28.
136. Litfin, *Paul's Theology of Preaching*, 70–71.
137. Litfin, *Paul's Theology of Preaching*, 75.
138. Litfin, *Paul's Theology of Preaching*, 112.
139. Litfin, *Paul's Theology of Preaching*, 82.

means by which people sought out both to form their beliefs and have their beliefs shaped through eloquence.

Along this line, Frank Hughes writes,

> It is clear from the study of the history of Greek rhetoric and its appropriation and development in Roman rhetoric that the elements of rhetoric were part of the culture that Paul lived in, that Paul was very possibly trained in rhetoric, and that several if not most of Paul's congregation were familiar with it. Rhetoric was present in Hellenistic culture, perhaps not every element in every city or school, but it was part of the culture of the cities of the early Roman Empire . . . so the issue is not whether Paul could have used rhetoric, but whether or not he would have wanted to do so.[140]

The Art of Greco-Roman Persuasion and Audience Reception

About the Greco-Roman world in which Paul ministered, Litfin says, "performance and delivery was arguably so inextricably linked that they were even synonymous, with both involving all aspects of how a speech was given to, and especially received by, its audience."[141] Audience reception could potentially determine the success or end of one's career as an orator.[142] Thus, it was customary for speakers to utilize "multiple means of delivery that was used to exploit their audience's reaction in the court of the Assembly for the optimum rhetorical effect."[143]

For this reason, "rhetoric monopolized secondary education and in this period the crest was probably reached in the number of students trained in declamation and in the influence of rhetorical study on literary composition."[144] In the first century, "the ideal orator continued to be an inspiration and a goal for thousands."[145] Eloquence could potentially "raise an orator to the heights and bestow on him every benefit of society."[146]

---

140. Hughes, "Paul and Traditions of Greco-Roman Rhetoric," 92.
141. Worthington, *Aspects of Performance*, 12.
142. Worthington, *Aspects of Performance*, 13.
143. Worthington, *Aspects of Performance*, 13.
144. Kennedy, *The Art of Rhetoric in the Roman World*, 428.
145. Kennedy, *The Art of Rhetoric in the Roman World*, 428.
146. Litfin, *Paul's Theology of Preaching*, 109.

Yet it was up to the audience to decide who or when an orator was successful, for they were the judge of eloquence.[147] According to Aristotle and Isocrates, "the identity of the audience shaped the rhetorical piece, and the opinion of the audience was key to the success of the speech."[148] Thus, the audience functioned as the final arbiter of Greco-Roman rhetoric oratory. Due to the role the audience's reception played in the rating of oratory's eloquence, "audiences were knowledgeable and eager to evaluate, to show their approval or disapproval."[149]

The audience of the Greco-Roman eventually became highly informed of the trade to a degree where it became a challenge for an orator to be discreet about rhetorical techniques.[150] "This is why so much attention was paid in ancient rhetorical literature to the mindset of the audience, to their belief systems, to their likes and dislikes, and to what will most likely win particular responses from them." Hence, understanding and consideration of audience reception was a critical aspect of culturally contextualized communication.

Going further than mere reception from the audience, Kathy Maxwell explains that ancient rhetors not only expected the audience to assess a persuasion but also were invited to participate.[151] Further, Maxwell cites evidence from rhetorical handbooks to indicate that a rhetor intentionally excluded some pieces from the persuasion, in order to facilitate audience participation.[152] She writes, "Part of the audience's responsibility was to supply information that the rhetor excluded. Of course, an accomplished rhetor would know the audience well enough to discern what that particular group knew or did not know."[153] Hence, audience reception and participation were essential part of Greco-Roman rhetoric.

---

147. Litfin, *Paul's Theology of Preaching*, 95.
148. Maxwell, "The Role of the Audience in Ancient Narrative: Acts as a Case Study," 171.
149. Litfin, *Paul's Theology of Preaching*, 98.
150. Litfin, *Paul's Theology of Preaching*, 100.
151. Maxwell, "The Role of the Audience in Ancient Narrative."
152. Maxwell, "The Role of the Audience in Ancient Narrative," 174–75.
153. Maxwell, "The Role of the Audience in Ancient Narrative," 180.

Aspects of Oratory and Speeches in Greco-Roman Rhetoric

In short, there is a role an audience plays in the entirety of speech through reception and participation; likewise, an orator has five tasks.[154] Eckhard Schnabel helpfully summarizes them:

> First, he has to find the relevant material, which includes arguments and proofs (*invention*). He collects the facts of the case (*materia*) and determines the nature of the case (*status*). Second, the orator composes the speech according to established rules (*disposition*). The speech begins with an introduction into the subject matter (*exordium*), which includes the effort to gain the interest of the audience (*attentum parare*) or even the goodwill of the audience (*captatio benevolentiae*). The next sections present the facts of the case as the basis of the following presentation (*narration*) and provides a review of the case and of the goals of the speech (*partition*). The central section of the speech contains the exposition of the case (*argumentation*), in which the orator presents the arguments for the case that he seeks to make (*probatio*) as well as the arguments that refute the case of the opposition (*refutation*). The speech finishes with a summation of the case and a direct or indirect charge or admonition (*conclusion* or *peroration*). Third, the orator formulates and writes down the speech (*elocutio*) using figures of speech such as rhetorical questions or irony, as well as appropriate tropes (metaphor, metonymy, hyperbole, allegory). Important qualities of rhetorical excellence are puritas (purity of expression), perspicuitas (*clarity*), aptum and decorum (appropriateness as regards the content and the goals of the speech), ornatus (ornamentation, embellishment), and brevitas (conciseness). Fourth, the orator memorizes the speech (*memoria*); reading a speech is regarded as inferior, a testimony to the ineptitude of the orator. Fifth, the orator presents the speech with appropriate modulation (*pronuntiatio*) and gestures (*actio*).[155]

Additionally, Heinrich Lausberg's magnum corpus *Handbook of Literary Rhetoric: A Foundation for Literary Study* explains that *argumentatio*, "the central, decisive part of the speech" is followed up by "at least one proof, but generally several proofs." These proofs in oratory are supported by two types of proofs: first, the inartificial proofs (*genus inartificiale probationum*), which presents argument without the help of rhetoric

---

154. Schnabel, *Paul the Missionary*.
155. Schnabel, *Paul the Missionary*, 344–45.

devices (through written or oral eyewitness statements and past decisions of the courts); and second, the artificial proofs or factual arguments (*genus artificiale probationum*), which are proofs deduced from the subject matter by rhetorical means with the help of intellectual reflection.[156]

The first type of artificial proof is *ethos*. Ethos seeks to gain a hearing by demonstrating that the orator is worthy of trust. Character, credibility, and relatability of the audience to the speaker are the factors that achieve the success of this proof. The second type is the *pathos*. The orator appeals to the audience's feelings or emotions strategically to win the hearers. The third type of artificial proof is *apodeixis*. This is a technique that aims to prove what is not certain by referring to what is certain or logical arguments. It is also referred to as the *logos* aspect of an argument.[157] These components are specifics to the oratory genre in Greco-Roman rhetoric.

Greco-Roman Rhetoric and Paul's Speeches

Ryan Carhart argues that Paul's *modus operandi* in Acts is to go to the synagogues of whichever city he enters and publicly engage in oratory or give speeches to the pagan audience.[158] Paul rhetorically reconfigures Israelite history to proclaim and also reason that Jesus is the fulfillment of Jewish expectations. In this ministry, Carhart claims that "Acts consistently presents Paul as an effective orator, either persuading his audience or riling them up with the content of his speeches." Paul's rhetorical prowess always generates a response from his audience, as the book of Acts consistently presents Paul as an orator *par excellence*.[159] Daniel Marguerat reaffirms John Lentz's appraisal on Paul as being a top-class orator possessing high rhetorical skill: "Paul the orator is at ease in all situations, be it in front of the Sanhedrin (Acts 22), Athenian philosophers (Acts 17), Roman procurators or King Agrippa (Acts 26). This feature is essential to the philosopher."[160]

---

156. Lausberg et al., *Handbook of Literary Rhetoric*, 345–46.

157. Schnabel, *Paul the Missionary*, 346.

158. Carhart, "The Second Sophistic and the Cultural Idealization of Paul in Acts," 192–93.

159. Carhart, "The Second Sophistic and the Cultural Idealization of Paul in Acts," 193.

160. Marguerat, *Paul in Acts and Paul in His Letters*, 67.

Rhetorical Features in Paul's Speeches

Are there rhetorical features in Paul's apologetic speeches? It may be useful to evaluate and see whether Paul's speeches in Lystra, at Areopagus, before Felix and Agrippa to see if one can detect the use of Greco-Roman rhetoric.[161] The use of Greco-Roman rhetoric in re-telling of Paul's speeches will indicate culturally contextualized communication.

Daniel Bock observes that Paul's speech in Acts 13 begins by Paul's invoking a resemblance of an orator. The speech itself "reflects a structure easily recognized by an audience familiar with conventions of ancient rhetoric."[162] He sees *exordium*, a brief comment to establish rapport and favor with the audience in Acts 13:16b and Acts 13:17–25 containing *narratio*, or a narration of history and statement of facts, *probatio* in Acts 13:26 in which the orator states a proposition, followed by *peroratio*, or an epilogue.[163] Bock explains that this division follows that of Quintilian.

Paul's speech at Areopagus reveals even greater clarity in this regard. The four identical rhetorical elements found in Acts 13 re-appear in the Acts 17 speech. Pervo also sees *exordium*, *propositio*, *probatio*, and *peroratio* in Acts speeches, which is in agreement with Dean Zweck.[164] Going further, Pervo asserts that Paul's speech before Agrippa features an unusual complexity. Paul's "style is relatively elevated here, in addition to the familiar alliteration, assonance, and rhyme, paronomasia, and effective repetition, and two optatives,"[165] indicating specific use of the rhetorical technique. Ben Witherington too confirms the use of Greco-Roman rhetoric as he states that this was to persuade his audience.[166]

Turning to Acts 24 and 26, Derek Hogan compares Paul's trial speeches, namely the one before Felix and the one before Agrippa, with two forensic speeches in ancient novels. He first introduces Quintilian's *Institutio Oratoria* as a point of reference, for this work is written in the first century, having the closest temporal proximity to the speeches in Acts and also because it features one of the longest and most detailed discussions

---

161. I will treat the selection of apologetics speeches in fuller detail in chapter 4 of this book.
162. Bock, *Acts*, 191.
163. Bock, *Acts*, 191.
164. Pervo and Attridge, *Acts*, 432.
165. Pervo and Attridge, *Acts*, 432.
166. Witherington, *The Acts of the Apostles*, 514.

of forensic speeches.[167] Quintilian provides the manual that offers a typical form of a forensic speech by dividing it into five parts: the *exordium* (introduction), *narratio* (statement of facts), *probatio* (proof), *refutatio* (refutation), and *peroratio* (conclusion). Hogan sees this to be a "common pattern although not universal among manuals."[168]

The two forensic speeches from the ancient literature that Hogan samples are Chariton's *Callirhoe* and Achilles Tatius's *Leucippe and Clitopho*. Upon evaluation, Hogan observes that Chariton's *Callirhoe* closely follow the rhetorical pattern set by Quintilian's model of forensic speeches, even though the length is shorter in the novel than what would have been written in real life.[169] On the other hand, speeches in Achilles Tatius's *Leucippe and Clitopho* "do not manifest reliance on the standard divisions given by Quintilian."[170] Hogan clarifies that this distinction is best explained by the temporal distinction—Chariton writing in the first century, whereas Achilles Tatius writing in the second-century after Second Sophistic emergence.

Moreover, this distinction implies that not all forensic speeches feature the same rhetorical technique. Yet, what becomes clearer in light of such assessment is that speeches in Acts do indeed skillfully use the features of Greco-Roman rhetoric to convey a message. For that reason, Luke's inclusion and treatment of Tertullus's speech are striking. In Paul's speeches before Felix, Tertullus gives his own forensic speech to accuse Paul. Tertullus's speech is largely made up of *exordium* that flatters Felix, yet his speech does not include *probatio*. Hogan writes,

> For a reader who knows anything about the rules of rhetoric, the lack of a *probatio* is a very telling sign. In this construction of Tertullus's speech, the writer of Acts may be signaling the weakness of the case against Paul. Tertullus would not omit proof unless he absolutely could not provide any. He seems unable even to fabricate any plausible evidence . . . The writer of Acts presents Tertullus a capable rhetor who has undertaken an impossible case. Later, unnamed Jews will have the same trouble when they make serious charges, but can offer no proof.[171]

---

167. Hogan, "Paul's Defense," 73–87.
168. Hogan, "Paul's Defense," 73.
169. Hogan, "Paul's Defense," 78.
170. Hogan, "Paul's Defense," 79.
171. Hogan, "Paul's Defense," 81.

As shown, a rhetorical feature is used to communicate a point in this speech. Yet another remarkable rhetorical feature appears and demonstrates this aspect of rhetorical communication. Paul next engages in skillful *narratio*, he proceeds to his *probatio*. Then, before Paul can continue with *peroratio*, Felix interrupts Paul. Hogan affirms that of the ten longest speeches in Acts, eight are either interrupted or concluded with a statement that the speaker had more to say. Hogan also introduces G. H. R. Horsley who argues that this technique was used by the writer of Acts to compensate for the brevity of the speeches given.[172]

However, alternatively, a number of scholars have weighed in on these interruptions to account for more than just brevity. Joshua Garroway contends that these interruptions are Luke's attempts to present speakers like Peter, Stephen, and Paul as "unassailable," not allowing the narrative to conclude with "scenes before opposing characters have been given the opportunity to formulate competing for remarks" because of Jesus's words in Luke 21:12–15 that promised that he would provide irrefutable words and wisdom in the future.[173] Dibelius argues that these frequent interruptions of speeches are designed to highlight the significance of the claim made just prior to the interruption, "in order to let the speech end at this important point and so to emphasize the meaning of the final words," citing parallels to ancient literature.[174] Similarly, Daniel Lynwood Smith argues that these interruptions are a "powerful literary and rhetorical device" that "serves to underscore the powerful impact of early Christian preaching," heightening the reception of the message.[175] Maxwell also notes that "incomplete, or abbreviated rhetorical elements in Acts" alludes to audience's participatory role.[176]

Undeniably, rhetoric was part of the culture of Paul's time. Frank W. Hughes points out that while not everyone may have been trained or skilled in rhetoric, yet Paul demonstrates eloquence as he sees fit. Hughes introduces Augustine's appraisal of Paul's rhetoric.

> Augustine's mentioning of the joining of *sapientia* (wisdom) and *eloquentia* (eloquence) not just once but twice, in reference to Paul's written work, speaks volumes about how a professional

---

172. Hogan, "Paul's Defense," 83.
173. Garroway, "'Apostolic Irresistibility' and the Interrupted Speeches in Acts," 738.
174. Dibelius, *Studies in the Acts of the Apostles*, 161.
175. Smith, "Interrupted Speech in Luke-Acts," 177–91.
176. Maxwell, "The Role of the Audience in Ancient Narrative," 180.

rhetorician in the fifth century evaluated the rhetoric of the apostle Paul.[177]

Paul intentionally employed Greco-Roman rhetoric to elevate his effect in his speeches. This illustrates his attempt to carry out culturally effective communication. Culturally effective communication produces a cultural connection, and fuels culturally contextualized apologetics.

Paul's Use of Greco-Roman Rhetoric in Speeches and Implications for Cultural Connection

Paul's speeches are laden with rhetorical devices. Rhetorical devices are present to communicate in a way that will convey meanings that will be illumined fuller because of cultural understanding. Communication that is taking place in the context of a cultural convention is rightly labeled enculturated communication. This is a communication method that optimizes symbols and forms that hearers know and appreciate. If this is so, then Paul is modeling enculturated communication and enculturated communication establishes a cultural connection with his audience.

CONCLUSION

Having observed Paul's use of non-canonical quotes and his use of Greco-Roman rhetoric, I conclude that Paul establishes cultural connection through his use of non-canonical quotes as a part of cultural points of contact. His enculturated communication appears in the form of Greco-Roman rhetoric. Establishment of cultural point of contact and enculturated communication help form a cultural connection. Therefore, Paul models a cultural connection. If this is so, how did Paul's culture process his communication? We explore Paul's cultural solidarity next.

---

177. Hughes, "Paul and Traditions of Greco-Roman Rhetoric," 86–87.

Chapter 3

Paul's Cultural Connection through Cultural Solidarity as the Wisdom Figure

IF PAUL EMPLOYED A CULTURAL POINT of contact and enculturated communication to establish connection to the culture, how did his culture connect to him? In other words, how did Paul's audience interpret his identity and role in light of their cultural context? In this chapter, I argue that Paul's cultural connection with his audience takes place through the development of cultural solidarity. Cultural solidarity, I argue, is developed through Paul presenting himself as a culturally identifiable figure.

Why does Paul's cultural connection merit research? Frances Young offers one of the answers to that question in *Biblical Exegesis and the Formation of Christian Culture*.[1] First challenging the eminence that the historical-critical approach has had in modern scholarship, Young asserts that we must retrace the way the Early Church community "received and appropriated" the bible, embracing "theology, praxis, and spirituality" in biblical interpretations that are often separated from the scholarship.[2] As

---

1. Young, *Biblical Exegesis and the Formation of Christian Culture*.

2. Young emphasizes that the role of receiving and appropriating the Scripture through "public community traditions embodied in liturgy." Young recognizes that such public community functioned as the key mode of reception: public reading and teaching. This ensured that the Word was heard in a context which produced reception in a meaningful way. Young, *Biblical Exegesis and the Formation of Christian Culture*, 3–4.

Young explicates the approach to the biblical interpretation of the immediate generation after the apostles, she argues,

> The scriptures came to be treated as an alternative body of literature, to be subjected to the same scholarly examination as the Greek classics, and to replace those classics in providing authoritative examples, quotations, and allusions for exploitation by Christian orators. Christian culture mirrored classical culture, but its discourse was formed by reference to another set of texts and stories—a novel intertextuality.[3]

Thus, Young advocates a need to retrace the Early Church's approach to biblical interpretation which does not neglect cultural connection.[4] Along this line, Gerd Thiessen also argues for the importance of a sociological perspective in interpreting the Scripture.[5] He is not alone in advancing the value of taking historical and cultural factors into the equation.[6] Hence, I too seek to investigate the way Paul was received and appropriated to the community and draw out the significance of such exploration.[7]

Paul's socio-cultural context greatly differs from that of early Jewish Christianity in rural parts of Palestine, and Paul's audience in the first-century Greco-Roman world had varying opinions on the newly "founded" Christian faith.[8] Some were hostile, some believed Christians were inferior

---

3. Young, *Biblical Exegesis and the Formation of Christian Culture*, 47.

4. Young also concludes that the aim of biblical interpretation was the formation of a new Christian culture, "a totalizing discourse."

5. Thiessen's first book, *Sociology of Early Palestinian Christianity*, takes the same approach. He interprets the development of the Jesus movement under the lens of two social roles in the movement: itinerant preachers and settled hearers. His next book that compiled his essays deals with Paul as his ministry is juxtaposed against the Jesus movement. See Theissen, *The Social Setting of Pauline Christianity*.

6. As listed in the introduction, Adolf Deissmann, Shirley Jackson Case, Abraham Malherbe, and more recently John Gager are among those who favor this approach.

7. Young writes, "The purpose of biblical exegesis, implicit and explicit, was to form the practice and belief of Christian people, individually and collectively. In so far as there was contention about belief or practice, the Bible was at the heart of the debate. But its most important contribution was that it provided a literature which shaped Christian discourse and fed the Christian imagination." Young, *Biblical Exegesis and the Formation of Christian Culture*, 299.

8. See Case, *The Social Origins of Christianity*; Harnack, *The Mission and Expansion of Christianity in the First Three Centuries*; MacMullen, *Christianizing the Roman Empire (A.D. 100--400)*; Meeks, *The First Urban Christians: The Social World of the Apostle Paul*; Troeltsch and Wyon, *The Social Teaching of the Christian Churches*; Kautsky, *Foundations of Christianity*.

to pagan philosophers, and some were confused.[9] Thus, the apostle had to present himself in a way that gains hearing through the framework of mind familiar to the Greco-Roman audience. As Judith Lieu points out, "awareness of sameness and difference, of a shared past and agreed values, of continuities and of boundaries, whether physical or behavioral, were all present, either implicitly or explicitly, as Greeks and Romans viewed themselves and others."[10] The same applied to the identity formation of Christians in Paul's world.[11] "More pertinently, the Christian rhetoric of identity, even when making universalist claims, is articulated in the terms also used in Greco-Roman ethnography and identity formulation."[12]

Then how did Paul accomplish this? This chapter contends that cultural solidarity is formed with his audience as Paul is depicted as a wisdom figure. It is also argued that due to the roles that wisdom figures played in promulgating new ideas and effectively persuading the audience, Paul's perception as such a figure is critical in making cultural connection with the audience. This chapter shows that before the Gentile audience, Paul appears as a philosopher-like figure—just like the rest of those who philosophized when introducing new philosophy or teachings. For the believers, Paul is a sage-like figure whose suffering provides the legitimacy and authentication of his status, without which would not have gained Paul reception or credibility. Through relatability and authority, Paul makes the necessary cultural connection with the audience to culturally contextualize the vindication of the gospel.

In fact, Ben Witherington asks whether one can categorize Paul as a sage or sophist. He observes that wisdom tradition has long been part of Jewish lives; though Jesus's wisdom treads new ground with revelatory wisdom.[13] He claims that "there is some important evidence that Paul not only self-consciously drew on Wisdom material in various ways, but also sometimes, when the occasion warranted it, presented himself as a

---

9. Wilken, *The Christians as the Romans Saw Them*. Wilken argues that the polemics against the Christians in the early days help fortify Christian identity. He discusses five well-known early critics of Christianity, namely, Pliny; Galen, the second-century Greek physician and scientist; Celsus; Porphyry; and Julian the Apostate.

10. Lieu, *Christian Identity in the Jewish and Graeco-Roman World*, 17.

11. Lieu, *Christian Identity in the Jewish and Graeco-Roman World*, 20.

12. Lieu, *Christian Identity in the Jewish and Graeco-Roman World*, 20.

13. Witherington, *Jesus the Sage*. Witherington articulates the source, the personification, and revelation.

prophetic sage."[14] However, Witherington's verdict is derived through his analysis of Paul's letters to Corinthians and Romans only and does not attempt to view it through his speech activities, as this chapter aims to show. Moreover, I explore Paul's potential perception as a philosopher and what cultural significance it may have had on the audience.

Based on this, in order to show Paul's cultural solidarity formation as a wisdom figure, a chronological survey of the various roles that sages and philosophers played as a wisdom figure played in the cultural context during Paul's era will be profitable. Consequently, the analysis of Paul's tribulation list, known as the *peristasenkataloge*, will further verify how his such list solidifies Paul's status as the wisdom figure. I now turn to the cultural understanding of sages first.

PAUL AS A WISDOM FIGURE IN GRECO-ROMAN CONTEXT

Emergence of Sage

Sages played a significant role all throughout the Hellenistic and Greco-Roman era.[15] The rising influence and function of the sage became meaningful not only in Greek culture but also in Jewish Antiquity as well.[16] Solomon, Job, and writers of Ecclesiastes and *Qoheleth* have also been categorized as sages.[17] Sophistic movement, Stoics, and philosophers too have also received such classification.[18] Thus, sages were not uncommon figures in both Jewish and Hellenistic culture.

"The term *hakam* means wise, *hokmah* wisdom, but these are not by any manes technical terms for a specific kind of information or literature."[19] Similarly, "the term 'sage' can have multiple meanings depending on the context;" it has multilateral usage across the Greek and Jewish, as well as

---

14. Witherington clarifies that this is not the chief way Paul identified himself; the apostolic calling came first. However, his analysis demonstrates ample evidence of Paul operating as a prophetic sage like unto a Ben Sira or the author of the Wisdom of Solomon in various ways. Witherington, *Jesus the Sage*, 296.

15. Perdue, *Scribes, Sages, and Seers*.

16. Uusimäki, "The Rise of the Sage in Greek and Jewish Antiquity," 1–29.

17. Blenkinsopp, *Sage, Priest, Prophet: Religious and Intellectual Leadership in Ancient Israel*.

18. Brouwer, *The Stoic Sage*.

19. Witherington, *Jesus the Sage*, 4.

Mediterranean culture.[20] Equally multilayered is the development of the social status of the wise in the Ancient Near East and the Greek culture.[21] Elisa Uusimäki persuasively argues that this idealized wisdom figure, a sage, is first conceptualized in the classical Greek world, but cultural collaboration in the Greco-Roman world has resulted in the emergence of a myriad of roles and images of a sage.[22] Hence, in the following, the term wisdom figure and sage will be used loosely and interchangeably. Now, to better grasp the general perception of wisdom figures in Paul's culture, a chronological survey is needed.

Sages in the Early Antiquity

From the Antiquity, more popular sages in the culture were seven sages of Greece, namely Thales of Miletus, Pittacus of Mytilene, Bias of Priene, Solon of Athens, Cleobulus of Lindus, Myson of Chen, and Chilon of Sparta.[23] Sages during in this culture functioned as poets, politicians, and performers.[24] Numerous illustrations and evidence present themselves to serve the fact that sages engaged in poetry, including those of Diogenes, Solon, and Thales, as well as other well-known sages of the Greek antiquity.[25] They were also highly involved in politics, and this is evidenced by the complex association with politics they underwent:

> Thales advised the Milesians not to ally themselves with Croesus, the king of Lydia . . . Solon was preeminently political . . . Like Solon, Pittakos laid down his office after a period of successful political organizing that included ordering the Mytilenean constitution. Chilon, as ephor, was involved in the political structure of Sparta. Periander was a tyrant. Bias is remembered by Herodotus as the one who proposed that Ionians band together and emigrate to

20. Uusimäki, "The Rise of the Sage in Greek and Jewish Antiquity," 2.

21. Perdue, *Scribes, Sages, and Seers*; G. B. Kerferd, *The Sophistic Movement*; Brouwer, *The Stoic Sage*.

22. Uusimäki does recognizes distinctives that are present in each culture. Uusimäki, "The Rise of the Sage in Greek and Jewish Antiquity."

23. Martin, "The Seven Sages as Performers of Wisdom," 108–28.

24. Martin illustrates these roles in his article.

25. Cavarnos, *The Seven Sages of Ancient Greece*; Reiner, "The Etiological Myth of the 'Seven Sages,'" 1–11; Stamatopoulou, "Hesiodic Poetry and Wisdom in Plutarch's Symposium of the Seven Sages," 533–58.

Sardinia. Thales also proposed Ionian federation at the Panionion, Herodotus notes.[26]

Among all the roles that sages played, the third role—a role as a performer comes to greater prominence for the current discussion. By performance, "it means a public enactment, about important matters, in word or gesture, employing conventions and open to scrutiny and criticism."[27] Multiple illustrations of a sage playing the role of a performer are found in ancient records: Thales rented all the oil mills and amassed a fortune in order to non-verbally demonstrate how easy it is to grow rich; Solon opened the graves of certain dead bodies to illustrate the victory of Salamis was by force alone not of right; Chilon and Pittacus "performed" deceitfully to eradicate their opponents.[28] As poets and performers, sages modeled by the Seven Sages of Greece communicated archaic wisdom not exclusively through verbal communications, but also through "gestural" and "ritual" involvement.[29]

Further Development

However, sage's roles begin to crystallize near Paul's time after the early Antiquity.[30] A few significant developments take place during this transitional period. Distinctions between wisdom, philosophy, sophists, and sage begin to take shape. Sophists are itinerant instructors who teach rhetoric, philosophers are paid professionally to teach wisdom, while the sage is further described as god-like, "righteous and holy and wise."[31] According to Greek tradition, sage maintains tranquility in all circumstances, someone to be emulated; in the Jewish tradition, not only are sages exemplary figures, but also responsible for the transmission of wisdom.[32] In Greek Jewish writing, sages are still the ones to be emulated, ones that embody

---

26. Martin, "The Seven Sages as Performers of Wisdom," 115.
27. Martin, "The Seven Sages as Performers of Wisdom," 115–16.
28. Martin, "The Seven Sages as Performers of Wisdom," 112–19.
29. Martin, "The Seven Sages as Performers of Wisdom," 119.
30. Uusimäki, "The Rise of the Sage in Greek and Jewish Antiquity," 4.
31. Uusimäki, "The Rise of the Sage in Greek and Jewish Antiquity," 4.
32. Uusimäki, "The Rise of the Sage in Greek and Jewish Antiquity," 11–14.

wisdom, and personification of virtuous living, all signaling changes in perception of sages throughout the cultural context of different periods.[33]

Sages as Philosophers

Prior to the death of Socrates in 399 B.C., Greek communities usually considered sages or wise men as those who possessed special talents; however, the proximity in which people accessed these wise men became more integrated into the society.[34] "The designation sage or wise man (*Sophos*) applied first and foremost to the philosopher."[35] This change affected the way people perceived sages in culture leading up to the New Testament era: first of these changes was the opportunity to teach at a higher level, often through institutionalized education in schools such as the Academy, the Lyceum, and other rhetorical schools.[36] "The concept of the philosopher who is the wise man is henceforward closely allied with the concept of the philosopher as a completely rational thinker."[37] Secondly, wise men again began to be identified as the ideal man—sages are thus not only philosophers with rationality but someone who functions as the ideal prototype of a human being.[38]

These characteristics of sages became dominant in both Stoicism and Epicureanism.[39] For Stoics, a wise man was the desired status, marked by the capability to carry out truly right actions, appropriate actions, along with a full understanding of what is it that makes them right; Epicureans, on the other hand, considered pleasure as the highest good, serving as the standard by which one judges everything that is good. For all Epicureans, "the ideal of the wise person was, of course, that of the ideal Epicurean

---

33. Uusimäki, "The Rise of the Sage in Greek and Jewish Antiquity," 15–17. Uusimäki does discuss variations in semantics, but basic notion of a wisdom figure remains the same.

34. Kerferd, "The Sage in Hellenistic Philosophical Literature (399 BCE-199 CE)," 319.

35. Gammie, "The Sage in Hellenistic Royal Courts," 149.

36. Kerferd, "The Sage in Hellenistic Philosophical Literature," 319.

37. Kerferd, "The Sage in Hellenistic Philosophical Literature," 320.

38. Kerferd, "The Sage in Hellenistic Philosophical Literature," 320.

39. Kerferd, "The Sage in Hellenistic Philosophical Literature," 321–23.

philosopher, and all later members of the school regarded this ideal as embodied above all in Epicurus himself."[40]

Sages in Hellenistic Courts

Now in Paul's time, it is important to note that sages possessed their unique places in Hellenistic royal courts. Royal courts served as a cultural center for kings.[41] It was a normative cultural custom that kings would attract leading philosophers, sculptors, painters, poets, philologists, physicians, natural scientists, historians, geographers, and mathematicians to the royal courts as tutors for their sons and librarians.[42] Among those, it was sages that engaged in philosophy before the kings. To illustrate:

> Diogenes Laertius records Theophrastus, the successor to Aristotle at the Lyceum, being invited to the royal court in Alexandria at the invitation of Ptolemy I Soter. Zeno, the founder of the Stoics, received an invitation to Antigonus II Gonatas, though he ended up sending two of his pupils, Persaeus of Citium and Philonides of Thebes. Epicureans too took place in Hellenistic courts. For instance, Philonides of Laodicea enjoyed the favor and earned hearings of Antiochus IV Epiphanes and Alexander Balas, whom also appealed before Demetrius for the freedom of his city.[43]

Moreover, these kings assembled what historians from antiquity labeled "friends" and "counselors" from wise sages.[44] Some of these are Demetrius of Phalerum who advised Ptolemy I, Sosibius who was labeled as "a friend of the king" and "highly influential adviser" of Ptolemy IV Philopator, and Agathocles, a partner with Sosibius.[45] Kings with their royal courts also included Jewish savants: Letter of Aristeas that covers the years between 187–192 records "the seventy-two young Jewish savants who utter wise apothegms in response to the king's queries on kingship, education,

---

40. Kerferd, "The Sage in Hellenistic Philosophical Literature," 321–23.
41. Gammie, "The Sage in Hellenistic Royal Courts," 148.
42. Gammie, "The Sage in Hellenistic Royal Courts," 148.
43. Gammie, "The Sage in Hellenistic Royal Courts," 148.
44. Gammie, "The Sage in Hellenistic Royal Courts," 151–52.
45. Gammie, "The Sage in Hellenistic Royal Courts," 152.

Cultural Solidarity as the Wisdom Figure

morality, and religion."⁴⁶ Kings philosophized and considered new ideas in their royal courts.⁴⁷

Sages as Central Figure in Religious and Philosophical Communication

In sum, sages, or those who functioned as sages or wise men, were perceived to embody the wisdom in their lives. But more importantly, they were seen as the transmitter of wisdom and virtuous living. As shown above, the role continued to uphold both exemplary and communicative functions over the years. Throughout the course of history, there was a presence of wisdom figures in the culture; at times sages were perceived as those who perform the wisdom, other times as the idealized figures, or an objection of emulation. Moreover, sages played the role of philosophers, and philosophers too were seen as sages. Sages were also expected to embody the wisdom. Culturally, sages communicated wisdom and truth before kings and emperors. These were the roles sages played during Paul's time.

Paul as Performer of Wisdom

If the sages had a distinctive role to play in royal courts as an orator, can Paul be attributed to playing that function? We now turn to Paul's ministry activities in Luke, particularly the Areopagus, the marketplace of philosophies, and royal courts. It will be demonstrated that Paul's public activities bear a striking resemblance to what a sage would perform in a given setting. Paul's audience then would have been able to make cultural associations with him.

Paul's Portrayal as a Philosopher

David Peterson observes that in the first century, the Council of the Areopagus functioned as "the effective government of Roman Athens and its chief court. As such, like the imperial Senate in Rome, it could interfere in any aspect of corporate life—education, philosophical lectures, public

---

46. Gammie, "The Sage in Hellenistic Royal Courts," 153.
47. Gammie, "The Sage in Hellenistic Royal Courts," 148.

morality, and foreign cults."⁴⁸ In short, Areopagus was a marketplace of ideas, also serving as a place of jurisdiction concerning religious and moral matters.⁴⁹ Paul walked into a place where contemporaneous wisdom figures, philosophers, and sages were gathering and exchanging ideas. Paul's presence in the Areopagus was sparked by the fact that they considered Paul to be a representative figure and a wisdom figure who would illumine other philosophers of the new teaching. "Areopagus was the very council before which such an effort to judge the introduction of new deity to be made, and there is evidence that this council functioned this way in the first century AD"⁵⁰

Paul's portrayal as a philosopher Ben Witherington echoes others when he writes, "the text seems to be presenting Paul as a new Socrates."⁵¹ Peterson, in agreement with Barnett, states, "Socrates, the archetypal philosopher of Athens, was always available for discussion with anyone willing to converse with him in the marketplace, and some have suggested that Luke intended an analogy with Socrates in his presentation of Paul's ministry here."⁵² The presence of philosophers such as Epicureans and Stoics added to Paul's perception as a "Socratic teacher" figure.⁵³ As shown, Paul carries out his speeches in Areopagus as any other sages would in that setting.

Beyond the significance of the location of Paul's activity, Daniel Marguerat proposes three reasons for the possibilities of seeing Paul as a Socratic figure: "the model of a moralist, an inspired man, or a witness for the truth in trail."⁵⁴ Marguerat inquires what would have prompted the first readers of Acts to identify the presence of the Socratic model in Acts. He discovers hints in Ephesus, Lystra, Athens, and the status of the Torah.⁵⁵

In Ephesus, Paul faces resistance and opposition from the Jews, leading him to change the location and set up a school. Marguerat does not see the depiction of the migration from a synagogue to school as an

---

48. Peterson, *The Acts of the Apostles*, 492.

49. Tino, "Paul's Greatest Missionary Sermon: A Lesson in Contextualization from Acts 17," 171.

50. Witherington, *The Acts of the Apostles*, 517.

51. Witherington, *The Acts of the Apostles*, 514.

52. Peterson, *The Acts of the Apostles*, 489–90.

53. Charles, "Engaging the (Neo) Pagan Mind," 47.

54. Marguerat, *Paul in Acts and Paul in His Letters*, 66–77.

55. Marguerat, *Paul in Acts and Paul in His Letters*, 66.

Cultural Solidarity as the Wisdom Figure

accidental detail.⁵⁶ In this episode found in Acts 13, he finds evidence of Paul's sage-like representation from the fact that a) a process of geographical separation from the synagogue is unfolding; b) the school vocabulary is strengthened by the triple mention of the term; c) the distinctive label of the Christian faith as the "Way" suddenly appears here; and d) the teaching provided in the school gathers a universal audience, namely Jewish and the Greeks. All of these signal a major shift and sets up Paul's identity on par as those philosophers running a school, inspiring teaching and exchanges, on the level of Greek philosophers.⁵⁷

In Lystra, Marguerat believes that the line of argument on divine transcendence, as well as divine accommodation to grant human happiness is "a motif that the first readers of Acts could connect to Socratic discourses."⁵⁸ Divine transcendence related to human happiness is the very characteristic of sages described earlier.

Marguerat's assessment continues with Paul's activity in Athens. He notes that 1) Socratic strategy aims at unmasking false scholars and forcing them to admit their ignorance; 2) the motif of divine mission; 3) Socratic rhetorical strategy, even though Paul's speech is cut off short, all evidence Paul's representation of wisdom figure.⁵⁹

Finally, as the last evidence of Paul's portrayal as the wisdom figure, Margeurat writes,

> It is understandable why Luke, in spite of his sharp and fierce picture of the 'Jews,' portrayed as enemies of Christians, ready with any misdemeanor to harm them, does not hide his admiration for the antiquity of the Law, for the piety of Israel and the importance of its ethical values. Attachment to the Law is thus given an identifying function. What is at stake is apologetic: by guaranteeing the Jewish cultural and historical treasure its survival in the Christian community, Luke wants to avoid that the new Christianity be accused of *superstitio nova ac malefica* (new, immature superstition). For Christianity, breaking with the Law runs the risk of looking like a religion without tradition, without a past—hence not legitimate.⁶⁰

---

56. Marguerat, *Paul in Acts and Paul in His Letters*, 67.
57. Marguerat, *Paul in Acts and Paul in His Letters*, 67–68.
58. Marguerat, *Paul in Acts and Paul in His Letters*, 69–70.
59. Marguerat, *Paul in Acts and Paul in His Letters*, 73–74.
60. Marguerat, *Paul in Acts and Paul in His Letters*, 77.

Cultural Contextualization of Apologetics

Paul's Role-Play as Sage in Royal Courts

Again, royal courts were placed where kings considered new ideas. As discussed in the section above, sages had their regular place in the royal courts. Although intellectual interactions were not the only activities in the royal courts, considering new ideas and exchange of wisdom was a frequent pursuit in Hellenistic royal courts.

Hence, Paul's appearance in the royal courts is culturally laden.[61] First, he is taken to Felix, the governor; then Paul seeks an audience with King Agrippa. It is true that Paul was on trial before Felix due to the accusations brought by several members of the Sanhedrin, the high priest, and their spokesman, Tertullus.[62] However, it is Paul who requests to see the emperor, instead of Jerusalem's religious court. In Acts 25:8–12, Paul requests to see the emperor himself. Even though Paul was accused of profaning the temple and agitating all the Jews throughout the world, he appealed that he would have an audience with the emperor instead of Jerusalem Sanhedrin court for the sake of his innocence. Porcius Festus who succeeds Felix sees Paul's case a religious matter and not a political one, and asks Paul if he would be willing to go to Jerusalem. Festus the Sanhedrin seems to believe that Jerusalem would be a more appropriate venue than a Roman court. Yet, Paul is adamant in speaking before the emperor.[63]

While the exact intention of Paul's request may not be readily disclosed through the Scriptures, it is undoubtedly clear what is taking place in the royal courts. Stanley Porter, along with numbers of other scholars, agrees that,

> Paul recognizes that he is making a defense before Agrippa. His statement that he is making a defense is especially appropriate at the beginning of his speech before Felix, but it is also probably appropriate before Agrippa in light of the circumstances, in which he defends himself, even if this is not a formal trial. The situation is probably that Festus has not given up his responsibility to make a decision in this matter, although he is apparently relying upon Agrippa to give him some kind of advice on what should be done with this perpetual prisoner, against whom there are no substantive charges. Paul apparently realizes this situation, as indicated not only by his address of Agrippa and his explicitly calling his

---

61. I will discuss this in length in the next chapter.
62. I am referring to Paul's account in Acts 22–26.
63. Acts 25:8–12

speech a defense, but also his re-casting his approach in the course of his speaking so that he refers to his speech as "bearing witness" in v. 22. Paul appears to have taken the initiative in light of the legal situation (note that he has already appealed to Caesar), and turned the context to his favor.[64]

Ruben Dupertuis argues that opposition is a central theme in Acts and that this centrality has the "narrative function of constructing the heroes of the narrative as 'true' philosophers."[65] He shows that the imagery of conflict between "the figure of philosopher at conflict with a ruler or an authority figure has a long history in Greek literature."[66] He believes that Paul's appearance in royal courts likewise indicates Paul's standing as a philosophical figure.

Dupertuis and Paul Sampley both recognize the importance of παρρησία in Acts' speeches attributed to Paul. Sampley refers to Demetrius who informs that an orator mainly had three ways to produce correction or affection towards the conduction of another person or a group: flattery, figured speech, and adverse criticism.[67] Among these types, παρρησία is the type that becomes the "keyword" in Paul's speech in royal courts.[68] παρρησία in the ancient world denoted the right of a citizen to make a free speech, but through the course of history leading up to the first-century, it came to characterize philosopher's bold speech against opposing ruling authorities.[69]

After surveying various literature to demonstrate this historical background, Dupertuis elucidates that the philosophers in this culture associated their παρρησία to a divine commission, Socrates being the chief example.[70] Moreover, he notices that philosopher's role in παρρησία was not limited to fulfilling divine commission, but their identity as a wisdom figure was fortified as their conflict resembled that of Socrates. "By the early

---

64. Porter, *The Paul of Acts: Essays in Literary Criticism, Rhetoric, and Theology*, 159–60.

65. Dupertuis, "Bold Speech, Opposition, and Philosophical Imagery, 153.

66. Dupertuis, "Bold Speech, Opposition, and Philosophical Imagery," 153.

67. Sampley, "Paul and Frank Speeches," 293–318.

68. Dupertuis, "Bold Speech, Opposition, and Philosophical Imagery," 153.

69. Dupertuis, "Bold Speech, Opposition, and Philosophical Imagery," 156.

70. Dupertuis, "Bold Speech, Opposition, and Philosophical Imagery," 158–59.

Roman imperial period, Socrates had become the pre-eminent martyr, the prototype of the philosopher unjustly accused, tired, and executed."[71]

Reminding the occurrence of the term παρρησία in Paul's address to Agrippa, Dupertuis argues that Paul's speeches in Acts invoke the presence of opposition typically exhibited in the philosopher of Paul's day. Divine commission, too, appears in Paul's bold speech to Agrippa as well, supplemented by the final scene in Acts 28:23–31 seemingly resembling Socrates's famous funeral.[72] Thus, Paul's appearance and speech in the king's court aims not at his own defense, but "bearing witness" according to Paul. He understands his time and place before the king to be one of "testifying what God has done" as found in verse 22. Such scenery invokes sages at the royal courts, and those contained in that scene would have made a cultural connection to the activities.

Paul's Role-Play as Itinerant Sage

Aaron Chalmers, in Exploring the Religion of Ancient Israel: Priest, Prophet, Sage, and People, explains that there were specific areas where Hebrew wisdom figures exercised their activities.[73] They were royal courts, schools, and the town gates.[74] Sages were known to be teaching, advising or counseling, arbitrating disputes, and composing documents.[75]

> People were specifically recognized for their wisdom, who held positions of leadership and who performed wisdom-oriented roles (such as teaching, advising and arbitrating disputes) would have been found within the capital city of each kingdom, and more specifically within the royal court and key educational centers.[76]

Craig S. Keener highlights such aspect of Paul. He explained that people of Paul's times "valued the rhetorical skill of being able to communicate relevantly to different audiences." When considering Paul communicates in synagogues (Acts 13:16–41), to farmers (Acts 14:15–17), and to the philosophically educated (Acts 17:22–31), it alludes the very image of a

---

71. Dupertuis, "Bold Speech, Opposition, and Philosophical Imagery," 159.
72. Dupertuis, "Bold Speech, Opposition, and Philosophical Imagery," 165.
73. Chalmers, *Exploring the Religion of Ancient Israel*.
74. Chalmers, *Exploring the Religion of Ancient Israel*, 68–42.
75. Chalmers, *Exploring the Religion of Ancient Israel*, 76–81.
76. Chalmers, *Exploring the Religion of Ancient Israel*, 87.

Cultural Solidarity as the Wisdom Figure

wisdom figure.[77] In other words, Paul speaks with rational force, speaks to varying audiences, and teaches at multiple locations; and such descriptions are descriptors for typical sages of this time.

Paul teaching in various locations functions to portray Paul as a sophist-like figure. Ryan Carhart argues that Luke "inscribes Paul into a sophist-like role that trades on the social eminence of sophists during this period."[78] Carhart deems that Paul's *apologiai*—defense speeches—functions the way analogous to the widespread use of the *apologia* tradition among Second Sophistic authors such as Lucian, Dio, and Apuleius. Thus, observing the traces of rhetorical and literary strategy found in Paul's speeches, Carhart too argues that Paul is seen as an "embodiment of the παιδεία of the Christian movement."[79] He writes,

> Luke stages a culturally authoritative figure in Paul who symbolically represents the παιδεία of the Christian community as it seeks to negotiate its own privileged identity in relation to both the past and current cultural, social, and political realities of the Greek-speaking world under the Roman Empire ... The version of Paul that Luke construct in many ways appears to emulate the public prominence of sophists during this period, such as Dio Chrysostom, and this characterization deliberately constructs an aura of παιδεία around Paul that rhetorically represents the παιδεία of Christianity in the text.[80]

Hence, during the era of the Second Sophistic, παιδεία represented the embodiment of culture, learning, and erudition. When considering Paul's travels throughout the Roman Empire, as expressed by his speeches, Paul's παιδεία activity becomes more visible in Paul's *apologia*.

John C. Lentz's dissertation lends support to this view. In his effort to reconstruct Luke's portrayal of Paul, Lentz argues that Luke aims to portray Paul as a man of high social status and moral virtue—the one to be emulated, bearing marks of social distinction. Although Marguerat qualifies this notion by reminding that Paul also was harassed, imprisoned, and beaten; yet, he agrees with Lentz's judgment. Lentz argues that Luke's aim in portraying Paul in a particular way was to attract non-Christians by

---

77. Keener, *The IVP Bible Background Commentary*, 376.
78. Carhart, "The Second Sophistic and the Cultural Idealization," 187.
79. Carhart, "The Second Sophistic and the Cultural Idealization," 187.
80. Carhart, "The Second Sophistic and the Cultural Idealization," 192.

holding up Paul as an example of cosmopolitan Christianity.[81] This takes place through Paul speaking to the Jews to argue for Christianity's continuity with Judaism, and to Greeks showing that Christians are law-abiding members of the Roman Empire.[82] There are "explicit and implicit status indicators given them by Luke" that allow the audience to affirm that "Paul of Acts was a man of such status and prestige that he could presume to influence the governor and arrange for his case to be heard by Nero in Rome."[83] Taken together with elite Jewish upbringing and education, Paul of Acts is a sophisticated representative figure. Considering that virtue was the hallmark of every exemplary philosopher, rhetoricians, poets, historians, and lawyers Paul is seen to be a model representative that pagan audience can admire. In short, Paul is that representative figure of the newly founded "way" called Christianity, an object of admiration and virtuous living. They are the main characteristics of sage-like figures and Paul symbolizes the very imagery.

Analysis and Implications for Cultural Connection

Paul's role-play as sage may not be explicitly outlined in the Scripture, but his role explicitly fits that of Greco-Roman sages. Paul plays the role of philosophers in Areopagus. Paul plays the role of sage appearing before kings and emperors in their royal courts. Paul also plays the role of a sage familiar to the ancient Israel community. All of these engenders greater receptivity, cultural solidarity, and thus the cultural connection.

SUFFERING PAUL AS SAGE FIGURE

Construction of Paul's cultural solidarity does not stop with his portrayal in royal courts or symbolism. If we grant Luke for Paul's portrayal as a wisdom figure, would Paul agree with such imagery? In the following, I argue that Paul indeed would agree with that intent. I argue that Paul evidences this position through his discussion of suffering. Moreover, this discussion propels his audience to perceive him as a wisdom figure.

---

81. Lentz, *Luke's Portrait of Paul*.
82. Lentz, *Luke's Portrait of Paul*, 139–52.
83. Lentz, *Luke's Portrait of Paul*, 170.

Cultural Solidarity as the Wisdom Figure

In order to assess this, one must first identify passages in which Paul himself discusses his own understanding of suffering and next decipher ways in which his suffering was interpreted in his cultural context. The former task—Paul's assessment of his own suffering—can be extracted by biblical exegesis on the passages that deal with Paul's suffering.[84] The latter task—public perception of suffering and its function—requires an exploration of Paul's cultural context. When the results of these two tasks merge, it will be demonstrated that Paul established cultural solidarity by authenticating his apostleship through suffering, at the same time being portrayed as a sage figure also through his suffering.

Among twenty-one places that Paul speaks of his suffering, a list of hardships, is also referred to as *peristasenkataloge,* take up the bulk of his discussion.[85] The fact that this appears as a type of form hints the existence of the underlying message; in other words, Paul's *peristasenkataloge* is not merely an appeal for empathy, but also a function.[86] In order to assess precisely what function it is, we must first analyze Paul's message.

As mentioned above, large portions of Paul's discussion of his suffering appears in a list format. Von Robert Hodgson identifies them as simple lists and antithetical lists.[87] Simple lists and antithetical lists are found as follows.

A careful analysis of these passages will provide necessary and critical clues to understanding what roles these sufferings play in Paul's formulation of cultural solidarity. It will reveal what Paul is aiming to communicate through suffering. I will begin with passages in the simple list and continue onto the antithetical list.

---

84. Kruse, *Paul's Letter to the Romans.* Kruse identifies 21 places: Rom 5:3; 8:35; 12:12; 1 Cor 7:28; 2 Cor 1:4, 8; 2:4; 4:17; 6:4; 7:4; 8:2; 13; Eph 3:13; Phil 1:17; 4:14; Col 1:24; 1 Thess 1:6; 3:3,7; 2 Thess 1:4,6

85. Hodgson, "Paul the Apostle and First Century Tribulation Lists," 59–80.

86. I will discuss this subject in detail in the latter part of this chapter.

87. Hodgson, "Paul the Apostle and First Century Tribulation Lists," 66–67.

Table 1. Simple List

Romans 8:35b	affliction, anguish, persecution, famine, nakedness, danger, sword
2 Corinthians 6:4b-5	afflictions, hardships, anguishes, blows, imprisonments, riots, fatigues, watchings, fastings
2 Corinthians 11:23–29	fatigues, imprisonments, blows, deadly circumstances, thirty-nine lashes, struck with rods, stoning, shipwreck, adrift at sea; danger from rivers, robbers, own people, Gentiles; danger in town, in countryside, on the sea, from false brethren; fatigue, toil, watchings, hunger, thirst, fastings, cold, nakedness, anxiety, concern for churches, weakness, scandal
2 Corinthians 12:10	weaknesses, insults, hardships, persecutions, anguishes

Peristasenkataloge: Simple List

Romans 8:35

This last part of Romans 8 contains Paul's conviction regarding God's triumphal vindication, care, and eternal love for God's people in Jesus Christ. In this section of Romans 8, Paul uses a question-answer pattern in which he first raises a question in his own words, then follows it up with a response that is found in the earlier traditional material. For this reason, Richard Longenecker believes the list of hardships contained in verse 35 to be an early Christian confessional, an expanded form that connects with Psalm 44:22.[88] He sees the suffering list here to denote "the list of potential obstacles to the love of God that is in Christ Jesus our Lord."[89]

Paul's suffering list serves to demonstrate two strands of thought: first, they appear to show Paul's personal identification with the suffering Christ, and secondly, this triumph over suffering is made available to all believers who are in Christ Jesus.[90] Paul is advocating that believers can stand as conquerors and victors, not based on their merit but on the One who did not spare His Own Son; and Paul's triumph over these suffering demonstrate such fact. Paul's list of suffering found in Romans 8:35b serves

---

88. Ps 44:22 "Yet for your sake we are killed all the day long; we are regarded as sheep to be slaughtered."

89. Longenecker, *The Epistle to the Romans*, 747.

90. Longenecker, *The Epistle to the Romans*, 758.

to heighten the climactic conclusion to the theme that has been building throughout the chapter.[91]

Colin Kruse notes that for Paul, suffering was the "ongoing and ever-present reality of his life" as well as the lives of his converts.[92] Schreiner further emphasizes that Paul here is not indicating that believers will be able to avoid suffering through the love of Christ. Instead, suffering will be the "means by which believers will be more than conquerors."[93] In essence, Paul's suffering list here functions to demonstrate believer's identification with Christ in hardships and victory; and to showcase the greatness of Christ's glory in love.

2 Corinthians 6:4b-5

Unlike the suffering list in Romans, Paul speaks of his own suffering here. In these verses, Paul expresses that the Corinthian church also experiences similar encouragement in the midst of afflictions, as they embrace and endure the same type of suffering as Paul did.[94] Guthrie sees the list here to having a logical flow of moving from more of a general list of suffering (in a great deal of endurance, in affliction, in crises, and in stressful situations), to more of a specific list of suffering (in beatings, in being put in jail, and in mobs).[95] In this escalating list of Paul's suffering, he commends himself as God's agent who both manifests God's work in him, as well as the one who perseveres through them all.[96] In other words, "afflictions in themselves do not commend anyone, but Paul's great endurance of afflictions does."[97] From Paul's perspective, suffering is not something to be avoided as a detour but is the main road in which he must travel to show qualification for the call.[98] Summing up, Paul sees suffering to be for the encouragement of the believers, the qualification for the call through endurance, and the manifestation of God's work in a physical sense.

---

91. Murray, *The Epistle to the Romans*, 330.
92. Kruse, *Paul's Letter to the Romans*, 464.
93. Schreiner, *Romans*, 464.
94. Guthrie, *2 Corinthians*, 326.
95. Guthrie, *2 Corinthians*, 326–28.
96. Seifrid, *The Second Letter to the Corinthians*, 277.
97. Garland, *2 Corinthians*, 307.
98. Garland, *2 Corinthians*, 307.

Cultural Contextualization of Apologetics

2 Corinthians 11:23–29

This section contains a variety of suffering, persecutions, and hardships endured by the apostle. This list is laden with rhetorical features including "lively style of colloquial speech," "a degree of fullness that seeks to overwhelm the readers with ringing tones and emphatic figures of speech," and "fullness and intensity conveyed through the carefully crafted placement of words."[99] All of these literary features serve to commend once again to the Corinthian believers and other churches that Paul is their "authentic messenger, founder, and guide."[100]

Contrary to those who attempt to falsely claim the title servants of Christ, Paul legitimates his authenticity through the list of suffering. Even though Paul believes it is absurd to boast in the magnitude of his suffering, he finds it inevitably necessary to combat those who claim to be superapostles of sorts.[101] "As Paul's brief description of his escape from Damascus further suggests, the opponent's self-commendation as an apostle was based on signs, wonders, and mighty deeds (11:30–33; cf. 12:12). However, strikingly, Paul's commendation is based on his weakness. Paul's credentials lie not in what he has accomplished but in what he has endured. Thus, his heightened list of suffering works to expose the falsity of others. Paul's suffering once again functions to legitimate him as the Apostle of Christ.

2 Corinthians 12:10

Paul wraps up his "Fool's Speech" in this section. This conclusion is marked by "this weaknesses" which encapsulates all the list of suffering and hardships endured and listed in all preceding verses. All of these hardships Paul suffers is said to have been "for Christ's sake" or on "Christ's behalf."[102] Through this concluding remark concerning the role suffering played and the meaning it had for him, Paul is advocating that they all were done in "Christ's interest" as well as done as part of "authentic ministry."[103] Furthermore, Paul stresses that a move from weakness to strength actually implies his "real and effective *koinonia* with Christ, in which the apostle

---

99. Martin, *2 Corinthians*, 561–68.
100. Martin, *2 Corinthians*, 570.
101. Garland, *2 Corinthians*, 498.
102. Guthrie, *2 Corinthians*, 597.
103. Guthrie, *2 Corinthians*, 597.

shares in Christ's power, even if that power remains the possession of Christ alone."[104]

Table 2. Antithetical List

1 Corinthians 4:10—13a	We are fools for Christ's sake, but you are wise in Christ. We are weak, but you are strong. You are held in honor, but we in disrepute. To the present hour we hunger and thirst, we are poorly dressed and buffeted and homeless, and we labor, working with our own hands. When reviled, we bless; when persecuted, we endure; when slandered, we entreat. We have become, and are still, like the scum of the world, the refuse of all things.
2 Corinthians 4:8–9	afflicted in every way, but not crushed; perplexed, but not driven to despair; persecuted, but not forsaken; struck down, but not destroyed
2 Corinthians 6:8–10	Through honor and dishonor, through slander and praise. We are treated as impostors, and yet are true; as unknown, and yet well known; as dying, and behold, we live; as punished, and yet not killed; as sorrowful, yet always rejoicing; as poor, yet making many rich; as having nothing, yet possessing everything
Philippians 4:12	how to be brought low, and I know how to abound; In any and every circumstance, I have learned the secret of facing plenty and hunger, abundance and need

Peristasenkataloge: Antithetical List

We now turn to Paul's antithetical suffering list. They mostly appear in his two letters to the Corinthians, along with one in Philippians.[105] I will continue to examine the passages to analyze Paul's own perception of suffering. The first antithetical list appears in 1 Corinthians 4:10–13a.

One of the more notable features of Paul's discussion of suffering found in 1 Corinthians 4:10–13a is Paul's suffering playing a vicarious role.[106] David Garland notices that the term περικάθαρμα (refuse: referring to that which is removed by cleaning; flighty residue or scum) and περίψημα (scrapings: which refers that are scrubbed off something) to have

---

104. Seifrid, *The Second Letter to the Corinthians*, 453.
105. They are 1 Cor 4:10–13a; 2 Cor 4:7–12, 2 Cor 6:8–10, and Phil 4:12.
106. Garland, *1 Corinthians*, 142–43.

special significance in this passage.[107] He explains that while they may be a popular form of "self-depreciation," it is more typical that those were terms "associated with human victims in rituals designed to ward off evil through an expiatory sacrifice."[108] Thus, the word-picture Paul uses here functions to depict Paul's ministry as seemingly having the appearance of a scapegoat that is despised as a sin-offering. In other words, Paul is using the term to highlight that in actuality, they are bringing conciliation with God to the whole city through their suffering.[109] Paul understands suffering as having a vicarious role for the sake of the believers.

Along with this vicarious understanding of suffering, Paul also employs this series of suffering to address the Corinthians' accusation. Thiselton argues that Paul lists his suffering here to reveal Paul following Jesus's example of non-retaliation.[110] He explains that this type of non-retaliation would have been regarded as "weak" or "unmanly" in the Roman and Greco-Roman world of Paul's day, yet Paul exhibits the counter-cultural model of Jesus.[111] Fee also agrees that the whole point of the passage is to urge Corinthians to "imitate him" so that they follow his "way of life in Christ Jesus."[112]

Moreover, with the backdrop of Stoic-Cynic traditions, Craig S. Keener opines that Paul's suffering would have spurred some disdain from affluent Corinthians for most people also regarded homeless and un-wealthy philosophers such as Cynics as weak and foolish beggars.[113] But, Paul is radically challenging such social convention precisely with his suffering list. To those Corinthians who valued wealth and status, Paul somewhat sarcastically suggests that they are inspired to be wiser and nobler than Christ's servant who brought God's wisdom and power through being a fool and preaching God's folly.

Thus, Paul uses suffering as an admonition against arrogance in Corinthian believers and provides evidence for his genuine apostleship again. Even the concurrent Stoic thinker Seneca would have cataloged series of suffering as being superior to wisdom founded upon comfort

---

107. Garland, *1 Corinthians*, 142.
108. Garland, *1 Corinthians*, 142–43.
109. Garland, *1 Corinthians*, 142.
110. Thiselton, *The First Epistle to the Corinthians*, 363.
111. Thiselton, *The First Epistle to the Corinthians*, 363.
112. Fee, *The First Epistle to the Corinthians*, 180.
113. Keener, *1—2 Corinthians*, 130.

and complacency.¹¹⁴ Considering how Corinthians' perception of power and Paul's differed, Paul "therefore employs both dissimulative ironies to unmask pretense and paradoxical irony to restore contact with reality in 4:8–13. Can the addressees really be wealthy monarchs, while the apostles are 'scum' living under a death writ?"¹¹⁵ Through this irony, Paul connects his suffering to Christ's affliction and demonstrates his genuine apostleship.

The suffering of the righteous is inevitably connected with the inauguration of the kingdom of God; and as an authentic apostle, he is in such a role through his suffering. Along this line, C. K. Barrett ties this suffering list to the teaching of Jesus, especially that in the Sermon on the Mount that states that blessed are those who are persecuted for righteousness sake.¹¹⁶ Given this fact, this theology of the cross displayed through suffering must result in acceptance of Paul's genuine apostleship.¹¹⁷ Hence, to sum up the analysis of the passage, Paul's suffering is for the benefit of the believers, for a demonstration of the authenticity of genuine apostleship, instruction of believers, and participation in Christ.

2 Corinthians 4:7–12

Paul here sees the suffering to be a jar of clay that carries the treasure which is the gospel. Suffering is how the power of the gospel is not only manifested but also advanced. "The idea of picturing humans as jars of clay as a metaphor for human weakness was common in the ancient world, including Qumran writing."¹¹⁸ Paul's suffering becomes a platform that readily displays God's power and glory.

Paul Duff adds to this notion by suggesting a possible allusion to the Greco-Roman "procession imagery." Duff takes the passage to be a metaphorical allusion to Greco-Roman religious procession. Such triumphal procession was a ritual laden with the celebration of military victory. It featured victorious general marching into the city—as in Roman triumphal parade—accompanied by his entourage, along with booties from the campaign and enemy captives in chains. Paul's suffering functions as those booties from the campaign in God's triumph. God is the victorious

---

114. Thiselton, *The First Epistle to the Corinthians*, 367.
115. Thiselton, *The First Epistle to the Corinthians*, 367.
116. Barrett, *A Commentary on the First Epistle to the Corinthians*, 112.
117. Fee, *The First Epistle to the Corinthians*, 181.
118. Hafemann, *2 Corinthians*, 182.

general and Paul's suffering enhances the glory of God in this processional imagery.[119]

There also is the Christological purpose of Paul's suffering. Hafemann explains that Jesus's suffering parallels that of Paul's. The power of God revealed through the life and crucifixion of Christ is the very power that is at work in Paul's suffering. "Here, too, the categories of Jesus's death and resurrection are used to interpret Paul's experience of suffering and sustenance, thereby demonstrating that his life mediates the knowledge of God to the world embodied in Christ."[120] In this manner, Paul is assured that his suffering is part of God's divine plan for the spread of the gospel. Paul correlates his suffering to be something divinely orchestrated, that his suffering —like the cross of Christ —performs a revelatory function. This literary device that features an antithetical list of suffering is used to highlight the antithesis of death and the life of Jesus Christ, as such are united in Paul. Thus for Paul, suffering is a means that proclaims the gospel in its beauty.[121]

Haffmann additionally notes that unlike suffering found in 1 Corinthians 4:8–14 where Paul's intent was instructional, here in 2 Corinthians 4:7–18, it is apologetic. Paul's calumniators had contemptuously described his bodily appearance as weak, and his speech is of no account (10:10; 11:6, 12:7), hoping to discredit his authority thereby.[122] Paul, however, is not discredited by his suffering. It rather becomes a means of identification with Christ.[123] A long line of God's righteous people who have always suffered—as the Sermon on the Mount reveals and Paul's juxtaposition of deliverance with distress recalls similar contexts in Scripture, especially of Thanksgiving Psalms.[124] In this sense, suffering is "the essential and continuing characteristic of apostolic service" for Paul.[125]

---

119. Duff, "Apostolic Suffering and the Language of Processions in 2 Corinthians 4:7–10," 158–65.
120. Hafemann, *2 Corinthians*, 182.
121. Martin, *2 Corinthians*, 228.
122. Barnett, *The Second Epistle to the Corinthians*, 142.
123. Garland, *2 Corinthians*, 227.
124. Seifrid, *The Second Letter to the Corinthians*, 206.
125. Guthrie, *2 Corinthians*, 259.

Philippians 4:12

Here in Philippians, Paul discusses yet another aspect of suffering. He not only "embraces the life similar to that of the Lord," but he has also learned to accept whatever circumstances that came to him regardless of the situation. Cynic life who intentionally chose to be in want only stands deliberately and sharply contrasted with Paul. Unlike the Cynic, Paul learned to be not just in want but also in plenty as well. He advocates that his relationship with the Lord is irrespective of material circumstances.[126] In this sense, it appears that Paul's suffering has been a pathway to a greater depth in discipleship and apostleship. Paul is explaining "not simply stating that he has experienced life at both ends of the economic spectrum, though this was true. Rather, as an amplification of verse 11b, he is explaining that he knows how to live in an appropriate manner under these contrasting circumstances."[127]

Paul has learned the secret of being content because of the "enabling power of Christ." This becomes more evident in the next verse that states "I can do all things in Christ who strengthens me."[128] Paul's ability to handle himself in both situations, including the one in suffering, comes from God's power. Therefore, Paul sees suffering to be an opportunity for discipleship, as well as a demonstration of God's power working in the lives of the believers.

2 Corinthians 6:8–10

Despite the fact that the believers in Corinth have failed to grasp this qualification, Paul uses the list of suffering to expose the quality of the true servant of God.[129] Paul Barnett observes the system of antithesis: by pitting "impostors" and "true," Paul rebuts his critics and opponents; in the antithesis of "unknown" and "known," Paul heightens what he previously claimed—countering those who refused to recognize Paul's apostolic vocation.[130] In the antithesis of "dying" and "we live," Paul's pattern of experience discloses Jesus, in the case of his death and resurrection; in the fourth

---

126. Fee, *Paul's Letter to the Philippians*, 433.
127. O'Brien, *The Epistle to the Philippians*, 521.
128. Silva, *Philippians*, 204.
129. Witherington, *Conflict and Community in Corinth*, 399.
130. Barnett, *The Second Epistle to the Corinthians*, 331.

antithesis, "punished" and "not killed," Paul testifies to God's power and mercy despite Paul's own shortcomings in the past; in "sorrowful" and "rejoicing," Paul contrasts human opinion of Paul against divine reality; in "poor" "yet making many rich," Paul again is alluding to Jesus Christ as the *imitation* of the Servant; and In the last antithesis, "having nothing" and "possessing everything," Paul denotes summation of eschatological blessing.[131]

Summary and Analysis of Paul's Self-Understanding of Suffering: Suffering as a Legitimation of Paul's Apostolic Ministry

Having surveyed and analyzed the above verses that contain Paul's suffering, we now can briefly summarize Paul's self-understanding of suffering before turning to analyze the cultural reception of his suffering and its role in the formation of cultural solidarity.[132] Certainly, Paul understands suffering to be integral to his ministry as an apostle.[133] "Paul also portrays his sufferings as part of his discipleship and apostolic vocation: they were part of his missionary activities and intrinsic to his calling."[134] Moreover, "Paul's conformity to the gospel is evident in his conformity to the sufferings of Jesus."[135] Synthetic analysis on Paul's suffering discourses illumines the messages he intended to communicate.[136] While they cannot be summed

---

131. Barnett, *The Second Epistle to the Corinthians*, 331–34.

132. Much more can be said regarding this topic. However, since the discussion must remain focused on cultural reception of Paul's suffering and its role in forming cultural solidarity, the treatment is kept minimal here.

133. Acts 9:15–16: "But the Lord said to him, "Go, for he is a chosen instrument of mine to carry my name before the Gentiles and kings and the children of Israel. For I will show him how much he must suffer for the sake of my name.""

134. Adewuya, "The Sacrificial-Missiological Function of Paul's Sufferings in the Context of 2 Corinthians," 89.

135. Koontz, "Apostolic Suffering in 2 Corinthians," 40.

136. Not only did Paul's suffering display God's glory, but it also demonstrated Jesus Christ. Union with Christ through suffering, God's mean to display His glory, and authentication of genuine apostleship altogether reveal Jesus Christ and His gospel. For Paul, his suffering is a continuous demonstration of Christ's humiliation, passion, and crucifixion. It is at the same time a sure proclamation of the ongoing power of resurrection, as well as of eschatological dominion. His suffering is a testimony to the ministry of the cross. See Proudfoot, "Imitation or Realistic Participation: A Study of Paul's Concept of 'Suffering with Christ,'" 140–60; Lambrecht, "Paul and Suffering," 47–67; Koontz, "Apostolic Suffering in 2 Corinthians"; Fredrickson, "Paul, Hardships, and Suffering,"

up in a few propositions; yet Paul's *peristasenkataloge* essentially serves to legitimize Paul's status as an apostle, in response to various attacks that challenged it.[137]

Paul suffered to defend his apostolic ministry, so that he may also defend the genuineness of the gospel; certainly, Paul did not see his suffering as a sign of divine judgment or disqualification.[138] Rather, his suffering was the very indication that he was carrying out true divine calling, naturally embedded in his apostolic call.[139] Thus, to withdraw from suffering was unfitting for Paul. In this sense, lack of afflictions would have discredited Paul; and accordingly, the gospel he was bringing to the Gentiles. He, therefore, withstood all types of accusations—both internal and external—for the sake of the gospel.[140] "Paul in effect calls into question not merely their stature as trusted heralds of the gospel but fundamentally the validity of their standing in Christ,"[141]

As seen throughout the epistles, Paul's opponents were set on undermining Paul's gospel ministry by contending that Paul and his companions are a "deluded groups of people who were exploiting people with selfish reasons through trickery."[142] Against this attack, Paul responds by stating that Thessalonians know of Paul's suffering. Hence, Gene Green sees Paul's discussion of suffering to be "Paul's apologetics for his character against negative criticism."[143]

In the same way, the hardship list in 2 Corinthians 11 functions as "rejoinder" to the "super-apostles" and their supporters in Corinth.[144]

172–97; Manus, "Apostolic Suffering (2 Cor 6:4–10): The Sign of Christian Existence and Identity," 41–54; Beker, "Suffering and Triumph in Paul's Letter to the Romans," 105–19.

137. Thomas Schreiner wrote an excellent section entitled, "Suffering and the Pauline Mission: The Means of Spreading the Gospel" in his book, *Paul, Apostle of God's Glory in Christ: A Pauline Theology*. In it, he argues that Paul sees suffering as the very means by which the gospel spreads. Suffering is not meant to be a subsidiary of his mission, but rather central to his ministry. His suffering validated his message, providing the evidence of the gospel. See Schreiner, *Paul, Apostle of God's Glory in Christ: A Pauline Theology*.

138. Schreiner, *Paul*, 87.

139. Acts 9:15–16: "But the Lord said to him, Go, for he is a chosen instrument of mine to carry my name before the Gentiles and kings and the children of Israel. For I will show him how much he must suffer for the sake of my name."

140. Kelhoffer, "Suffering as Defense," 127–43.

141. Kelhoffer, "Suffering as Defense," 129.

142. Hendriksen, *Second Corinthians*, 59.

143. Green, *The Letters to the Thessalonians*, 111.

144. Kelhoffer, "Suffering as Defense," 133–34.

Kelhoffer states that in 2 Corinthians 11–12, Paul offers six responses to his critics, whom he construes as false apostles and agents of Satan (2 Cor 11:13–15), and his intent is "not to convince his opponents but rather to persuade the Corinthians that he—and not these other apostolic claimants—deserves their loyalty."[145] Therefore, Paul is seeking a way to connect to his audience as a figure that they can place their trust and loyalty—as a means to build cultural solidarity.

ANALYSIS OF PAUL'S AUDIENCE

Now we turn to inquire how Paul's cultural context interpreted suffering. I suggest that the answers to these questions disclose that suffering Paul was perceived as a wisdom figure. The following analysis will demonstrate how Paul's suffering thus functions again not only to establish solidarity through the legitimization of his apostleship but also to portray him as a representative figure of the newly found philosophy called Christianity.[146] But first, how did the ancients understand suffering?

Suffering in the Ancient Culture

L. Gregory Bloomquist cites Lefkowitz as he paints the backdrop to Paul's world: "Mediterranean antiquity was marked by a profound pessimism concerning life. This was true for inhabitants of the Levant or Egypt, of the Homeric period or Augustan Rome, of the world of Jesus or the world of Paul."[147] Such pessimism, frequented by sufferings arising from famine, war, and epidemics was a subject matter sages attempted to address.[148] Suffering was seen as a "prelude and herald" of death.[149] In the face of suffering and death, ancient wise men informed the public of their view: Plato, Epicurus, Lucretius ferociously reminded them of their predicament; Stoics, along with Epicureans, taught them to be indifferent; and other extant writings encouraged them to see it as being educational.[150] "Seneca conceives of

---

145. Kelhoffer, "Suffering as Defense," 134.

146. I discuss how Christianity was firstly regarded as another superstition, pagan religion, or philosophy in the later part of this book.

147. Bloomquist, "Subverted by Joy," 271.

148. Bloomquist, "Subverted by Joy," 271.

149. Bloomquist, "Subverted by Joy," 271.

150. Bloomquist, "Subverted by Joy," 272.

suffering as valuable and even necessary for testing, refining, and instructing a person in the path of virtue."[151]

For this reason, suffering was not a mere consequence of fate but was considered to be carrying out a function.[152] Along with the prevalence of pessimism mentioned above, equally abundant is the use of the tribulation list in ancient literature.[153] Hodgson cites Schrage drawing attention to "copious use of tribulation lists" in the intertestamental literate to demonstrate that "the apocalyptic frame of reference for such list is congenial to Paul."[154] He cites 2 Enoch 66:6 where the seer offers the following as specific terms of discipleship: "walk, my children, in long-suffering, in meekness, honesty, in provocation, in grief, in faith . . . in illness, in abuse, in wounds, in temptation, in nakedness, in privation."[155] Similarly, *Testaments of Joseph* 1:4–7 contains an antithetical type list where the patriarch speaks of his life:

> These my brethren *hated* me, but the Lord *loved* me: They wished to *slay* me, but the God of my fathers *guarded* me: They *let me down into a pity* and the Most High *brought me up* again: I was sold into *slavery* and the Lord of ah made *me free*: I was taken into *captivity*, and His strong hand *succoured* me. I was beset with *hunger*, and the Lord Himself *nourished* me.[156]

In the like manner, a greater abundance in paralleling tribulation lists appear in Stoics and Greco-Roman sophists.[157] David DeSilva asserts that there are forms of simple verbal parallels, extended verbal parallels, conceptual parallels, use common imageries, and use of common forms to illustrate Paul's extensive parallelism with that of the Stoa.[158] Robert Bultmann asserts that Paul's list of suffering stems from popular

---

151. Tabb, *Suffering in Ancient Worldview*, 68.

152. Tabb analyzes the role of suffering in formation of one's view on God, human nature, human predicament, solution to that predicament, and eschatology. See Tabb, *Suffering in Ancient Worldview*, 69.

153. Hodgson argues that against the traditional research that identified parallel between Paul's list with that of Stoics or Jewish apocalyptic writing, argues that the list stems from widespread literary convention including Josephus, Mishnah, and Nag Hammandi library. See Hodgson, "Paul the Apostle and First Century Tribulation Lists."

154. Hodgson, "Paul the Apostle and First Century Tribulation Lists," 160.

155. Hodgson, "Paul the Apostle and First Century Tribulation Lists," 168.

156. Charles, *The Apocrypha and Pseudepigrapha of the Old Testament in English*.

157. Bultmann, *Der Stil Der Paulinischen Predigt Und Die Kynisch-Stoische Diatribe*; DeSilva, "Paul and the Stoa."

158. DeSilva, "Paul and the Stoa," 549–64.

philosophies of the Greco-Roman world. His position has been one of the major positions historically; and he finds the conceptual antithesis—Stoic who is suffering yet in happiness—resembling Paul's rhetorical use of the suffering list.[159]

> Two examples from Epictetus will show the likeness of foe Pauline and Stoic lists. Arguing for indifference to all things, Epictetus says that, "if one wants to define life's circumstances as hardships ... what hardship is involved when that which has come into being is destroyed? The instrument of destruction is a *sword*, or a *wheel*, or the *sea*, or a *tile*, or a *tyrant*. What concern is it to you by what road you descend to the House of Hades?" Or again, comparing Epicureans, Peripatetic, and Stoics, Epictetus fashions an antithetical list to drive home his point: "Show me a man who though sick is happy, though in danger is happy, though dying is happy, though condemned to exile is happy, though in disrepute is happy. Show him! By the gods, I would fain see a Stoic!"[160]

Paul's use of the suffering list again invokes familiarity with those who are aware of the rhetorical features and thoughts of Stoicism.

Hodgson argues that the use of the tribulation list is not limited to the above samples; it is much wider.[161] To illustrate, the Jewish historian Josephus also provides related material in his records as well. Josephus's writings not only feature such an antithetical list of suffering, but it also matches the content of the list.[162] For instance, aspects of hardships uttered in 2 Corinthians 11:23–29 are "hunger, thirst, danger at sea;" and *Antiquities* III. 2.2 shows Moses speaking to the Israelite by pointing out God's provision despite "famine and thirst, things that are in their own nature insuperable; and also against mountains, and that at sea."[163] *Antiquities* IV.6.6 has Balaam not being able to curse Israelites because "it is true no entire destruction can seize upon the nation of the Hebrews, neither by war,

---

159. Manus, "Apostolic Suffering (2 Cor. 6:4–10): The Sign of Christian Existence and Identity," 46.

160. Hodgson, "Paul the Apostle and First Century Tribulation Lists," 67.

161. He argues that "history of religions background for Paul's tribulation list is broader than the one generally found in relevant modern commentaries, monographs and articles."

162. Hodgson, "Paul the Apostle and First Century Tribulation Lists," 70.

163. Hodgson, "Paul the Apostle and First Century Tribulation Lists," 71.

nor by plague, nor by scarcity of the fruits of the earth, nor can any other unexpected accident be their entire ruin."[164]

As shown, the wide availability of the list of suffering found in other cultural contexts heightens the possibility that Paul's suffering engendering cultural solidarity between Paul and his audience. The above survey shows that the format of the list is not unique to Paul. A format readily identifiable in other cultural contexts generates familiarity with the audience.

Suffering as a Legitimation of Paul

Equally important to the wide availability of the paralleling material is the meaning and function of such lists. John T. Fitzgerald, in his study of *peristasenkataloge*, argues that contemporaneous of Paul would have considered suffering as a test that reveals truly virtuous sage.[165] Out of the array of options, he too believes Paul's list of suffering parallels most closely with Stoic and Cynic sage, arguing that Stoic sage of Seneca, Musonius, and Epictetus as the best context for understanding Paul's use of the catalogs.[166] More importantly, Fitzgerald writes,

> Since *peristaseis* constitute a test of human character, they have both a revelatory and a demonstrative function. The man with little or no integrity collapses under the weight of his burdens. His *persitaseis* reveal and prove his deficiencies as a person. The *proficiens* (the one who makes progress), by contrast, shows greater strength of character in dealing with his hardships, so that his *persitaseis* reveal his progress, what he is becoming. Since they help to form his character, they play a crucial role in his παιδεία. For the sapiens (sage or wise man), however, *persitaseis* no longer have this educative character. They provide the proof that he is educated. Consequently, they exhibit who he is, what he has become.[167]

Therefore, as Fitzgerald regards those who endure hardships and overcomes them have a credential of a sage. Paul's audience would have perceived Paul's *persitaseis* in this light. Paul's connection to the culture takes place through Paul's communication of his suffering. Through the calmness of the sage in the midst of suffering, or at times expressing

164. Hodgson, "Paul the Apostle and First Century Tribulation Lists," 70.
165. Fitzgerald, *Cracks in an Earthen* Vessel.
166. Fitzgerald, *Cracks in an Earthen* Vessel, 30.
167. Fitzgerald, *Cracks in an Earthen* Vessel, 115.

contempt or gratitude, if sufferings are understood as given by Fate, they demonstrated virtue.[168] Sages' steadfast endurance of hardships were perceived to be exemplary and worthy of praises. Therefore, the enumeration of hardships in catalogs magnifies renders sages all the more impressive and praiseworthy.[169]

Dorothea Bertschmann reaffirms this valuation. She elucidates that Stoic philosopher Epictetus perceives suffering to be a "training to ultimately show clam in the face of death for such calmness will be the greatest witness to God who created him as a rational being."[170] For Epictetus, suffering is a means by which God potentially activate true-self, leading to become a fuller human.[171] With this cultural background, Paul's audience may have processed the reality of suffering to be a litmus test of the worthiness of an authoritative figure.

David Fredrickson offers an additional perspective on Paul's suffering list's cultural association with Paul's audience. Another function of expressing the sage's endurance was to demonstrate his philanthropy.[172] Epictetus and Lucian's work depicts this notion, but it is clearer when Dio Chrysostom separates himself from other philosophers who disassociate themselves with the crowd to avoid danger; instead, participation in suffering produced comradery and friendship.[173] Fredrickson explains that philosophers placed limits on how much philosophers were to actually join in suffering; however, "in spite of these limits imposed by some philosophers, we find the complete sharing of adversity, even pain, sorrow, and grief to be a commonplace pertaining to friendship."[174] Furthermore, the ultimate demonstration of such friendship was the willingness to suffer death for another. He explains that literary sources from Paul's time gained great popularity in the first century.[175] Therefore, Paul's audience would also have potentially seen Paul's hardship list as evidence that he can be trustworthy enough to share friendship.

168. Fitzgerald, *Cracks in an Earthen* Vessel, 70–85.
169. Fitzgerald, *Cracks in an Earthen* Vessel, 107–14.
170. Bertschmann, "What Does Not Kill Me Makes Me Stronger," 9–20.
171. Bertschmann, "What Does Not Kill Me Makes Me Stronger," 18.
172. Fredrickson, "Paul, Hardships, and Suffering," 176.
173. Fredrickson, "Paul, Hardships, and Suffering," 178.
174. Fredrickson, "Paul, Hardships, and Suffering," 178.
175. Fredrickson, "Paul, Hardships, and Suffering," 178.

Another cultural association the suffering list may have evoked Paul's audience is battle scars. Jennifer A. Glancy introduces the role visible scars play in the Roman discourses, by explaining that scars caused by battle were a common ingredient for rhetoric.[176] Wounds and scars left on the body as a result of battle were frequent sources of boasting.[177] Glancy writes that "Paul boasts of beatings both for strategic reasons" and the "Corinthians, habituated to a first-century corporal idiom.[178] Glancy refers to various texts to confirm that "throughout Greek and Roman literature, scars incurred in combat serve as inscribed images of excellence and manly virtue." "Within the Roman *sermo corporis*, the vocabulary of battle scars—and display of battle scars—was finely calibrated."[179] The audience in Paul's culture was in the habit of interpreting the list of tribulation demonstrated on the body to prove one's authoritative status.[180]

Suffering Paul's Cultural Solidarity

However, Glancy argues that Paul, though employs the same rhetorical tool, tells a different story: the message Paul carries on his physical body is not the one of a victorious battle, but of whipping, akin to that of Jesus.[181] Paul "perceives that in his marked body the story of Jesus's passion is legible; he thus has both tactical and theological reasons for boasting of his publicly humiliating beatings."[182] Therefore, Paul's suffering specifically authenticates his ministry as the apostle that walks in the footsteps of his Master.[183] For Paul, every aspect of Christ-event is bearing witness—His incarnation,

---

176. Glancy, "Boasting of Beatings (2 Corinthians 11:23–25)," 99–135.

177. Glancy explains that suffering caused by whipping would have been perceived as "the archetypal mark of dishonor." She writes, "Flogging was the most commonly practiced species of corporal punishment. The ability to order a whipping signaled a person's dominance over another; the inability to resists a whipping, the dishonor of the person whipped. Within an idiom that was distinctively though not uniquely Roman, corporal punishment was routinely associated with slaves; vulnerability to corporal punishment signaled servility . . . Dishonorable bodies were whippable; honorable bodies were not." Glancy, "Boasting of Beatings (2 Corinthians 11:23–25)," 108.

178. Glancy, "Boasting of Beatings (2 Corinthians 11:23–25)," 135.

179. Glancy, "Boasting of Beatings (2 Corinthians 11:23–25)," 106.

180. Glancy, "Boasting of Beatings (2 Corinthians 11:23–25)," 103–7.

181. Glancy, "Boasting of Beatings (2 Corinthians 11:23–25)," 108–35.

182. Glancy, "Boasting of Beatings (2 Corinthians 11:23–25)," 127.

183. This authentication springs from Paul's union with Christ.

circumcision, transfiguration, suffering, death, burial, resurrection, ascension, glorification, and future appearing—none is dissociated from the body.[184] Thus for Paul, suffering is a display of Jesus's death; deliverance from it is a display of Jesus's life; to put in another way, "death and life are personified in Paul."[185] For Paul, "living a self-giving life in participatory suffering with Christ is the model for ministry, a personification and a living witness of Christ's sufferings."[186] Hence, Paul listing his experiences of physical beating is thus performing as a means to legitimate his apostolic call.

Summing up, the audience of Paul's message was familiar with *peristasenkatalogue* in various shapes and forms. In the Greco-Roman culture, the list alluded to a virtuous sage who possess greater tranquility and wisdom than those average citizens. These wise and virtuous sages' endurance in hardships produced philanthropy with those who are all too familiar with the hardships of life. Moreover, the list of suffering experienced in Paul's body aims to inform how to accurately perceive Paul as an apostle.

CONCLUSION: CULTURAL CONNECTION IN APOLOGETICS

Therefore, it can be demonstrated that Paul's ministry activities invoke the role that sages played in various aspects of cultural context, all of which are familiar to his audience. Though whether Paul intended to present himself as such is debatable, Paul's audience has all the necessary indicators to associate him as a wisdom figure. Paul's rhetorical use of *peristasenkataloge* also aids his audience to locate him in their cultural context as the one who has legitimate authority, particularly a sage who demonstrates virtuous living, philanthropy, and apostolic call. Paul's ministry activities recorded in Luke, coupled with Paul's own writings on the tribulation lists, offers a specific portrayal of himself as the wisdom figure easily identifiable and relatable in the cultural context.

Hence, Paul cultivates cultural solidarity with his audience. To be exact, Paul's cultural connection takes place through the forging of cultural solidarity as a wisdom figure. But how does this finding relate to Paul's

---

184. See Barnett's discussion of this subject in Barnett, *The Second Epistle to the Corinthians*.

185. Hodge, *An Exposition of the First Epistle to the Corinthians*, 101.

186. Adewuya, "The Sacrificial-Missiological Function of Paul's Sufferings," 89.

culturally contextualized apologetics? It forms a cultural connection with the audience—just as Paul's use of non-canonical quotes and Greco-Roman rhetoric as cultural point of contact and enculturated communications do. Paul appear as a wisdom figure to the Gentile audience, and such identification allows the audience to better situate the newly found teaching called Christianity. Paul appear as a sage-like figure to the believers, and such identification grants him legitimacy as an authoritative figure, consequently adding greater weight to his message. Through the forging of cultural solidarity, Paul's relatability and authority enhance cultural intelligibility of the audience, establishing yet another form of cultural connection. How do these factors appear in Paul's apologetics ministry? I explore this subject next.

Chapter 4

Cultural Contextualization of Paul's Apologetics Speeches

We must now investigate how the features of cultural contextualization, specifically cultural connection and cultural solidarity, appear in Paul's apologetics speeches. The analysis of Paul's apologetics in speeches will aid in determining what model can be outlined by apologetics speeches attributed to Paul. My argument is twofold: 1) Paul's apologetics speeches consistently respond to cultural objections to the Christian faith, thus modeling a way culturally contextualized apologetics can be carried out; 2) delineation of elements found in Paul's apologetics speeches uncovers a scheme akin to kerygmatic speeches of the apostles: the common factors patterned in Paul's apologetics speeches are cultural connection, cultural solidarity, a defense of the Christian faith from cultural objection by presenting the virtue of the Christian life, and exposition of the resurrection.[1]

---

1. In this book, I use the phrase "virtue of the Christian life" to denote the presentation of the Christian life as an attractive alternative to cultural objections. I use the term "virtue" to simply indicate a sense of general excellence in character and being that includes exemplary morality. I mean the term to encompass the kind of living that is most worthy and satisfactory. Paul's familiarity, given the cultural context, with the concept of virtue and its philosophical significance and status may be a possibility. However, I do not wish to argue that the apostle's calling for a virtuous life, as delineated by the ancient philosophy, constituted a major component of Paul's preaching scheme, though may be an interesting topic to pursue. I am simply using the term to represent good, upright living and being. For more technical sense of the term, see Crisp, "Virtue Ethics."

In order to substantiate my first argument, I will first identify apologetics speeches targeted to the Gentiles out of all the speeches in Acts, and conduct a biblical exegesis with special attention to their cultural context. With this selection of speeches, I will survey their socio-cultural interpretations to decipher the ways in which Paul develops a response to cultural objections against the Christian faith.[2] Next, after affirming the existence of a patterned scheme in kerygmatic speeches of the apostles, I will demonstrate how each of the apologetics speeches attributed to Paul likewise contain cultural connections (via cultural point of contact and cultural solidarity as the previous chapters of this book has already laid out), the presentation of the Christian life as an appeal or a defense, and the exposition of Christ's resurrection. This analysis will lead to the conclusion that Paul models a culturally contextualized apologetics in his apologetics speeches.

ANALYSIS OF PAUL'S APOLOGETICS SPEECHES

Identification of Apologetics Speeches

In order to analyze Paul's speeches in their socio-cultural context, I will first identify which of Paul's speeches count as apologetics in nature, then outline arguments contained in those speeches. There are thirteen speeches attributed to Paul in the book of Acts.[3] They are as shown in Table 3:

---

2. For sociological reading of Paul in Luke, important works include Porter, *Paul in Acts*; Cilliers Breytenbach, *Paul's Graeco-Roman Context*; DeSilva, "Paul and the Stoa : A Comparison," 549–64; Bauckham, *The Christian World around the New Testament*; Deissmann, *Light from the Ancient East*; Forell, *The Proclamation of the Gospel in a Pluralistic World*; Gager, *Kingdom and Community*; Hubbard, *Christianity in the Greco-Roman World*; Meeks, *The First Urban Christians*; Meeks, et al., *The Social World of the First Christians*, Rowe, *World Upside Down*.

3. Bruce, *The Speeches in the Acts of the Apostles*; Soards, *The Speeches in Acts*.

Table 3. List of Paul's Speeches in Acts

Acts 13:16b-41, 46–47	Paul's Speech at Antioch of Pisidia
Acts 14:15–17	The Speech of Barnabas and Paul at Lystra
Acts 17:22–31	Paul's Speech in the Areopagus
Acts 18:6b-d	Paul's Speech to the Corinthian Jews
Acts 20:18b-35	Paul's Speech to the Ephesian elders
Acts 21:13b-c	Paul's Speech to the Disciples in Caesarea
Acts 22:1, 3 to 21	Paul's Speech to the Jerusalem Jews
Acts 23:1b, 3, 5, 6b	Paul's Speech before the Council
Acts 24:10b-21	Paul's Speech before Felix
Acts 25:8b, 10b-11	Paul's Speech before Festus
Acts 26:2–23, 25–27, 29	Paul's Speech before King Agrippa
Acts 27:10b, 21b-26, 31b, 33b-34	Paul's speech(es) during the Sea Voyage to Rome
Acts 28:17c-20, 25b-28	Paul's speech to the Roman Jewish leaders

For the benefit of the current discussion, research is limited to apologetics speeches targeted to the Gentiles. Moreover, even if the speech does not have a form of public sermon or homily, if it contains any evangelistic value or content related to apologetic arguments, I have included them in my analysis. To note, I include Paul's speech before Felix and King Agrippa because both contexts involve the Gentiles rather than Jews.[4] I will thus omit from this study the speeches that do not possess merit or characteristic for the sake of this book. Under this filter, Paul's recorded the speech to the Corinthians Jews in chapter 18, his speech to the elders in chapter 20, Paul's speech to the disciples in chapter 21, and series of events following the sea voyage in chapter 27 and 28 are excluded since they do not meet the proposed criteria. Based on this, I will now analyze Paul's speeches found in Acts 14, 17, 24, and 26, in light of their background context in pursuit of socio-cultural interpretation that illumines Paul's approach to responding to cultural objections.

---

4. Porter, *Paul in Acts*, 161. George Kennedy agrees with this judgement. He points out that Acts 26:23 and 22:21 both mention the Gentiles right before ensuing interruption.

The Speech of Paul and Barnabas at Lystra 14:15–17

This incident provides one of the rare examples from Luke concerning how the apostles went about preaching the gospel to purely pagan audiences.[5] Unlike the Gentiles who were accustomed to messages proclaimed from Jewish synagogues, Paul's audience here had no familiarity with God of Israel.[6] The initial reaction from the people in Lystra is to mistake Paul for Hermes and Barnabas for Zeus. The reason Lystrans identify Paul as Hermes is that typically Hermes's role is to speak.[7] Lystrans are convicted that the gods have come down in the human form.[8] Furthermore, it was customary for the priest of Zeus to bring oxen and garlands to the gates to offer sacrifice.[9]

Cultural Context

Charles Talbert points out that "mistaking impressive humans for deities was common in antiquity" and cites Chariton's *Chaereas and Callirhoe*, Xenophon's *Ephesian Tale*, and Josephus's *Antiquities*.[10] This idea is evident in *Odyssey* as well: "holy gods, in the form of wandering foreigners, taking on various forms, often go through countries and cities, that they may see mortal's foolish misdeeds as well as piety."[11] Correspondingly, when mortals fail to recognize these traveling deities that visited cities and villages that came in human form, they were subject to divine wrath.[12]

Particularly in Lystra, there is a more specific cultural context to be considered. According to Ovid in *Metamorphoses*, Zeus and Hermes visited a region called Phrygia, not too far from Lystra.[13] Philemon and Baucis, an aged couple from the region, were the only ones that showed hospitality to Zeus and Hermes, while the rest of the people were annihilated for their lack of. Talbert explains why later on, Philemon and Baucis are deified:

---

5. Bruce, *Commentary on the Book of the Acts*, 276.
6. Bruce, *Commentary on the Book of the Acts*, 276.
7. Lüdemann, *Early Christianity According to the Traditions in Acts*, 161.
8. Acts 14:11.
9. Acts 14:13
10. Talbert, *Reading Acts*, 133.
11. Talbert, *Reading Acts*, 133.
12. Talbert, *Reading Acts*, 133.
13. *Metamorphoses* 8:626–724

there is a shred of "archaeological evidence for a cult of these two gods, dating from about AD 250 has been found near Lystra. If the locals had failed to honor the gods on their previous visit, they would not repeat their mistake."[14]

John Pilch adds another dimension to the cultural context. He argues that interpreting Luke's language of sickness and healing in terms of his own culture generates more accurate and fuller reading, providing greater detail in seeing the text in a proper cultural context.[15] Under this lens, he argues that health is defined as "a state of complete well-being, not the restoration of individual activity or performance," contrasted with the modern, Western, and scientific perspective.[16] In other words, Luke's healing stories are essentially concerned with a state of wholeness that involves not just one's physical mobility or individual activities.[17] The healing that serves as a backdrop to Paul's speech at Lystra affirms "the biblical culture's acceptance of spirits as operative and interfering in human affairs, validating a division of human ailments into those involving malevolent spirits and those attributable to the spirit know as God."[18]

Issues in Cultural Objection

Beyond mere archaeology, the current cultural issue at hand is a potential syncretism of magic and paganism.[19] Hans-Josef Klauck argues that Paul's speech in Lystra interconnects with the episodes regarding the Jewish magician Bar-Jesus, the Samaritan magician Simon, the poor Philippian slave-girl with the spirit of divination, the unlucky Jewish exorcists in Ephesus, as well as those in Athens and Malta.[20] When Christianity is faced with magic and pagan idolatry, it comes down to the battle of who is more powerful.[21] In this regard, there is a "certain danger of confusing magic with Christian miracles, therapies and exorcisms, and, still worse, of taking Christian belief for a more powerful manifestation of magic;" and

---

14. Talbert, *Reading Acts*, 133.
15. Pilch, "Sickness and Healing in Luke-Acts," 181–209.
16. Pilch, "Sickness and Healing in Luke-Acts," 190.
17. Pilch, "Sickness and Healing in Luke-Acts," 209.
18. Pilch, "Sickness and Healing in Luke-Acts," 209.
19. Klauck, "With Paul in Paphos and Lystra," 93–108.
20. Klauck, "With Paul in Paphos and Lystra," 100.
21. Klauck, "With Paul in Paphos and Lystra," 100.

CONTEXTUALIZATION OF PAUL'S APOLOGETICS SPEECHES

the same confusion appears in the reaction of Lystrans.[22] Along this line, Craig Keener writes,

> Polytheism was more intellectually fashionable in many circles than was monotheism: (This is because) it represented the views of the dominant culture. It was undoubtedly difficult to give up polytheism; deities or spirits were associated with entrances to the home, with trees, and with personified virtues; for Romans, spirits were associated with families and even individuals. Beliefs about and thus feelings involving deities pervaded people's daily lives and habits; their experience seemed continuous and second nature. To give up polytheism was to surrender an entire worldview associated with virtually everything familiar that surrounded its devotees.[23]

Response to Objections

Paul's speech at Lystra contains the following argument: 1) You must turn to a Living God, who is also the Creator, 2) You failed to realize that in the past, and 3) All of Creator's provisions are evidence of his existence.[24] Keener notes that rhetorically speaking, the brevity of this speech is deliberative and summative.[25] Luke Timothy Johnson sees the speech to be an extension of the "paradigmatic character of the healing narrative," but only this time to a completely pagan audience.[26] In other words, this speech principally contains what Luke would summarize as the essential components contained in the apostle's responses to the pagan audience. In short, the speech contains Luke's natural theology and the discussion of the "Living God" as a refutation.[27]

Paul's main response to the cultural objection is that "even in the face of ignorance and rebellion, God has not left Himself without testimony."[28]

22. Klauck, "With Paul in Paphos and Lystra," 101–3.
23. Keener, *Acts*, 2163.
24. The outlines are mine, but I closely follow that of Craig S. Keener.
25. Keener, *Acts*, 2158.
26. Johnson and Harrington, *The Acts of the Apostles*.
27. Keener finds parallel in Rom 1:19–25. "In Romans, the revelation in nature makes humanity morally responsible for idolatry (1:18–23), but this revelation contrasts with the revelation in the gospel, which provides salvation (1:16–17)." Keener, *Acts*, 2158..
28. Peterson, *The Acts of the Apostles*, 410.

Against the danger of syncretism, Paul is asserting that God's goodness evidenced by the benefits of God's providence and provision is the very mark of God's character that sets him apart from the magic and pagan idols.[29] It is also the reason that pagans must turn away from worthless idols and honor him as God: Peterson sees that this discussion of God's character "is a biblical foundation for evangelism in a culture where fundamental presuppositions about God and nature and the meaning of human existence need to be challenged."[30] This characterization of God stands in stark contrast to the pagan understanding of their idols.

Furthermore, Keener explains that Gentiles were agnostic about the nature of the deity, but rejected the multiplication of deities corresponding to human characteristics or needs.[31] Thus, humans making images in their own likeness, the mythical portrayals of some immortals staying old, various human activities, injustice, violence, and crime were topics of potential ridicule; therefore in this setting, Paul is rivaling the concept of the "Living God" over against polytheistic dead gods.[32]

Paul's Speech at Areopagus: Acts 17:22–31

Acts 17 contains arguably the most popular and thorough apologetics preaching from Paul. A wide array of research has been carried out on this speech regarding its content.[33] Other studies treat the rhetoric.[34] The speech

---

29. Peterson, *The Acts of the Apostles*, 410.
30. Peterson, *The Acts of the Apostles*, 411.
31. Keener, *Acts*, 2159.
32. Keener, *Acts*, 2165.
33. To cite some: Dibelius, *Studies in the Acts of the Apostles*; Winter, "On Introducing Gods to Athens: An Alternative Reading of Acts 17:18–20,"; Jipp, "Paul's Areopagus Speech of Acts 17:16–34 as Both Critique and Propaganda,"; Bailey, "Acts 17:16–34"; Schnabel, "Contextualising Paul in Athens: The Proclamation of the Gospel before Pagan Audiences in the Graeco-Roman World," 172–90. Given, "Not Either/Or but Both/And in Paul's Areopagus Speech," 356–72; Gray, "Implied Audiences in the Areopagus Narrative," 205–18; Gärtner, *The Areopagus Speech and Natural Revelation*; Shields, "The Areopagus Sermon and Roman 1:18: A Study in Creation Theology," 23–40; Conzelmann, "Address of Paul on the Areopagus," 217–30; Sandnes, "Paul and Socrates: The Aim of Paul's Areopagus Speech," 13–26; Rowe, "The Grammar of Life: The Areopagus Speech and Pagan Tradition," 31–50; Gangel, "Paul's Areopagus Speech," 308–12.
34. To cite some: Dibelius, *Studies in the Acts of the Apostles*, 17; Zweck, "The Exordium of the Areopagus Speech, Acts 17:22,23"; Winter and Clarke, *The Book of Acts in Its Ancient Literary Setting*; Gray, "Implied Audiences in the Areopagus Narrative"; Given,

has generated much research on its missional implications as well.[35] In this speech, Paul addresses the audience at the Areopagus who is known for religious fervor, as he is invited to speak on the new idea about God. Out of this plethora of writings, I will mainly focus on cultural response from Paul against cultural objections towards the Christian faith.

Cultural Context

Among many, one of the distinctive features of the Hellenistic world was its philosophical diversity and religious syncretism.[36] Moreover, a feature that accompanied this philosophical and religious phenomenon was the imperial cult.[37] In other words, "perhaps the most dominant form of Hellenistic pluralism Paul encountered came in the form of the Greek pantheon."[38] Mystery and magic cults along with a plethora of idols and gods were pervasive throughout Paul's world. It indeed was "pluralism *par excellence*."[39] Numbers of historical records indicate that "significant politico-religious changes occurred in Athens with the coming of Rome

---

"Not Either/Or but Both/And in Paul's Areopagus Speech"; Joseph Pathrapankal, "From Areopagus to Corinth (Acts 17:22–31; I Cor 2:1–5): A Study on the Transition from the Power of Knowledge to the Power of the Spirit," 61–80.

35. To cite some: Lotter and Thompson, "Acts 17:16–34 as Paradigm in Responding to Postmodernity"; Winter, "Introducing the Athenians to God: Paul's Failed Apologetic in Acts 17?" Strandenaes, "The Missionary Speeches in the Acts of the Apostles and Their Missiological Implications"; Charles, "Engaging the (Neo) Pagan Mind: Paul's Encounter with Athenian Culture as a Model for Cultural Apologetics (Acts 17:16–34)"; Strait, "The Wisdom of Solomon, Ruler Cults, and Paul's Polemic against Idols in the Areopagus Speech," 609–32; Mărculeț, "Elements of Inculturation in Saint Paul's Speech from Areopagus," 28–48; Mauro, "Witnessing Lessons from the Areopagus," 186–95; Aarde, "Reading the Areopagus Speech in Acts 17 from the Perspective of Sacral Manumission of Slaves in Ancient Greece," 47–58. Flemming, "Contextualizing the Gospel in Athens: Paul's Aeropagus Address as a Paradigm for Missionary Communication," 199–214; Schnabel, "Contextualising Paul in Athens."

36. Lotter and Thompson, "Acts 17:16–34 as Paradigm in Responding to Postmodernity," 697.

37. Lotter and Thompson, "Acts 17:16–34 as Paradigm in Responding to Postmodernity," 697.

38. Lotter and Thompson, "Acts 17:16–34 as Paradigm in Responding to Postmodernity," 697.

39. Lotter and Thompson, "Acts 17:16–34 as Paradigm in Responding to Postmodernity," 698.

to the East"—the introduction of the imperial cult.[40] Athens long enjoyed having prominence in deciding whether these imperial gods should be honored in Greece.[41]

Within Athens, another important aspect of the cultural context comes from the fact that Areopagus is a testing ground. "The approval or disapproval of new gods being added to the Athenian Pantheon continued to set a precedent for other Greek cities."[42] Talbert points to a text such as *Lives of Eminent Philosophers* by Diogenes Laertius that illuminates the cultural status of Areopagus as a "regular scene for the trial of a philosopher."[43] At the Areopagus, "the imperial high-priest may have been the person who moved the motion . . . The Council of the Areopagus would have been the body responsible for initiating action for the assimilation of the new god."[44] In this context, Athenians would have seen Paul was a herald of either foreign deities or imperial cult. Nature and the role Areopagus played in the cultural context confirm the fact that "Paul was seen by his hearers to be announcing new deities to the Athenians."[45]

Notably, the concept of "trial before the philosophers" carried a heavy cultural significance in the context of Paul's Areopagus speech: "In a culture that values, in matters of religion, the old and the traditional, the charge of newness and strangeness constitutes the ultimate refutation of religion."[46] Even if pagan philosophers dislike or disagree with teaching, it was vindicated by its tradition. For this reason, Tacitus expresses his disdain for Jewish rites but confesses that Jewish worship is "vindicated by antiquity."[47] Therefore, Athenians' interest in entertaining new ideas was a severe deviation to the typical cultural mindset but was fueled by curiosity. Hence, "the Athenian Areopagus is portrayed by Luke as effete intellectuals violating their own behavior the very standard they are charged to protect."[48]

Thus, Paul's speech here in Areopagus would have been perceived either as the "initial legal instrument in the process of admission of new

40. Winter, "On Introducing Gods to Athens," 75.
41. Winter, "On Introducing Gods to Athens," 75.
42. Winter, "On Introducing Gods to Athens," 73.
43. Talbert, *Reading Acts*, 160.
44. Winter, "On Introducing Gods to Athens," 79.
45. Winter, "On Introducing Gods to Athens," 80.
46. Talbert, *Reading Acts*, 160.
47. Tacitus, *History* 5.5
48. Talbert, *Reading Acts*, 161.

imperial gods and goddess," or "like Socrates, on trial before the most revered tribunal in the ancient world, demonstrating the incongruity that exists between the Christian movement's understanding of God and the polytheism."[49] Socrates reportedly instructed Athenians through trial about true religion, and Paul is seen to be conducting the same here.[50] Gerd Lüdemann observes that Socrates "argued with the representatives of philosophical schools, who accused him of introducing new gods."[51] Lüdemann again highlights Luke's assessment that Areopagus is the "best-known place of judgment in Athens, mentioning it for the narrative effect in order to produce a worthy scene for Paul's speech."[52] He also suggests that the word Areopagus has two options in meaning: first, the hill of Ares; and second, the legal authorities. Considering Luke's emphasis and the significance the location has in the narrative, Lüdemann believes the latter is more accurate.[53]

Issues of Cultural Objection

Drew Strait argues that Paul's criticism of objects of worship and listing of precious materials "is not a politically innocuous speech act when reading alongside the Wisdom of Solomon."[54] He contends that Luke is confronting "the iconic spectacle of gods and imperial authority with the gospel of the Lord of all—a worldview that is incompatible with the euergetic visual culture underlying the visibility of gods and kings."[55] The presence of the imperial cult constitutes a political dimension as part of the cultural objection present in the scene. Hence, Strait argues that "the imperial family's cosmogonic associations with traditional gods in Athens illustrate how Paul's allusive rhetoric could include a political dimension."[56]

---

49. Jipp, "Paul's Areopagus Speech of Acts 17" 574.
50. Keener, *Acts*, 2625.
51. Lüdemann, *Early Christianity According to the Traditions in Acts*, 189.
52. Lüdemann, *Early Christianity According to the Traditions in Acts*, 190.
53. Lüdemann, *Early Christianity According to the Traditions in Acts*, 190.
54. Strait, "The Wisdom of Solomon, Ruler Cults, and Paul's Polemic against Idols," 610.
55. Strait, "The Wisdom of Solomon, Ruler Cults, and Paul's Polemic against Idols," 610.
56. Strait, "The Wisdom of Solomon, Ruler Cults, and Paul's Polemic against Idols," 616.

Response to Objections

Paul responds to cultural objections in several ways. To begin, Paul corrects the error of the imperial cult and dismantles its foundation. Bruce Winter contends that Paul initially aims to clarify who exactly "the unknown God" is, of whom they have an inscription, but is preparing for a seismic confrontation against pagan culture and its worldview.[57] At odds with Dibelius's ill-advised argument that the speech is essentially a monotheistic sermon with a Christian message attached at the end, Paul's discussion of the nature of God cannot be separated from Christological message, for such a nature of God is attested through the resurrection.[58] Winter writes,

> (Paul) cites the resurrection of Jesus from the dead as the 'proof' given by this deity to all mankind (31b). That they mocked him at this point is explicable. The august Council of the Areopagites had been founded on these words: 'When a man dies, the earth drinks up his blood. There is no resurrection (anastasis)' (Aeschylus, *Eumenides* 647–48). Here, Paul contradicted the very principle on which this ruling body of Athens had been established to judge those guilty of crimes. They believed that offenders could not be left for judgment in the afterlife because there was no resurrection from the dead. Judgment, therefore, had to be passed before the death of the accused. This had been the traditional remit of the Areopagus until the coming of Rome when matters of a criminal nature were transferred to the jurisdiction of the governor of the province. The Athenian audience who had cast Paul in the role of a herald seeking to introduce new deities to Athens would have realized at this point in the speech that it was neither he nor his 'God' was seeking to secure their official *imprimatur*. Rather, Paul was announcing that a judicial role which they had traditionally fulfilled was suddenly reversed.[59]

The risen Jesus is proclaimed as the supreme Judge before whom all must give an account for, and this is direct defiance to the cultural norm.

Then, Paul, recurrently and strategically employing the language of his audience and pagan understanding of philosophy introduces the superiority

---

57. Winter, "Introducing the Athenians to God," 46.

58. Dibelius's assessment appears in his often-cited chapter, "Paul on the Areopagus" See Dibelius, *Studies in the Acts of the Apostles*. Also see Dionne, "La Figure Narrative de Dieu Dans Le Discours à Lystre (Ac 14,15–17)," 101–24.

59. Winter, "Introducing the Athenians to God," 47.

of the Christian distinctive.[60] Joshua Jipp argues that there are two congruent agendas in Paul's speech at the Areopagus: the first is to "narrate the complete incongruity between the Christian movement and the Gentile religion" and the second is to "exalt the Christian movement as comprising the best features of Greco-Roman philosophical sensibilities and therefore as a superior philosophy."[61] "Though the theology of the Areopagus speech is refracted through the monotheism of an altar to an unknown god, its criticism—within its own framework—is ultimately toward all gentile religiosity."[62] Paul takes over the "topics, tools, and scripts of Greco-Roman philosophy, particularly matters of true worship and piety" to in fact reveal the Athenians' ignorance and superstition regarding deity while transitioning into a proclamation of God's identity.[63] In essence,

> Paul engages in a critique of his audience with respect to superstition and idolatry by using Hellenistic philosophical tools and by Hellenizing biblical traditions. In so doing, he demonstrates that his movement's beliefs about God not only demonstrate it to be legitimate but even prove it to be a superior form of religion. The Christian movement embodies the philosophical elite's ideals better and more consistently than do the Athenians. Luke thereby fuses Septuagintal traditions with Hellenistic philosophy regarding monotheism, worship of images, and anthropology both to critique and to legitimate.[64]

Paul's intention is to present Christianity as a superior worldview, which is now evidenced by his testimony of Jesus's resurrection. He challenges the pagan understanding of the nature of God and their epistemology.[65] Paul's speech aims to ultimately "break the connection between God and the world that underwrites pagan religion" by "reshaping of the reader's religious imagination by placing its theological foundation in the transcendence of the Creator God over the world of images."[66] Paul's introduction of Israel's God is both transcendent and immanent—as Christ is God-Man:

---

60. Jipp, "Paul's Areopagus Speech of Acts 17," 2012.

61. Jipp, "Paul's Areopagus Speech of Acts 17," 568.

62. Strait, "The Wisdom of Solomon, Ruler Cults, and Paul's Polemic against Idols in the Areopagus Speech," 616.

63. Jipp, "Paul's Areopagus Speech of Acts 17," 576–78.

64. Jipp, "Paul's Areopagus Speech of Acts 17," 576.

65. Jipp, "Paul's Areopagus Speech of Acts 17," 581.

66. Rowe, *World Upside Down*, 36.

this duality of God's transcendence and immanence renders Christianity unparalleled to any other worldview found in the cultural context.[67]

Yet another approach Paul takes in response to the cultural objection is to highlight the incompatibility of idolatry to the divine nature. "The link between God and humanity through this concept of generation allows Paul to dismiss idolatry as foreign to the divine nature, and aptly places the creatures in its creaturely relation to the Creator."[68] Paul overturns their logic: if humans are offspring of God, one should be allowed to surmise that divinity does not consist of material substance, or represented by gold, silver, or any other forms crafted by human hands.[69]

Paul's Speech before Felix: 24:10b-21

Paul stands before Felix for his defense. Many have identified this speech as forensic in form.[70] Paul stands before the social and political notables of Palestine, the Roman procurators, and the Jewish King. Here Tertullus makes a formal accusation against Paul, citing charges of stirring up a riot and profaning the temple. This formal courthouse accusation sets the setting for Paul's speech in Acts 24.

Cultural Context

According to Bruce Malina and John Pilch, legal proceedings in the ancient world were not known to guarantee justice.[71] "Just as U.S. legal proceedings are concerned with winning, in parallel fashion, ancient Mediterranean legal proceedings were concerned with dishonoring one's opponents." In fact, someone who was not able to avoid a legal proceeding was considered a failure; all the more if one could not afford to bribe the judge.[72] In fact, Michael Gray-Fow suggests that this may well be the reason Paul waited

---

67. Jipp, "Paul's Areopagus Speech of Acts 17," 581.
68. Porter, *Paul in Acts*, 121.
69. Porter, *Paul in Acts*, 121.
70. Tajra, *The Trial of St. Paul*; Neyrey, "The Forensic Defense Speech and Paul's Trial Speeches in Acts 22–26: Form and Function," 210–24; Sherwin-White, *Roman Society and Roman Law in the New Testament*; Talbert, *Perspectives on Luke-Acts*.
71. Malina and Pilch, *Social-Science Commentary on the Book of Acts*, 162–63.
72. Malina and Pilch, *Social-Science Commentary on the Book of Acts*, 162.

until Festus succeeded Felix, rather than directly appealing his case to Caesar.[73]

Along this line, Tacitus and Josephus both annotate the terrible reputation Felix had among the Romans.[74] Tacitus says Felix was "backed by vast influence, believed himself to be free to commit any crime," and "practiced every kind of cruelty and lust, wielding the power of a king with all the instincts of a slave."[75] Josephus pronounces that during Felix's administration, Jewish social chaos reached new heights. Felix's administration responded to riots in Caesarea, killing many Jews and property plundered in the process of subjugating the crowd. The result was the Jewish delegation pleading the case against Felix before Nero.[76]

Issues of Cultural Objection

Paul here again opens with the usual complimentary *exordium*.[77] "Though the setting was that of Paul's defense before the Jewish charges, the result was invariably Paul's witness to Christ. For this witness, the resurrection was primary."[78] The cultural objection present in this scene is exposed by Tertullus. Harry Tajra explains that Tertullus's aim is to convince Felix that Paul's "preaching was causing a public disturbance in the constituted Jewish communities through the empire and that the imperial authorities could not remain indifferent to such subversive activity."[79] This is reflecting the fact that the governor may be reluctant to convict Paul purely on religious charges. Tajra draws attention to the fact that Tertullus's polemic "highlights the political ramifications of Paul's deeds."[80] In other words, Christianity is represented as a new faith outside Judaism. There is a clash of culture and worldview from orthodox rabbinic tradition.[81]

---

73. Gray-Fow, "Why Festus, Not Felix? Paul's Caesarem Appello," 473–85.
74. For a fuller treatment on Felix's background, See: Brenk and Rossi, "The 'Notorious' Felix, Procurator of Judaea, and His Many Wives (Acts 23—24)," 410–17.
75. *Annals* 12.54; *Histories* 5.9, as cited by Malin and Pilch.
76. Talbert, *Reading Acts*, 205.
77. Bruce, *Commentary on the Book of the Acts*, 468.
78. Polhill, *Acts*, 477.
79. Tajra, *The Trial of St. Paul*, 121.
80. Tajra, *The Trial of St. Paul*, 121.
81. Tajra, *The Trial of St. Paul*, 122.

Tertullus's charge against Paul concerns with socio-cultural context as well. Tertullus refers to Paul as λοιμός, a pest or a pestilent fellow, but the term more accurately describes Tertullus's sentiment is a "public enemy."[82] Malina and Pilch explain that the term would connote contagion, and an agitator, and a ringleader of the faction.[83] A faction centered on a particular person—such as Jesus of Nazareth during Tertullus's lifetime—continued to exist but by Paul's time, it has morphed into a new form.[84] Tertullus viewed a newly formed faction that is centered on Jesus to be engaging in on-going conflict with other factions as he saw it develop into a group-centered coalition or party.[85]

Coupled with this agitation, Felix would not have viewed Paul's faction as a legitimate religion. Rome boasted general tolerance regarding relations with the realm of the deity; therefore, the matter at hand for Felix was the veracity of Paul's claim that Jesus of Nazareth died but was alive.[86] Malin and Perch again write that the issue handled in Felix's court was their local, cultural code of conduct, observing that "in the ancient, Greco-Roman world, a just or upright person was someone who knew and played by the specific cultural rules of the game in his cultural context."[87]

Response to Objections

Paul follows up his *exordium* and *probatio* with his *refutation*.[88] In this section, Paul dismisses the charges brought against him, specifically the charge that Paul was the ring-leader of the Nazarenes.[89] The way Paul is able to prove his opponent wrong is first by "readily admitting his association with them."[90] Paul, responding to the cultural objection raised by

---

82. Malina and Pilch, *Social-Science Commentary on the Book of Acts*, 163.

83. Malina and Pilch, *Social-Science Commentary on the Book of Acts*, 163.

84. Malina and Pilch further explain how factions centered in Jesus of Nazareth stood in conflict with many Judeans.

85. Malina and Pilch, *Social-Science Commentary on the Book of Acts*, 162–63.

86. Malina and Pilch, *Social-Science Commentary on the Book of Acts*, 166.

87. Malina and Pilch, *Social-Science Commentary on the Book of Acts*, 164–66.

88. Bruce W. Winter, "Official Proceedings and the Forensic Speeches in Acts 24–26," in *Book of Acts in Its First Century Setting*, ed. Bruce W. Winter and Andrew D. Clarke (Grand Rapids: Paternoster Press, 1993), 325.

89. Winter, "Official Proceedings and the Forensic Speeches in Acts 24–26," 325.

90. Winter, "Official Proceedings and the Forensic Speeches in Acts 24–26," 325.

Tertullus, declares that he has worshipped the God of "our fathers" and never deviated from believing both the Scripture and the resurrection of the just and the unjust, "even as his accusers did."[91] Paul's mention of "God of fathers" indicates that in Paul's mind, he has never left Judaism.[92]

Paul recognizes that certain Jews from Asia formed the revolting crowd and brought accusations against him. "When he entered the Temple there was no crowd or uproar, so if this group has a charge against him, they should appear before Felix, too. The only statement that he shouted out was that he was on trial for the resurrection of the dead."[93] The implication Paul has in mind is that "their competence to act as witnesses or accusers were restricted to that examination which Claudius Lysias had permitted,"[94] as he aims to "draw the parameters for the Jews present, including the high priest, to act in a legal way before Felix and bring a criminal charge which could be sustained in a court of law."[95] Paul thus aims to dismantle the challenge brought before him.

Further, as Loveday Alexander argues, the trial of Paul not only attests to Paul's innocence but also "embodies an inclusive political vision that is profoundly subversive of the imperial order."[96] She opines that one be mindful of a double audience: those who Paul addresses during the Roman tribunal and the "third-level audience"—the readers who hear above and behind the dramatic audiences inscribed in the text.[97] "What Luke shows us is a Paul solidly rooted in the political realities of his day, a Paul who knows how to survive within an oppressive system and who will use all the weapons at his disposal to do so."[98] Paul has both the rhetorical capabilities and the Roman citizenship to not only to navigate through the bureaucracy of the imperial system, but also to "demonstrate an ultimate allegiance that transcends the real, but strictly limited, the authority given to earthly rulers."[99]

---

91. Winter, "Official Proceedings and the Forensic Speeches in Acts 24–26," 325.
92. Tajra, *The Trial of St. Paul*, 127.
93. Porter, *Paul in Acts*, 157.
94. Winter, "Official Proceedings and the Forensic Speeches in Acts 24–26," 326.
95. Winter, "Official Proceedings and the Forensic Speeches in Acts 24–26," 326.
96. Alexander, "Luke's Political Vision," 283.
97. Alexander, "Luke's Political Vision," 287.
98. Alexander, "Luke's Political Vision," 287.
99. Alexander, "Luke's Political Vision," 290.

Paul's Speech before King Agrippa: Acts 26:2-23, 25-27, 29

The speech marks the culmination and climax of Paul's defense in 21–26. This is Paul's summary of the Christological message conveyed in the book of Acts.[100] Paul explains that the reason for the bond and chains is his unwavering commitment to the fact of the resurrection of Jesus Christ. Paul here is "not operating in the usual forensic mode; in other words, Paul is not offering attacks on opponents or extended rebuttals of charges. It is a broader appeal - more of an *apologia pro vita sua*."[101] In essence, Paul is not offering a defense of himself against political charges; rather he is presenting a positive case for his understanding of newly found salvation message in God's work in Christ testified by His resurrection.

Cultural Context

Herod Agrippa II was the great-grandson of Herod the Great, and thus for Luke, a figure who was halfway between Rome and Judaism.[102] King Agrippa, a "half Judean by genealogy," but more so by his "Hellenistic Judean enculturation," he would have much familiarity when customs and controversies of Judeans.[103] "True to the agnostic nature of Mediterranean cultures, Judeans were continually involved in never-ending discussions and disputes as is reflected in much later rabbinic literature."[104] Comparatively, Romans were highly suspicious and fearful of secret societies, secret rites, and secret teachings; thus, there may be a hint of intention in Paul reminding Agrippa of his familiarity with Israelite tradition and the Prophets.[105] Furthermore, charging a philosopher as being made was common to antiquity, Dio Chrysostom being one of the examples—hence, madness due to learning denoted that one was in elevated social status.[106]

Social status was a cultural factor Paul was ready to employ. By Paul's time, the right of appeal was made available to all Roman citizens living

---

100. Witherington, *The Acts of the Apostles*, 735.
101. Witherington, *The Acts of the* Apostle, 736.
102. Kilgallen, "Paul before Agrippa (Acts 26:2-23), 170.
103. Malina and Pilch, *Social-Science Commentary on the Book of Acts*, 167.
104. Malina and Pilch, *Social-Science Commentary on the Book of Acts*, 167.
105. Malina and Pilch, *Social-Science Commentary on the Book of Acts*, 167.
106. Malina and Pilch, *Social-Science Commentary on the Book of Acts*, 170.

Contextualization of Paul's Apologetics Speeches

in the provinces.[107] Records of Tacitus and Pliny tell of incidents where Roman citizens charged with various offenses receive an opportunity to plead their case before the emperor. "The right to appeal was reaffirmed by the promulgation in Augustus's reign of the *Lex Iulia de vi publica et private* . . . Paul knows his rights and uses them for his protection."[108] Festus sets a date to entertain the case in Caesarea; and his decision is "based on a fundamental Roman principle (*ethos*), that the accusers must appear in person to make their case against the accused, and that the accused must be allowed an opportunity (*topos*) for self-defense (*apologia*)."[109]

Issues of Cultural Objection

King Agrippa was a "man who could speak intelligibly to the Romans of things Jewish."[110] He was the great-grandson of Herod the Great: thus for Luke, he is a figure that represents a link between Rome and Judaism.[111] Indeed, Agrippa "could speak like a pagan theologian," yet was highly Romanized.[112] Combination of these two cultural background information, along with the accuser's practical need, the objection against Paul and his message of the resurrection is "couched in political terms."[113] In other words, it is packaged as a political issue; yet at the heart, it is an objection to the proclamation of the resurrection.

Response to Objection

Paul responds to mainly two charges: first, that Paul believes in the resurrection from the dead. To the first charge, Paul's logical strategy is not to stay on the defensive but to get on the offensive.[114] Paul contends that he is not causing dissension; instead, he argues that Christian belief in the

---

107. Talbert, *Reading Acts*, 209.
108. Talbert, *Reading Acts*, 209.
109. Alexander, "Luke's Political Vision," 284.
110. Rowe, *World Upside Down*, 83.
111. Kilgallen, "Paul before Agrippa (Acts 26:2–23), 170.
112. Rowe cites Josephus recording Agrippa's confession concerning the shifting of the goddess to be responsible for fortune and fate. He also cites Braund, *Rome and the Friendly King*.
113. Rapske, *The Book of Acts and Paul in Roman Custody*, 151.
114. Soards, *The Speeches in Acts*, 122.

resurrection is a fulfillment of the promise given to their ancestors and the Twelve Tribes—the resurrection is "what the Twelve Tribes must hope for if they hope to have what was promised to our fathers. Paul thus challenges both Sadducee and pagan to reevaluate their convictions about the resurrection of the dead."[115]

Cultural Responses in Paul's Speeches: Conclusion

Paul's apologetics speeches are given in cultural context. They concern themselves with addressing the cultural objection—whether implied or explicit. C. Kavin Rowe affirms that the complex, and at times confusing, convergence between paganism and Christianity conveyed "the clash between the exclusivity of the Christian God and the wider mode of pagan religiousness."[116] To be exact, it essentially is not merely a minor adjustment of cultural practices, but involves "an extraction or removal from constitutive aspects of pagan culture and a concomitant cultural profile that rendered Christians identifiable by outsiders."[117] Paul's speeches aimed at cultural intelligibility, culturally contextualized its message, all the while crystallizing the gospel to pagan ears.

PRELIMINARY THOUGHTS ON SCHEME OF APOSTOLIC SPEECHES

Having considered how Paul's speeches address the issues arising from a cultural context, I now turn to observe it from a wider vantage point: does Paul's culturally contextualized apologetics occur as a strategy? I suggest that it does. I argue that, akin to kerygmatic speeches found in Acts, Paul's apologetics speeches operate as a scheme. In other words, cultural connections via cultural point of contact and cultural solidarity, as well as responses to cultural objections via the virtue of Christian life and exposition of the resurrection, consistently emerge out of Paul's apologetics speeches. To illustrate, I will re-survey the apologetics speeches to detect elements of the scheme proposed above. But before, a few preliminary discussion is due

---

115. Kilgallen, "Paul before Agrippa (Acts 26:2–23)" 176.
116. Rowe, *World Upside Down*, 17–18.
117. Rowe, *World Upside Down*, 18.

regarding the role of audience, scheme in kerygmatic speeches, and scheme in apologetics speeches.

Double Audience

Studies have investigated various literary features and functions of the speeches in the book of Acts and produced valuable insights.[118] They help the modern-day reader gain greater discernment regarding Luke's intention and its application in the present day. Correspondingly, interpretation of Acts with literary sensitivities enables modern-day readers to make the distinction between Luke's primary audience and a secondary audience.[119] In the following, I make the distinction between the two by denoting the primary audience as those who are physically present in Paul's speeches narrative; whereas, the secondary audience encompasses Theophilus, those audiences in the first century, and all those who read the narrative in consequent years.[120] Mark Given advocates the importance of such distinction, arguing that historical-critical hermeneutics fail to detect Luke's intention without taking the implied reader into the interpretation.[121] Patrick Gray also asserts, "Close attention to Luke's compositional technique reveals the ways in which the Areopagus narrative is not aimed at a monolithic Gentile audience but rather engages multiple implied readers."[122] This awareness enables a deeper understanding of how the speeches were organized as a whole. To this end, the schemes in kerygmatic speeches illumine the way the speeches in Acts operate.

Schemes in Kerygmatic Speeches

C. H. Dodd clarifies the term *kerygma* by singularizing the act of preaching apart from the content. He writes, "Though the word is translated as

---

118. Long, "The Trial of Paul in the Book of Acts: Historical, Literary, and Theological Consideration"; Evans, *Ancient Texts for New Testament Studies*; Talbert, *Reading Acts*; Winter and Clarke, *The Book of Acts in Its Ancient Literary Setting*.

119. Loveday Alexander uses the expression, 'third-level audience' and Patrick Gray, "implied audience."

120. Loveday Alexander and C. Kavin Rowe sees speeches in Acts as literary elements that move forward the narrative.

121. Given, "Not Either/Or but Both/And in Paul's Areopagus Speech."

122. Gray, "Implied Audiences in the Areopagus Narrative," 205.

preaching, it signifies not the action of the preacher, but that which he preaches, his 'message.'"[123] He continues to pinpoint the teachings that include either ethical instruction or exposition of theological doctrine to be separate from a public proclamation of Christianity to the non-Christian world. Dodd clarifies that the term "preaching the gospel" denoted a specific type of preaching that aimed at producing converts, as much as handing down the teaching of Jesus was important.[124]

Dodd's line of reasoning is profitable to the argument set forth by this book in three aspects. Dodd argues the following: first, Paul did not preach out of a vacuum; instead, he had received *kerygma* from the tradition that constituted his proclamation. Second, though fragmentary evidence limits a fuller comprehension of Paul's *kerygma*, at least Paul's *kerygmatic* preaching demonstrates a different bent to the ones found in Peter's preaching. In other words, there is a distinctive Pauline *kerygma* that is different than Jerusalem *kerygma*. Third, *kerygma* functioned as a foundation; and others including Paul built superstructures on top of it. In other words, the contents of *kerygma* operated as one of the parts in each preaching Paul proclaimed.

Martin Dibelius detects that speeches in Acts all possess "a similar, well-planned outline whose sections are frequently repeated and only accidentally change their order." He writes, "Thus we have the right to speak of a scheme which the author consciously accepts and which consists of the following: *kerygma* or message, scriptural proof, an exhortation to repentance."[125] Dibelius recognizes that these may appear in short sentences or two, yet both the repetition and similarity in tone proves to be unmistakable.[126] More importantly, he claims that such a constitution of repeated materials is "intentional."[127] There is a scheme that moves the speeches in Acts.

Richard Bauckham agrees with Dodd's and Dibelius's analysis while qualifying it with his own suggestions. He argues that indeed the scheme constitutes the form of Acts speeches and that they take on more variations than Dibelius suggested. Bauckham stresses the flexibility and variability found in the speeches by stating, "The form was hospitable to variation and

---

123. Dodd, *The Apostolic Preaching and Its Developments*, 7.
124. Dodd, *The Apostolic Preaching and Its Developments*, 8.
125. Dibelius, *From Tradition to Gospel*, 16–17.
126. Dibelius, *From Tradition to Gospel*, 17.
127. Dibelius, *From Tradition to Gospel*, 17.

innovation."[128] Moreover, Bauckham argues and illustrates if elements such as kerygmatic summaries functioned as a scheme, early Christian literature should reflect its function.[129] It appears that the pattern is already visible in speeches in Acts.[130] Now the question arises: is there a pattern in Paul's apologetics speeches?

THE SCHEME IN PAUL'S APOLOGETICS SPEECHES

Bertil E. Gärtner believes the answer to whether there is a pattern in Paul's apologetics speeches is positive. He argues that "Areopagus speech can legitimately be considered a typical exemplar of the first Christian sermons to the Gentiles."[131] Eduard Schweizer equally notices the consistencies patterned after the exemplar sermon: "With due recognition of differences in contents, a far-reaching identity of structure" is present in speeches in Acts.[132] "Many verbal, thematic, and structural connections connect the words and deeds of the three principal actors, Jesus, Peter, and Paul."[133] Schweizer also observes "a largely parallel structure" between Paul's speech in Acts 14 and Acts 17: (1) direct address, (2) a misunderstanding pointed out, (3) reference to the proclamation of the apostles, (4) call to repentance, and (5) passages from Scripture, as those common factors.[134] He stresses that even when compared to other speeches, the structure is present: the

---

128. Bauckham, "Kerygmatic Summaries in the Speeches of Acts," 190.

129. Bauckham, "Kerygmatic Summaries in the Speeches of Acts."

130. Strandenaes argues for the occurrences of common structures in all of Acts speeches. The missionary speech (the kerygma) i: 2:22–40; ii: 3:17–26; iii: 4:9–12; iv: 5:30–32; v: 10:37–43; vi: 13:27–41; vii: 14:15d-17; viii: 17:24–31. The kerygma is sometimes introduced by addressing the audience once more; i: 2:22; ii: 3:17; iii: nil; iv: nil; v: nil; vi: 13:26; vii: nil; viii: nil, and by including the following three elements (not necessarily in the same order): (a) A short summary of the life, death, and resurrection of Jesus, or an account of Gods work and its relevance i: 2:22–24, (31–36); ii: 3:13–15, 18–21; iii: 4:10; iv: 5:30–32; v: 10:37–42; vi: 13:27–31; vii: 14:15–17; viii: 17:24–28a. (b) Proof from Scripture or scriptures - quotation and exposition; i: 2:25–36; ii: 3: 22–26; iii: 4:11; iv: nil; v: 10:43; vi: 13:32–37; vii: nil; viii: 17:28b. (c) An admonition: call for repentance; i: 2:37–40; ii: 3:17–21; iii: 4:12 (indirectly); iv: 5:31 (indirectly); vi: 13:38–41; vii: 14:15c; viii: 17:29–31. Strandenaes, "The Missionary Speeches in the Acts of the Apostles and Their Missiological Implications."

131. Gärtner, *The Areopagus Speech and Natural Revelation*, 71.

132. Schweizer, "Concerning the Speeches in Acts," 210.

133. Zwiep, *Christ, the Spirit and the Community of God*, 164–65.

134. Schweizer, "Concerning the Speeches in Acts," 212–13.

only significant mode of change is the audience.[135] Depending on the audience, "*Christo*logical kerygma is replaced by the *theo*logical one wherever a typical Gentile congregation is listening" (italics his).[136]

In like manner, I argue and show that there is a scheme that is common to Paul's apologetics speeches to the Gentiles, as shown in table 4.

Table 4. Scheme of Paul's Culturally Contextualized Apologetics Speeches

Elements	Acts 14	Acts 17	Acts 24	Acts 26
Cultural Point of Contact	v.17	v.22, 28	v.10	v.2–3
Cultural Solidarity	v.15a	v.23	v.17–18b	v.4–5
Virtue of the Christian Life	v.15b	v.30	v.11–13, 16	v.19–21
Exposition of Resurrection	v.15?[137]	v.31	v.21	v.23

The scheme consists of patterned elements, namely a cultural connection, cultural solidarity, the discussion of the Christian life as an alternative to their culture, and an exposition of the resurrection. To elaborate, I contend that one of the *kerygma*-like messages that repeatedly appear in Paul's apologetics speech is the virtue of the Christian life. This forms Paul's response to cultural objection includes, and is an effort to draw attention to, the anthropological side in Christian faith. Moreover, as part of the scheme, Paul's apologetics speeches consistently contain an exposition of the resurrection. The following now demonstrates these elements in Paul's apologetics speeches.

Acts 14

Cultural Point of Contact

Paul's proclamation about God establishes the cultural point of contact. "The monotheistic language may well be addressed directly at a belief in Zeus as the creator God, reflecting beliefs held in southern Asia Minor

---

135. Schweizer, "Concerning the Speeches in Acts," 214.
136. Schweizer, "Concerning the Speeches in Acts," 214.
137. See my discussion below on "Living God."

CONTEXTUALIZATION OF PAUL'S APOLOGETICS SPEECHES

at the time, and reflected in the way Paul and Barnabas were met by the Lystrans."[138] Creator God's benevolent provision on human beings given through nourishment and gladness is revelation self-attested in nature.[139] Richard Rackham asserts,

> Paul here uses the method of accommodation. He starts with a doctrine they would readily accept—creation by God; he appeals that evidence which would be most obvious to country folks—the witness of nature; and he makes use of their present state of feeling—the gladness and joy of a festival.[140]

Cultural Solidarity

Porter remarks that there is "an appeal to the commonality of human nature" in this speech.[141] Paul answers his own rhetorical question, "Why are you doing these things?" by emphatically stating that they all are of the same human nature: "Here appeal to a common human nature points to a common conception of humanity, with common origins, common destiny, and common functions."[142] Despite the fact that the audience of Paul's speech here is Gentiles, there is no division at all. Porter writes, "Paul attempts to erase any distinctions, and places all of humanity on common ground."[143]

Johnson comments that "such unsophisticated religiosity provides Luke the opportunity to have Paul and Barnabas appear both as genuine

---

138. Porter, *Paul in Acts*, 139.

139. Lenski, *The Interpretation of the Acts of the Apostles*, 580.

140. Rackham, *The Acts of the Apostles*, 233.

141. Porter, in discussing the speech at Lystra, makes two important observations and assessments. First, though this speech is shorter than others, it nevertheless demonstrates that the speech is "surprisingly consonant with other speeches by Paul in Acts." The second is that because this is not Paul's and Barnabas's first missionary visit, positively presupposing that they have already encountered a variety of situations similar to the one at Lystra, one can give "credence to the idea that (even if) the words are not those of Paul, but those of the author only, it is still significant to note that he has put into Paul's mouth words that are consistent with Paul's other missionary speeches." This hints the presence of a kerygma-type material present in apologetics speeches. Porter, *Paul in Acts*, 137.

142. Porter, *Paul in Acts*, 138.

143. Porter, *Paul in Acts*, 139.

philosophers who reject attempts at deification."[144] Mikeal Parsons also opines that "Luke employs (with variation) the literary *topos* of the self-disclosing sage whose commitment to wisdom and truth compels him to full disclosure in order to guard against misimpressions regarding his powers."[145] He cites Dio Chrysostom's discussion of the proper response to the crowd's excessive admiration: "(1) He should tear his garments; (2) he should leap forth naked upon the public highways; (3) thus he will prove to all the world that he is no better than any other man," arguing that the actions of Paul and Barnabas "closely correspond to the literary topos of what the sages should do."[146] The tearing of garments and rushing out functions as "a symbolic gesture of 'self-disclosure,' and an 'ocular demonstration' that the sage has nothing to hide."[147]

A Virtue of the Christian Life[148]

Due to the brevity of the speech, this element is the least visible; but nevertheless is included as part of the scheme. To demonstrate that life in Christ is worth the living instead of living for the vain idols, Paul and Barnabas present the call to repentance. They also present identities as the disciples that bring good news rather than those gods whose visitations may be a threat.[149] This clarification is given in other speeches and frequented in reports of the disciple's activities.[150] The good news—Christ's redemption that opened a way to enter into the life in Christ—is "explained in a striking manner" as Paul calls them to turn from worthless things to the living God.[151] Rowe asserts that the speech here does not merely communicate a

---

144. Johnson and Harrington, *The Acts of the Apostles*, 251.

145. Parsons sees this to perhaps respond to the second century criticism that labeled Christianity as a movement populated by "credulous and uneducated rustics. Lucian, for example, charged, 'if any charlatan or trickster, able to profit by occasions, comes among them, he quickly acquires sudden wealth by imposing upon such simple folk. Such characterization of Christianity as a movement drawing primarily on the *hoi polloi* extends back even into the first century." Parsons, *Acts*, 201.

146. Parsons, *Acts*, 201.

147. Parsons, *Acts*, 201.

148. Acts 14:15b states, "And we bring you good news, that you should turn from these vain things to a living God."

149. Soards, *The Speeches in Acts*, 89.

150. Soards, *The Speeches in Acts*, 89.

151. Soards, *The Speeches in Acts*, 89.

new idea about God or correct a minor behavioral issue; instead, "Luke's call through the mouths of Paul and Barnabas is not simply an admonition to tweak a rite or halt a ceremony. It contains, rather the summons that simultaneously involves the destruction of an entire mode of being religious."[152]

Exposition of the Resurrection[153]

At first glance, the speech does not seem to explicitly mention the death and resurrection of Jesus Christ. This may be due to the fact that the speech is abruptly interrupted, or the stop is deliberate.[154] Whatever the case may be, Lightfoot is correct in recognizing that in the phrase "Living God," "the stress is laid on the attributes, not the person," finding a correlation to 2 Corinthians 3:3 where the contrast there is between a dead letter and a "Living God."[155] The phrase "Living God" signifies an exposition of Christology, and possibly the resurrection, for "in Luke-Acts, salvation flows from the Living Jesus."[156] The resurrection "functions both to provide the means by which salvation may flow from Jesus and define the nature of the ultimate victory over death."[157]

To substantiate this, Christian Dionne argues that though the speech may not readily demonstrate the element of the kerygma, theology embedded in expositions of the "Living God" in the Lystra speech presupposes kerygmatic tradition.[158] If one takes kerygma to be the proclamation of Jesus become Christ and Lord and Savior of the world by virtue of his resurrection, since such affirmations are founded on theology of God, it would be inaccurate to argue that theology in the speech is foreign to kerygma—even if it is not overtly visible.[159] Dionne believes that "living God" who manifests himself in creation and provision constitutes

---

152. Rowe, *World Upside Down*, 21.
153. Acts 14:15 states, "a Living God"
154. I discuss the interruptions of speeches in chapter 2.
155. Lightfoot and Witherington, *The Acts of the Apostles*, 186.
156. Talbert, *Reading Luke-Acts in Its Mediterranean Milieu*, 125.
157. Talbert, *Reading Luke-Acts in Its Mediterranean Milieu*, 125.
158. Dionne, "La Figure Narrative de Dieu Dans Le Discours à Lystre (Ac 14,15–17)," 122
159. Dionne, "La Figure Narrative de Dieu Dans Le Discours à Lystre (Ac 14, 15–17)," 123.

fundamental dimensions of the Christian faith, especially to those who are not familiar with monotheism in Lystra.[160]

Acts 17

Cultural Point of Contact[161]

Paul, as in his Lystra speech, again establishes the common ground with his hearers through the use of natural theology. His logical strategy is to "begin with the epistemological assumptions of its hearers, building on a common understanding of the cosmos, yet climaxing in the fullest self-disclosure of the Creator—the resurrection of the God-man."[162] As in Acts 14, there is "a general willingness to mix concepts and thoughts forms from Gentile thinking in order to make contact for the gospel with the non-Jewish mind."[163] Thus, Paul's statement, "I perceive that in every way you are very religious," contains *captatio* with its reference to an Athenian altar that "frees the speaker of the suspicion of introducing alien deities to Athens, and furnishes a point of contact for the proclamation of one God."[164] In sum, "acts of creation and evidence of his presence and benevolent acts in their past history" function as the point of contact and reference.[165]

Hans Conzelmann renders the use of the term "news" to be significant.[166] Since the Christians did not "emerge as a new religious community within Judaism, but continued to consider themselves Jews," their message did not inform 'new' ideas about God; instead "proclaimed a new

---

160. Dionne's view can be summarized as follows: "An application of the principle of the characterization of persons from the practice of narrative analysis enables us to discern the 'portrait' of God painted by Paul. Three principle characteristics of the narrative figure of God emerge from the discourse: a creator God, source of all that exists; a God who is present in and through history in the quest for meaning by peoples and nations; a providential God who gives human beings all their needs for subsistence." Dionne, "La Figure Narrative de Dieu Dans Le Discours à Lystre (Ac 14,15–17)," 124.

161. Acts 17:22b states, "Men of Athens, I perceive that in every way you are very religious."; Acts 17:28, "for '"In him we live and move and have our being'; as even some of your own poets have said, '"For we are indeed his offspring."

162. Charles, "Engaging the (Neo) Pagan Mind," 55.

163. Shields, "The Areopagus Sermon and Roman 1," 37–38.

164. Zweck, "The Exordium of the Areopagus Speech, Acts 17," 102.

165. Strandenaes, "The Missionary Speeches in the Acts of the Apostles," 351.

166. Conzelmann, "Address of Paul on the Areopagus," 220.

message."[167] Conzelmann argues that Paul's discussion of *one* God, over against idols, is certainly not only new to the Jews, but is also shown to establish a point of contact with the Greeks as Paul reminds that this idea of God is not new or foreign even to them.[168] "With Luke, this point of contact does not imply a degree of compromise between the old and the new religion. On the contrary, it means that monotheistic thinking has carried through resolutely."[169]

Moreover, Athenians' religious (or philosophical) fervor serves as another point of contact. "Here the opening point of contact is the religiosity of the Athenians themselves."[170] This mention of Athenians' religiosity works both to praise them and at the same time refute them, establishing a connection with them.[171] "The inscription 'to the unknown God', when taken literally, is thus to be read not as a commendation of the Athenians' theological penetration but instead as Athenian self-testimony to their need for the kind of knowledge that comes with Paul's preaching."[172]

Another way cultural connection via enculturated communication takes place in this speech is exemplified in the use of rhetoric. As discussed in the earlier section of this book, the meaning of the use of Greco-Roman rhetoric is not negligible in Paul's world.[173] Countless commentators have detected features of Greco-Roman rhetoric within Paul's speeches.[174] But others have suggested the use of rhetoric in the way the speech is situated in the larger narrative.[175] Karl Sandnes argues that the audience reaction to the speech—the request for further information—is part of the rhetorical strategy in forming the speech as *insinuation*.[176] He explicates that an ending to the speech at the Areopagus is designed to model Socrates and more importantly to move the audience to inquire more—something equivalent

---

167. Conzelmann, "Address of Paul on the Areopagus," 220.
168. Conzelmann, "Address of Paul on the Areopagus," 220–21.
169. Conzelmann, "Address of Paul on the Areopagus," 221.
170. Flemming, "Contextualizing the Gospel in Athens," 202.
171. Zweck, "The Exordium of the Areopagus Speech, Acts 17," 102–3.
172. Rowe, "The Grammar of Life," 41.
173. See chap. 2 of this book.
174. To cite some notable works: Witherington, *The Acts of the Apostles*; Winter and Clarke, *The Book of Acts in Its Ancient Literary Setting*; Bock, *Acts*; Bruce, *Commentary on the Book of the Acts*.
175. Sandnes, "Paul and Socrates," 17.
176. Sandnes, "Paul and Socrates," 17–18.

to today's click-bait.[177] As previously discussed, the use of rhetoric as a communication method help establish a connection with the audience.

Cultural Solidarity[178]

Luke Timothy Johnson writes that "no ancient reader could miss the piquancy of a wandering Jewish preacher confronting the cultured sages of Athens."[179] He also observes the importance of Luke's rendering of the scenery that functioned as the "emblem" and a carefully crafted "set-piece" in re-telling the speech:

> The presence of statues and shrines everywhere, including those to 'anonymous gods' which in fact gave the Athenians precisely the reputation for 'piety/superstition' that Paul ascribes to them; the ubiquitous presence of the philosophers always ready for a debate, especially one picked with a religious 'proclaimer' who frequented the agora and confronted passers-by there, some of these philosophers notoriously skeptical of religious claims (the Epicureans), some of them more cautiously open (the Stoics); the traditions associated with Socrates—the charge of inculcating 'foreign gods,' and the hearing before the Areopagus—Luke gets all of this as vibrantly as any sketch in Lucian of Samosata.[180]

Luke goes the distance to set the scene in a way that will situate the speech at a precisely apt cultural location. Downing suggests that "Luke's references to Athens and to the philosophical tradition it represents are frequent in Josephus." Acknowledgment of the Athenians' religiosity, the trial of their heroes, and the caricature of philosophy at Athens are such commonality.[181] Luke's portrayal of the scene operates to invoke cultural solidarity.

---

177. Sandnes also cites Tannehill to be in agreement that the last words of the speech has a function. See Tannehill, *The Narrative Unity of Luke-Acts*.

178. Acts 17:23 states, "For as I passed along and observed the objects of your worship, I found also an altar with this inscription: 'To the unknown god.' What therefore you worship as unknown, this I proclaim to you."

179. Johnson and Harrington, *The Acts of the Apostles*, 318.

180. Johnson and Harrington, *The Acts of the Apostles*, 318.

181. Downing, "Common Ground with Paganism in Luke and in Josephus," 546–59.

Contextualization of Paul's Apologetics Speeches

A Virtue of the Christian Life[182]

C. Kavin Rowe advocates for a reading of this speech with the exploration of "the interconnection between intellection and life in ancient theology and philosophy."[183] He asserts that Paul's speech at the Areopagus actually reveals "fundamentally different grammars for the whole of life" that creates conflict with the pagan view.[184] He argues that most modern interpreters have erroneously endorsed the notion that this speech was an indicator that "pagans may not yet have attained to fullness of Christian knowledge, but inasmuch as (the non-canonical quotes) testified to the truth, they were doubtless on the way."[185] Rowe argues that the "common vocabulary" employed by Paul and the pagans is not meant to suggest "theological commensurability."[186] In other words, "Paul's Areopagus speech is not a paean of the Greek intellectuals or spiritual achievement. It is instead the presentation of an alternative pattern of life."[187]

Paul presents the repentant life as the alternative to the pagan way of living. This alternative pattern of life is marked by "a shift from the 'unknown God' to a knowledge of him, moving into and inhabiting the way of life constituted by repentance and the recognition of the identity of the man who was raised from the dead."[188] Rowe writes,

> Luke's method of telling the story of Paul's speech does not lead him to articulate narratively a manner of thinking that would—were it to exist—encompass both Stoicism and Christianity as total ways of life, a kind of general or more comprehensive grammar that would transcend intellectually the particularities of Christian language about the world (or Stoic language—or whatever). To the contrary, Luke recognizes the conflict and confrontation that occurs when irreducibly particular patterns of life offer irreducibly different ways of being.[189]

---

182. Acts 17:30 states, "The times of ignorance God overlooked, but now he commands all people everywhere to repent."
183. Rowe, "The Grammar of Life," 33.
184. Rowe, "The Grammar of Life," 33.
185. Rowe refers to C.K. Barrett as an exception, but argues that John Calvin Rowe, 33.
186. Rowe, "The Grammar of Life," 34.
187. Rowe, "The Grammar of Life," 35.
188. Rowe, "The Grammar of Life," 45.
189. Rowe, "The Grammar of Life," 49–50.

Exposition of the Resurrection[190]

Paul's speech at the Areopagus announces that there will be a day of judgment, confirmed by the resurrection. Verse 31 makes a "total differentiation from any Hellenistic idea of determinism, a concept congenial to the Stoic group."[191] This judge will be "a man," and his resurrection affirms the identity. "The idea of Judgment was not foreign to the auditorium;" yet on the side of the Greek philosophy, people questioned how God the just Judge can overlook such prevalent evil behavior.[192] However, Paul here exposits the resurrection and proclaims that God is the Just Judge, "different from Epicurean gods or those gods with human weakness from Homer literature and even different from the Jewish concept of God, seen very often as nationalistic and partial."[193] The resurrection not only proves that Jesus is Just Judge, but the event also is a call to repentance. Paul calls the Gentiles to repentance as he did to the Jews; and this is the only rightful response to the appointment of Jesus as the Judge of the living and the dead, which is now confirmed by the resurrection.[194] The exposition of the resurrection leads to the discussion of the Just nature of God and eschatological vision.

Acts 24

Cultural Point of Contact[195]

Michael Kochenash suggests that Luke characterizes Paul in a way that will invoke imagery familiar to his readers. He contends that Paul's conversion narrative functions in a way that enables the readers to view whoever opposes Paul's Gentile mission triggers the image of those who opposed Dionysus.[196] Moreover, Kochenash explicates that reversal of the role—going from the one who persecuted Jesus to now being persecuted

---

190. Acts 17:31 states, "Because he has fixed a day on which he will judge the world in righteousness by a man whom he has appointed; and of this he has given assurance to all by raising him from the dead."

191. Mărculeț, "Elements of Inculturation," 46.

192. Mărculeț, "Elements of Inculturation," 46.

193. Mărculeț, "Elements of Inculturation," 46–47.

194. Johnson and Harrington, *The Acts of the Apostles*, 319.

195. Acts 24:10b states, "Knowing that for many years you have been a judge over this nation, I cheerfully make my defense."

196. Kochenash, "Better Call Paul 'Saul,'" 433–49.

for the sake of Jesus—"indicates to readers with the appropriate cultural competence that opposition to Gentile inclusion is akin to Pentheus's opposition to Dionysus—and will incur comparable consequences."[197] The image of a paralleling figure helps establish a cultural connection with both the primary and the secondary audience.[198]

Cultural Solidarity[199]

"Against the backdrop of hostility, corruption, and time-serving, Paul's character emerges as truly philosophical."[200] Paul is depicted as being knowledgeable in legal proceedings, making full use of his privileges as he needs to.[201] This depiction provides an important clue to Paul's cultural solidarity as a relatable figure.[202] Jerome Neyrey questions where Luke imagined Paul fitted into different social statuses and concludes that Luke finds Paul among the social elites.[203]

Such a conclusion is drawn after first mapping out the levels of social stratification according to the work of Gerhard Lenski, then analyzing where Paul may be located.[204] Neyrey argues that Paul "appears as a retainer to the elites of Jerusalem and as a person who can speak eloquently to Greek philosophers, Roman proconsuls, and Jewish kings." Although the narrative does not inform the reader whether Paul indeed had his meeting with the emperor, "at least on the narrative level, Paul is a suitable person

---

197. Kochenash, "Better Call Paul 'Saul,'" 449.

198. Paul's use of Greco-Roman rhetoric, particularly *captio benevolentae*, also takes place in this verse as a cultural connection. But I do not include deeper interpretation since I discuss is in chapter 2 in greater detail.

199. Acts 24:17–18a states, "Now after several years I came to bring alms to my nation and to present offerings. 18 While I was doing this, they found me purified in the temple, without any crowd or tumult."

200. Johnson and Harrington, *The Acts of the Apostles*, 423.

201. Johnson and Harrington, *The Acts of the Apostles*, 423.

202. Wayne Meeks, Michael Theissen, and John Lentz have offered valuable analysis on Paul's social standing. See Meeks, et al., *The Social World of the First Christians*; Gerd Theissen, *The Social Setting of Pauline Christianity*; Lentz, *Luke's Portrait of Paul*.

203. Neyrey, "Luke's Social Location of Paul, 251–79.

204. Lenski identifies various social stratification in the Greco-Roman world. They are rulers, governing class, retainer class, merchants, priests, artisans, and expendables. See Lenski, *Power and Privilege*.

to appear before the emperor."[205] Paul also clearly encounters the governing class consisting of Jewish elites and the Roman authorities.[206] Coupled with "the perspective of honor articulated in cultural anthropology serving to give reliability to the intuitive perception that Luke perceives and presents Paul as a person of considerable honor and social status," Paul establishes cultural solidarity with his audience in the court. For this reason, "Luke has nothing against having Paul considered the representative of Christianity."[207]

A Virtue of the Christian Life[208]

Paul "argued that he had taken great pains to have a clear conscience both before God and man as he had always done."[209] Paul's "purpose in coming to Jerusalem was a commendable one and endorsed by Rome who provided an armed escort for Jewish collections."[210] William Willimon summarizes Luke's position: "Our movement is best understood as a branch of faithful Judaism which, like the Pharisees, believes in the resurrection; and we can work within the Empire to accomplish our purposes."[211] Winter cites William Long who contends, "It is the appearance of the word 'conscience' that makes his confession a real proof, for the word means that he has a conscious record of his past acts, his awareness of having done good or bad."[212] In short, Paul's civic behavior is highlighted to respond to a cultural objection made against him.[213]

---

205. Neyrey, "Luke's Social Location of Paul," 260.

206. Acts 22–26.

207. Haenchen, *The Acts of the Apostles: a Commentary*, 659.

208. Acts 24:11–13 states, "You can verify that it is not more than twelve days since I went up to worship in Jerusalem, and they did not find me disputing with anyone or stirring up a crowd, either in the temple or in the synagogues or in the city. Neither can they prove to you what they now bring up against me."; Acts 24:16 states, "So I always take pains to have a clear conscience toward both God and man."

209. Winter, "Official Proceedings and the Forensic Speeches in Acts 24–26," 325.

210. Winter, "Official Proceedings and the Forensic Speeches in Acts 24–26," 325.

211. Willimon, *Acts*, 174.

212. Long, "The Trial of Paul in the Book of Acts," 233.

213. This pattern, as I will discuss in the consequent chapter, appears repeatedly in the subsequent generations of apologists.

Exposition of the Resurrection[214]

The resurrection that propels the "new faith" is exposited here as "not a treason to the old," but "the bond which holds the two together."[215] Paul connects the "hope in God" with the resurrection, both reminding the reader what the original charge against Paul was, and to draw attention to the eschatological hope.[216] Pharisees had disputed whether the righteous and the unrighteous will both be resurrected, as opposed to the righteous alone; and the topic served as a defining element of Pharisaic theology.[217] Yet, "As the guiding principle of Paul's life, resurrection along with its corollary, judgment, provides an incentive for the moral life. Living with a sense of ultimate accountability before God fosters having a good conscience before God and the world."[218]

Acts 26

Cultural Point of Contact[219]

Johnson believes that Paul's final defense in Acts 26 can be labeled "Christianity's first real *apologia* before the sophisticated Greek world."[220] He draws attention to not only the length, but elegantly crafted structure of the speech that is enabled by the use of "elevated diction, subtle syntax, and paranomasia that would have delighted Hellenistic rhetoricians, possessing just the qualities desired for an aristocratic audience."[221] Haechen too sees the unusual word order in *captio benevolentiae* to indicate "the elegant

---

214. Acts 24:21b states, "It is with respect to the resurrection of the dead that I am on trial before you this day."
215. Haenchen, *The Acts of the Apostles*, 659.
216. Holladay, *Acts*, 451.
217. Holladay, *Acts*, 451.
218. Holladay, *Acts*, 451.
219. Acts 26:2–3, "I consider myself fortunate that it is before you, King Agrippa, I am going to make my defense today against all the accusations of the Jews, especially because you are familiar with all the customs and controversies of the Jews. Therefore I beg you to listen to me patiently."
220. Johnson and Harrington, *The Acts of the Apostles*, 440.
221. Johnson and Harrington, *The Acts of the Apostles*, 440–41.

language of this speech," again signifying cultural connection taking place through the enculturated communication.[222]

Cultural Solidarity[223]

More than mere elegance, Paul's speech to King Agrippa contains heavy use of theological language, Osvaldo Padilla suggests that this is "actually part of the strategy; for the point of the speech is that Paul's case is a matter of theological dispute, not breaking of Roman law."[224] Paul states that the reason he is standing before Agrippa is because of Paul's proclamation of the resurrection.[225] Yet, "Paul is a Pharisee, and the resurrection from the dead as the future hope is exactly what Pharisees preach."[226] Paul essentially states that "his life from the beginning has been spent among his people and in Jerusalem;" in other words, Paul speaks as a cultural insider.[227]

Paul's cultural status as a lifelong figure in Judaism elevates to new heights as Paul discusses his conversion experience. Dennis Hamm tracks Paul's conversion accounts in Acts 9, 22, and 26, finding that blindness and its healing have both symbolic intent and constitute a theme that runs throughout the entirety of Luke-Acts.[228] Paul's loss of vision and restoration narrative is repeated, and it meets a "stunning variation" in Acts 26.[229] "What had been, in Acts 9, language referring to Saul's physical blindness and recovery has become, after a muting in Acts 22, a metaphor for the conversion of those to whom Paul is sent in the description of Acts 26."[230] Hamm sees this to be symbolic in that this light fulfills Isaiah's vision that

---

222. Haenchen, *The Acts of the Apostles: A Commentary*, 682.

223. Acts 26:4–5 states, "My manner of life from my youth, spent from the beginning among my own nation and in Jerusalem, is known by all the Jews. They have known for a long time, if they are willing to testify, that according to the strictest party of our religion I have lived as a Pharisee."

224. Padilla, *Acts of the Apostles*, 190.

225. Acts 26:6–8 states, "And now I stand here on trial because of my hope in the promise made by God to our fathers, to which our twelve tribes hope to attain, as they earnestly worship night and day. And for this hope I am accused by Jews, O king! Why is it thought incredible by any of you that God raises the dead?"

226. Padilla, *Acts of the Apostles*, 190.

227. Haenchen, *The Acts of the Apostles: a Commentary*, 682.

228. Hamm, "Paul's Blindness and Its Healing," 63–72.

229. Hamm, "Paul's Blindness and Its Healing," 66.

230. Hamm, "Paul's Blindness and Its Healing," 67.

anticipated Israel's covenant vocation to be a light to the nations.[231] In this light, Paul presents himself in a way that forges cultural solidarity.

Dale Allison Jr. renders that the series of Paul's conversion narrative that appears in Act 9:1–9, 22:6–11, and 26:12–18 as the result of received tradition or a "story that likened Paul's vision of Jesus to Ezekiel's vision of the anthropomorphic form of the Lord."[232] Allison confirms the parallel between Paul's inaugural call with that of Ezekiel by pointing to the fact that the revelatory voice utters the same words, both men fall to the ground upon beholding a supernatural light, and both Paul and Ezekiel dramatically emphasize the heavenly brilliance in their respective prophetic inauguration experiences.[233] Paul's Damascus road experience enables the perception of Paul as an authoritative figure from the tradition.

A Virtue of the Christian Life[234]

With the discussion of his loyalty to Judaism and obedience to the heavenly vision, again Paul makes the connection that repentance leads to a life lived in accordance with God's nature. Howard Marshall believes this is reminiscent of both Paul's earlier speeches and Peter's message to the Jews: "The stress on producing practical evidence of repentance is paralleled in the preaching of John the Baptist."[235] As in other speeches attributed to Paul, the call to repentance is a call that involves life.[236] Darrell Bock writes,

> Paul was not an antinomian. He did not believe that someone who had faith could do whatever one wished without concern for God's moral standards. So here he also exhorts his audience to live, in response to grace, in a way that produces fruit reflecting the change of direction called for by forgiveness. This is not a third responsibility, since the term πράσσοντας (performing) is a present participle, making the performing of deeds something that

---

231. Hamm, "Paul's Blindness and Its Healing," 71.

232. Allison Jr., "Acts 9:1–9, 22:6–11, 26:12–18: Paul and Ezekiel," 807–26.

233. Allison further notes the voice, literary parallels, and series of actions paralleled in both accounts.

234. Acts 26:19–21 states, "Therefore, O King Agrippa, I was not disobedient to the heavenly vision, but declared first to those in Damascus, then in Jerusalem and throughout all the region of Judea, and also to the Gentiles, that they should repent and turn to God, performing deeds in keeping with their repentance."

235. Marshall, *The Acts of the Apostles*, 291.

236. C. Kavin Rowe makes an excellent case for this in his book, *World Upside Down*.

happens alongside, and simultaneously with, the other elements, in dependence upon repenting and turning.[237]

Exposition of the Resurrection[238]

In these verses, the exposition of the resurrection has a new variation. Here, Paul uses a unique phrasing not found in other apologetics speeches: 'Christ was the first to experience the resurrection from the dead.'[239] Unlike the other occurrences that read, "Christ was raised," this is reminiscent of Peter's claim that Christ is the "Author of Life."[240] "The first to experience resurrection life, Christ is the pioneer of transcendent Life for everyone else."[241] Paul "proclaims light not only by the fact that through his resurrection he 'brings life and immortality to light'—hitherto the resurrection was only a matter of hope and faith—but by mediating as Son the forgiveness of sins."[242] Again, the speech contains an exposition of the resurrection—keeping the structure, while varying its implication.

CONCLUSION

Paul models culturally contextualized apologetics in his speeches. His apologetics speeches do not contain theoretical or theological propositions alone; instead, they respond to various cultural assumptions and objections the audience possesses. They are demonstrated uniquely in each of Paul's apologetics speeches. On a larger scale, though, Paul's apologetics speeches demonstrate a capacity for cultural contextualization by operating with a scheme. Similar to the way kerygmatic speeches have been detected, Paul's apologetics speeches also reveal a scheme that provides a structure. The structure, or scheme, constitutes the elements of cultural connection (through the use of cultural point of contact and enculturated communication) and a response to cultural objection (through the presentation of the

---

237. Bock, *Acts*, 719.

238. Acts 26:23 states, "that the Christ must suffer and that, by being the first to rise from the dead, he would proclaim light both to our people and to the Gentiles."

239. Holladay, *Acts*, 479.

240. Holladay, *Acts*, 479.

241. Holladay, *Acts*, 479.

242. Haenchen, *The Acts of the Apostles*, 688.

Contextualization of Paul's Apologetics Speeches

Christian life as an appeal as well as the expositions of the resurrection). All of Paul's apologetics speeches consistently feature these elements, validating the proposed argument. Hence, Paul models culturally contextualized apologetics in his speeches.

Chapter 5

Cultural Contextualization of Second-Century Apologists

Did Paul's model of culturally contextualized apologetics continue to function as a model after the apostle? I aim to demonstrate that indeed the first generation of apologists that came after Paul did use it as such. The next generation of apologetic works in the second century includes the work of Aristides, Athenagoras, Justin Martyr, Irenaeus, Tatian, Melito of Sardis, and the Epistle of Diognetus. They left a legacy of defending the Christian faith, and in it, they continued to employ the scheme set forth by the apostle.

In order to assess whether the apologetics works of the second-century figures engage in Paul's model of cultural contextualization of apologetics, I will look for parallels between Paul's model and that of the second-century apologists. As delineated in previous chapters, Paul's scheme consists of cultural connections and responses to cultural objections. Cultural connection constitutes a cultural point of contact, enculturated communication, and cultural solidarity. The key strategy, according to Paul, in responding to the cultural objection is to highlight the virtue of the Christian life and to proclaim the resurrection as having an appropriate implication.

In what follows, each of the second-century Greek apologists' main arguments and their cultural context is discussed. Then, the analysis looks for evidence of cultural connection through the cultural point of contact, enculturated communication, or cultural solidarity. Next, the investigation surveys the content of each apologist's works to evaluate whether the work uses virtue of the Christian life or the exposition of the resurrection as an appeal. This analysis will demonstrate that the second-century apologetics that came immediately after Paul utilized the same apologetics model. I begin with Aristides.

ANALYSIS OF APOLOGETICS OF ARISTIDES

Apology of Aristides is referred to as the earliest extant *Apology* for the Christian faith.[1] It is generally accepted that the *Apology* is intended to be addressed to Caesar Titus Hadrianus Antoninus.[2] Aristides's notable feature of his apologetics is his discussion of the eternity of God the Creator, a refutation of paganism, and presentation of Christian faith as a source that leads to an honorable life.[3]

Brief Outline of Apologetics Argument

Aristides's *Apology* constitutes the following argument.[4] The orderly disposition of the world successfully reveals the existence of God.[5] However, various groups of human beings respond to such a fact in different ways.[6] Barbarians, instead of worshiping the true God as the real power behind all creation, worship material bodies such as the earth, fire, water, winds, or the sun.[7] The Greeks worship gods that are all subject to human weaknesses and temptations. Their gods are not worthy of worship.[8] The Jews are better off than the rest of the human race because at least their faith is monotheistic. However, their cultic practice often includes worship of

---

1. O'Ceallaigh, "'Marcianus' Aristides, on the Worship of God," 227–54.
2. Edgar and Oliphint, *Christian Apologetics Past and Present*.
3. See the introduction to Aristides in Edgar and Oliphint.
4. Aristides, *Apology*. I was able to access the copy of J. Rendel Harris's translation of Aristides's *Apology* printed in 1891 from Chongshin Theological Seminary in Yangyi, Korea. Hereafter after all citations will be given as *Apo*.
5. *Apo.*, 1.
6. *Apo.*, 2.
7. *Apo.*, 3–7.
8. *Apo.*, 8–13.

angels, Sabbaths, and moons.⁹ The Christians alone "come nearer to truth and genuine knowledge than the rest of the nations."¹⁰ They model such moral life that they are far from various immorality such as adultery, fornication, or embezzlement; and instead, they honor parents, show kindness, and are pure.¹¹ All the human race will one day soon stand in judgment before God, thus those who utter vanity and hostility towards Christians must be silenced.¹²

Cultural Context

To properly locate the cultural milieu, one must begin by considering a historical-critical issue surrounding the *Apology*, which has generated varying opinions.¹³ It has led some to even argue that the *Apology*, though Eusebius and Jerome point to Aristides as the author, is written by a proselyte to Hellenist Judaism, arguing that it is "not at all as an *Apology* but primarily a counterattack upon polytheists and their religious notions and secondarily, as a defense of the monotheistic worship and the morals of the Jews."¹⁴ The problem arises due to the fact that key passages related to Jewish-Christian relations contained in *Apology* 2.2–4 and 14.1b–15.2 contain significant differences between Greek and Syriac versions of the text.¹⁵ More specifically, the Greek version of the text features a threefold vision of human kinships that compare Christians to Jews and polytheists, while the Syriac includes a fourfold division that places Christians next to Jews, barbarians, and the Greeks. The existence of Armenian and Egyptian textual traditions worsened the complication.¹⁶ While meaningful efforts have been made to reconstruct the original text by way of harmonizing the texts, the Syriac translation is widely recognized as the best preservation of the text.¹⁷ Discovery of a Syriac manuscript in 1889 by J. Rendel Harris has

---

9. *Apo.*, 14.
10. *Apo.*, 15.
11. *Apo.*, 16.
12. *Apo.*, 17.
13. Rutherford, "Reinscribing the Jews," 61–91.
14. G. O'Ceallaigh, "'Marcianus' Aristides, on the Worship of God," 227.
15. See Rutherford, "Reinscribing the Jews."
16. Rutherford, "Reinscribing the Jews," 65–67.
17. The Greek version of the Apology was introduced to the world through the legend of Barlaam and Ioasaph, a popular and influential medieval romance. However, in

greatly contributed to such verdict, as well as consequent interaction with J. A. Robinson.[18]

Aristides, not unlike Paul, presents his case before the emperor. Prior to Harris's discovery of the Syriac text, one of the primary starting points for the Apology of Aristides was Eusebius and Jerome. Eusebius carries two references to Aristides in *Chronicon* and *Historia Ecclesiastica*, which substantially repeat the same content.[19] It states that "Aristides of Athens, a philosopher of our faith, gave to Hadrian apologetic entreaties at his command."[20] Moreover, Eusebius writes in his *Ecclesiastical History* "Aristides also, a faithful disciple of our religion, has left an Apology of the faith dedicated to Hadrian."[21] Eusebius and Jerome both mentioning Hadrian as a recipient allows one to conclude that the Apology was given during Hadrian's reign as emperor of Rome. However, the surfacing of the Syriac version offered a new piece of information. The second superscription to the title contained Emperor Antoninus Pius as the recipient and the full name of the author—Marcianus Aristides.[22]

Such information generates controversies concerning the dating of the Apology. However, the greater concern for the current topic is the fact that Aristides delivers the argument to the emperor as a philosopher. There may be two options available in terms of the recipient. Harris suggests two options: either Aristides journeyed to Rome to present his Apology; or that Antoninus made some unrecorded visit to the East, though Harris favors the latter. He writes, "It is conceivable that it may have been presented to the Emperor, along with other Christian writings, during an unrecorded visit of his to his ancient seat of government in Smyrna."[23] Such a view is more popular.[24] Whatever the truth may be, it does not alter the fact

---

1889, J. Rendel Harris unearthed a Syriac manuscript in the monastery of St. Catherine on Mount Sinai; and consequently led many to conclude that the text sourced Barlaam's medieval romance. Rutherford also makes a compelling case based on comparative textual studies to contend that the Syriac text carries the authoritative weight. All publications on Aristides I consulted recognize the fourfold categorization found in the Syriac rather than the Greek text.

18. Harris, *The Apology of Aristides on Behalf of the Christians*.
19. Wolff, "The Apology of Aristides," 238–39.
20. Carriker, *The Library of Eusebius of Caesarea*.
21. See Carriker, *The Library of Eusebius of Caesarea*.
22. Wolff, "The Apology of Aristides," 240.
23. Harris, *The Apology of Aristides on Behalf of the Christians*, 17.
24. Cross, *The Early Christian Fathers*, 17.

that Aristides aims to carry out his apologetics before the emperor as Paul equally intended in Acts.

These conflicting sources make it difficult to place Aristides's Apology at a precise point in time. However, there are clues.[25] Robert Grant explains that if Eusebius is not mistaken, then it is conceivable that the Apology was delivered at the same time as Quadratus. The occasion surrounding the visit to the emperor with Quadratus could have been to entertain issues surrounding the saviors contrasted with the true Savior. Or, if Eusebius is indeed mistaken and the Syriac version correctly marks the recipient, then "it is possible that the *Apology* grew out of a need to respond to the famous rhetorician Fronto, who was consul suffectus in 143."[26]

Cultural Connections in Aristides

Cultural Point of Contact

Though the exact cultural context is uncertain, Aristides's *Apology* nevertheless establishes a cultural connection in a number of ways. To start, Aristides's discussion of the concept of God functions as a cultural point of contact. Aristides begins his apologetic message by marveling at the beauty of creation, immediately pointing to God as the power as well as the "mover" of all.[27] He asserts that "God is not born, not made, an everabiding nature without beginning and without end, immortal, perfect, and incomprehensible."[28] Aristides also emphasizes that God is truly independent, not requiring anything from anyone while all human beings "stand in need of Him."[29]

Aristides's apologetics starts with such common ground—his initial move is to establish a foundation that will serve as a point of contact. Nickolas P. Roubekas argues that Aristides's *Apology*'s beginning essentially is a theorization of origins of religion as a universal phenomenon.[30] He writes,

---

25. Grant, "Chronology of the Greek Apologists," 25.
26. Grant, "Chronology of the Greek Apologists," 25.
27. *Apo.*, 1.
28. *Apo.*, 1.
29. *Apo.*, 1.
30. Roubekas, "Unexpected Encounters," 1–16.

> Aristides appears to be offering a theory of the origins of religion based on an unexpected encounter with God via the observation any person may experience by paying attention to the perfection of the world. This type of epistemic justification, which is fundamentally philosophical and empirical, functions as a theory of origins of religion across time and space . . . [31] Already in the first century B.C., Cicero argued as such regarding the existence of a divine power that sets everything in motion, whereas the idea of an unmoved mover was articulated by Aristotle in the fourth century B.C. As such, the combined design and cosmological argumentation for theism that Aristides promoted in his *Apology* were already known among the Roman intelligentsia.[32]

Robert M. Grant too acknowledges that these opening lines of Aristides's *Apology* are "conventional Middle Platonic theology."[33] Moreover, he explains how not only the opening words of Aristides but also the fourfold categorization function as even more cultural points of contact. Grant writes,

> His discussion reflects the widespread interest in the history of religions in the early second century. Philo of Byblos had translated the ancient Phoenician author Sanchuniathon, many of whose statements about religion have been confirmed by materials from Ugarit, and during Hadrian's reign widespread concern for oriental religions was met by such works as Plutarch's treatise *On Isis and Osiris* and the lost book of Pallas *On the Mysteries of Mithras*. Hadrian himself used themes from Egyptian religion for his villa at Tivoli.[34]

Furthermore, Aristides's fourfold categories have a unique role as well. Traditionally, the class distinctions in Aristides's *Apology* were viewed as functioning to highlight the superiority of Christians over against Jews, Greeks, and Barbarians. While such categorization of human species does fulfill that role, the emphasis on differences in the groups also highlights "cultural kinship."[35] The *Apology* chapters 2 through 17 classifies similarities and differences among the four varied human groups based on their collective response (or lack of) to the knowledge of true God. Thus, this

31. Roubekas, "Unexpected Encounters," 8.
32. Roubekas, "Unexpected Encounters," 15.
33. Grant, *Greek Apologists of the Second Century*, 45.
34. Grant, *Greek Apologists of the Second Century*, 37.
35. Rutherford, "Citizenship among Jews and Christians," 3–26.

categorization is based not just on the ethnicity of a group, but a religious response that ultimately stems from the cultural composition.[36] Aristides concludes that amongst these cultural kinships, Christians are the "model kinship" that responds ideally in light of true knowledge of God.[37] Yet, all four species as cultural kinship share the same obligation to properly respond to cosmopolitan God. Aristides hence utilizes fourfold classification to accentuate the cultural point of contact.

Enculturated Communication

Aristides's cultural connection also takes place through enculturated communication. J. Rendel Harris sheds a light on this. Harris states,

> When the Greek world began to absorb the Christian idea, it was natural that defense should be written: the model for such composition were abundant and were a part of the study of every educated man. It was easy to recast old matter or to imitate famous speakers of bygone times, to say nothing of the charm which the Greek mind naturally found in the many-sidedness of the defense of the new people, and in holding up the newly-dropped crystal of the Faith, like a gem with many facets, into the light of popular and philosophical scrutiny.[38]

Thus, Aristides making culturally appropriate and effective methods of communication. In fact, Aristides's *Apology* precisely employs the same literary genre that is culturally acceptable and widely popular.[39] P. Lorraine Buck contends that Aristides's *Apology* shares such remarkable similarities with Plato's *Apology* that "the only real adaptation which that apologist make to this literary genre was that necessitated by changes to the political and judicial systems between the fifth century B.C. and the second century AD"[40]

---

36. Rutherford, "Citizenship among Jews and Christians," 17.
37. Rutherford, "Citizenship among Jews and Christians," 18.
38. Harris, *The Newly Recovered Apology of Aristides*, 5.
39. Buck, "Second-Century Greek Christian Apologies Addressed to Emperors."
40. Buck, "Second-Century Greek Christian Apologies Addressed to Emperors," 6.

CONTEXTUALIZATION OF SECOND-CENTURY APOLOGISTS

Response to Cultural Objections through Life in Christ

A Virtue of the Christian Life

Aristides's apologetics argument from the virtue of the Christian life is evident. The entirety of chapter 15–17 comprises such an argument. In chapter 15, Aristides draws attention to various moral aspects of Christians. Not only do Christians show kindness to strangers and judge rightly, they also make friends with oppressors and enemies.[41] Harris particularly notes the fact that the writing even features a positive mention of women and Christian's care for the poor.[42] Aristides argues that such moral life best corresponds to the true nature of God when he asserts that Christian's knowledge and trust in God the Creator, as well as receiving of divine commandments that are now engraved upon the minds, and eschatological hope is what propels the moral life of the Christian faith.[43]

Exposition of the Resurrection

Aristides's *Apology* contains a brief mention of Christ's resurrection, but it is nevertheless symbolic in that it encapsulates the beginning and the end of the work.[44] Aristides introduces a creed-like confession of faith in the beginning by uttering a series of descriptions that Jesus was "born of the race of the Hebrews," also the "incarnate God, died, was buried."[45] Aristides continues by informing the emperor that "they say that after three days he rose and ascended to heaven."[46] Aristides closes his *Apology* by stating "that they appear before the awful judgment which through Jesus the Messiah is destined to come upon the whole human race."[47] The exposition does not appear in its full force, but functions as part of the Christian creed.

---

41. *Apo.*, 15.
42. Harris, *The Newly Recovered Apology of Aristides*, 55–77.
43. *Apo.*, 15.
44. *Apo.*, 2 and 17, which is the closing chapter.
45. *Apo.*, 2
46. This perhaps is meant to denote a third-person objective viewpoint, reinforcing the idea that Aristides himself was not formerly a believer either.
47. *Apo.*, 17.

ANALYSIS OF APOLOGETICS OF ATHENAGORAS

Next, I turn to Athenagoras. "The principal manuscript of Athenagoras describes him in its title as an Athenian and a Christian philosopher."[48] With two works entitled *Legatio* and *De Resurrectione*, Athenagoras aimed to demonstrate God's existence from the harmony of the cosmos. He argued that his existence is seen through God's works in creation, beauty, and harmony found in it. For Athenagoras, hints of divine art and all of these components point to the necessity of a Creator. He also refutes charges of atheism and incest brought upon Christians by arguing that Christians do worship Trinitarian God and that Christian teachings actually do not allow immoralities as charged.

Brief Outline of Apologetics Argument

Legatio[49]

Athenagoras opens with the plea to the emperor "Marcus Aurelius Antoninus and Lucius Aurelius Commodus" for the fair treatment of the Christians.[50] He explains that his aim is to rebut three charges made against Christians, namely atheism, Thyestian feasts, and Oedipodean intercourse.[51] He clarifies that Christians are not atheists but worship one God, further claiming that order, harmony, and arrangement of the world produces "impressive signs conducive to piety."[52] He cites various philosophers and external sources to remind them there is only one God while highlighting the absurdity of polytheism and bringing attention to the testimony of the prophets and the Christian worship of the Trinity.[53] Athenagoras asserts that the moral teachings of the Christians dismiss the charge brought against them and inconsistency of those who accuse them.[54] Athenagoras's refutation against various angelic beings appears next along

---

48. Crehan, *Embassy for the Christians (and) The Resurrection of the Dead*, 6.
49. Roberts, et al., *The Ante-Nicene Fathers*. Hereafter after all citations will be given as *Leg*.
50. *Leg.* 1.
51. *Leg.* 3.
52. *Leg.* 4.
53. *Leg.* 6–10.
54. *Leg.* 11–14.

with other errors that exist outside of the Christian faith.[55] Athenagoras concludes by reasserting the elevated morality of the Christians and the need to be fairly judged.[56]

De Resurrectione[57]

Athenagoras wishes to build a case for resurrection by utilizing a unique mode of argument. Typically, "dissertations concerning the truth always take precedence of those in defense of it; but, for the purpose of greater utility, the order must be reversed, and arguments in defense of it precede those concerning it."[58] Athenagoras argues that the resurrection is not impossible if God is the Creator.[59] He then refutes the arguments against his claims and further presents support for God by showing that not only is God able to cause resurrection, but also resurrected bodies are different than the current ones.[60] Athenagoras further argues that it is absurd to argue against resurrection based on men's impotence and God's unwillingness.[61] Athenagoras continues by constructing his argument based on the nature and purpose of human beings and concludes by discussing the requirements of divine providence and judgment.[62]

Cultural Context

During a time when Christians' loyalty to the empire garnered much doubt, Athenagoras's *Legatio* appears.[63] In terms of a timeline, even though the work is devoted to "Marcus Aurelius Antonius and Lucius Aurelius Commodus," who are called "victors over the Armenians and the Sarmatians," Grant cites the fact that the coinage does not use the title Armeniacus after the death of Lucius Verus, and dates the writing to be after 176, before the summer

---

55. *Leg.* 15–29.
56. *Leg.* 32–37.
57. Athenagoras, *Legatio and De Resurrectione*. Hereafter after all citations will be given as *DeR*.
58. *DeR.* 1.
59. *DeR.* 2–3.
60. *DeR.* 4–8.
61. *DeR.* 9–10.
62. *DeR.* 11–25.
63. Grant, "Chronology of the Greek Apologists," 28.

of 177. This entails that Athenagoras is writing under the joint rule of the two emperors.[64]

Cultural Connection in Athenagoras

Cultural Point of Contact

Athenagoras "seems absolutely at ease when dealing with the poets and philosophers."[65] He cites multiple philosophers and poetries, demonstrating a vast array of cultural connections. Athenagoras's cultural connections are precisely what allow him to stand out as an apologist who "attenuated Christianity by accommodating to the Greek culture."[66] Athenagoras's apologetics contains a plethora of references to material from pagan culture, which function as multiple cultural points of contact.

The first of these cultural points of contact is found in Athenagoras's use of proverbs. "Greek education began with proverbs, and it is natural to find them in Athenagoras."[67] In chapter 12 of *Legatio*, Athenagoras employs a tale from the *Iliad*, "Sleep and death are twins;" and a sentence, "Those who test the quality of honey and whey can tell if the whole is good by tasting one small sample."[68] Another occurrence takes place in chapter 34; "The harlot presumes to teach the chaste woman;" and "They swallow up whoever comes their way, the stronger possessing the weaker."[69] Considering how emperors were highly familiar with a vast array of proverbial expressions, it becomes evident that Athenagoras uses them to establish a cultural point of contact, aiming to establish a cultural connection.[70]

Second, Athenagoras quotes familiar poets and also alludes to them. Robert Grant summarizes,

> Most of his quotations come from Homer, seventeen from the *Iliad* against only three from the *Odyssey*, and two of the three are closely connected. There are also two from the Orphic literature,

---

64. Grant, "Chronology of the Greek Apologists," 28.
65. Carrington, *Christian Apologetics of the Second Century in Their Relation to Modern Thought*, 29.
66. Richardson, *Early Christian Fathers*, 296.
67. Grant, *Greek Apologists of the Second Century*, 103.
68. *Leg.* 12.
69. *Leg.* 34.
70. Grant, *Greek Apologists of the Second Century*, 103.

three from Hesiod, and four from unidentified tragedians; one apiece from Aeschylus, Pseudo-Sophocles, and Pindar; and eight from the more popular moralist Euripides.[71]

Third, Athenagoras makes cultural connections through literature, history, and arts. In *Legatio* chapter 28, Athenagoras demonstrates his knowledge of Classical mythology as he refers to "Alexander and Hermes Trismegistus" as part of the theosophical literature of his time.[72] He further showcases his familiarity with pagan religious literature as he provides quotes from Jewish *Sibylline Oracles* and "Apollodorus" in *Concerning the Gods*.[73]

Fourth and finally, Athenagoras utilizes an impressive array of philosophy to construct his cultural point of contact. He draws from Aristotle, Stoics, Plato, Empedocles, and Pythagorean. Chapter 6 of *Legatio* contains Athenagoras's explicit use of cultural point of contact. He introduces Philolaus who claims that "all things are included in God as in a stronghold, teaches that He is one and that He is superior to matter;" Lysis and Opsimus who define God as the "ineffable number;" Pythagoreans who assert that "God is a unit;" and finally mentions Plato and Aristotle.[74] Chapter 22 contains the words of Empedocles and chapter 31 reminds people of Socrates's death.

As shown, Athenagoras apparently is versed in ancient philosophy and he uses it to forge a cultural connection that will result in greater reception from the audience. Crehan writes,

> His technique in developing an argument is manifestly Platonic: there is the analogy from agriculture and the manual arts brought in to suggest lines of thought; the derivation game is played in the manner of the *Cratylus*, and in the account of the digestive process—which Athenagoras finds himself involved in when facing difficulties alleged against the resurrection of the body—the behavior of stronger and weaker forces in attacking or retiring before the attacker is very much like that of the rival forms described in the *Phaedo*. Stock Platonic themes, like the attack on the poets as teachers of immorality and the value of the argument from design,

---

71. Grant, *Greek Apologists of the Second Century*, 103.
72. Barnard, *Athenagoras*, 50.
73. Grant, *Greek Apologists of the Second Century*, 104.
74. *Leg.* 6.

are used where there is no possibility of conflict with Christian thought.[75]

Athenagoras's intention in employing such a wide range of different cultural points of contact is to "vindicate the credibility of Christianity."[76] "In the width of classical knowledge and mastery ad subtle adoption of the Platonic tradition, he saw how the traditional arguments of the Academy and the Stoa could be utilized in the service of Christian truth."[77] As a Christian philosopher, Athenagoras positions prophets and inspiration of the Scripture above any other outside sources.[78] Yet at the same time, he "constructs his community's theology with an artistic flair that selectively and critically weaves together both pagan and Judeo-Christian sources; so that he might win a hearing from both his imperial and ecclesiastical audience."[79]

Enculturated Communications in Athenagoras

Athenagoras utilizes eloquent rhetorical style to gain a greater hearing. "The arrangement of his material is clear and his argument moves with cogency. His rhythmic style, patterned after that of the Atticists, betrays the self-conscious rhetorician."[80] His use of notable descriptions, references to mythology and history serve the purpose of holding the reader's attention; and his "intention to give his *Apology* the air of a speech which was actually delivered" comes through.[81] He demonstrates familiarity with Homer, Plato, and Herodotus, thus enhancing his cultural presence. Frequent references to florilegia were a common and current practice of rhetoricians, and Athenagoras frequents them.[82]

Athenagoras's rhetorical performance via enculturated communication augments hearing and creates cultural solidarity as well. Such an endeavor is demonstrated by the "conciliatory loyalist approach" in the

---

75. Crehan, *Embassy for the Christians (and) The Resurrection of the Dead*, 15.
76. Barnard, *Athenagoras*, 50.
77. Barnard, *Athenagoras*, 50.
78. Bingham, "'We Have the Prophets,'" 211–42.
79. Bingham, "'We Have the Prophets,'" 242.
80. Richardson, *Early Christian Fathers*, 292.
81. Richardson, *Early Christian Fathers*, 292.
82. Richardson, *Early Christian Fathers*, 294.

Legatio.[83] Appropriate to the genre, Athenagoras adheres to the form of speech through the use of "encomium on the emperor."[84] In *Legatio*, chapters 16 and 30, Athenagoras makes six references to imperial intelligence and two to their devotion to scholarship, and praises even the preceding Roman emperors when he mentions "the philanthropy shown by their ancestors to their subjects;" and "such statements are typical of patriotic oratory."[85]

Response to Cultural Objections through Life in Christ

A Virtue of the Christian Life

Athenagoras, like Paul and Aristides, responds to cultural objections through the life in Christ as an appeal. Athenagoras informs the emperor that the teachings that bring up the Christians are commands that say, "Love your enemies; bless them that curse you; and pray for them that persecute you."[86] He is essentially arguing that the Christian doctrines on morality benefit the society as a whole. Helen Rhee provides helpful insight as to how the appeal from the virtue of the Christian life helped build culturally contextualized apologetics in the second century. She writes,

> Given the pervasive reality of the imperial cult and the perilous predicament of Christians, the Apologists found themselves in a delicate position. They carefully weighed the balance between Christian denial of the imperial cult and their expression of loyalty to the Empire. Just as they denied the accusation of atheism and redefined it, they also disavowed the charge of political subversion and treason, and redefined true loyalty from the Christian perspective. They attempted to break the complex web of *pax deorum*, *mos maiorum*, *pax Romana*, and imperial cult and tried to reconfigure the web with the Christian God, Christian loyalty, and *pax Romana*. Their approach reveals one of ambivalence but eventual unity between Church and Empire.[87]

---

83. Grant, *Greek Apologists of the Second Century*, 100.
84. Grant, *Greek Apologists of the Second Century*, 101.
85. *Leg.* 30.
86. *Leg.* 11.
87. Rhee, *Early Christian Literature*, 164.

Athenagoras also praises the chastity of the Christians as he pits Christians' sexual morality against the pagan practice. Instead of adultery, abomination, or fornication, Christians' sexual practices, Athenagoras argues, stands out from the rest of the world. This is the standard approach the second-century apologists engaged in to demonstrate the superiority of Christian sexual morality: "Demonstrating the Christian lifestyle as consistent with the best of Greco-Roman sexual ethics against the popular practices." Using an appeal from the Christian life with superior sexual morality helps the audience "move on to the claim of a higher standard with the basic agreement in mind."[88] Moreover, such a presentation helped "gain acceptance and respect from the pagan elites."[89]

Exposition of the Resurrection

Apart from *De Resurrectione*, Athenagoras's major discussion on the resurrection appears in chapter 36 of the *Apology*.[90] Athenagoras's exposition explicates the reason for Christian behavior.[91] The resurrection of the living and the dead, though the text does not explicitly mention Christ, is tied to the existence of coming judgment; and this alludes to Paul's exposition of the resurrection at the Areopagus.[92] Hence, Athenagoras again exposits the resurrection to remind the reader of the eschatological viewpoint. Fairweather writes:

> Athenagoras challenges unbelievers to show that such a thing is either impossible for God or contrary to his will, proceed to answer definite objections brought against the doctrine and then argues

---

88. Rhee, *Early Christian Literature*, 117.
89. Rhee, *Early Christian Literature*, 156.
90. I outline the argument of *De Resurrectione.* in the section above.
91. "Who, then, that believes in a resurrection, would make himself into a tomb for bodies that will rise again? For it is not the part of the same persons to believe that our bodies will rise again, and to eat them as if they would not; and to think that the earth will give back the bodies held by it, but that those which a man has entombed in himself will not be demanded back. On the contrary, it is reasonable to suppose, that those who think they shall have no account to give of the present life, ill or well spent, and that there is no resurrection, but calculate on the soul perishing with the body, and being as it were quenched in it, will refrain from no deed of daring; but as for those who are persuaded that nothing will escape the scrutiny of God, but that even the body which has ministered to the irrational impulses of the soul, and to its desires, will be punished along with it, it is not likely that they will commit even the smallest sin."
92. Paul proclaims that the Risen Jesus will be the Just Judge all will face in Acts 17.

for it primarily from the divine purpose in man's creation, and the nature of man as so created, and secondarily from the providential reward or punishment due to each man in accordance with righteous judgment, and from the chief end of human existence.[93]

ANALYSIS OF APOLOGETICS OF JUSTIN MARTYR

Cultural Context

Now I turn to Justin Martyr. Eusebius lists eight writings attributed to Justin Martyr, yet many are either completely lost or falsely attributed.[94] Out of these, many works of apologetics that makeup Justin's apologetic anthology are *The First Apology*, *The Second Apology*, and *Dialogue with Trypho the Jew*, though of these only fragments survive.[95] Justin Martyr is notable in his usage of a legitimate type of *ad hominem* argument.[96] Justin was known to have been influenced by Stoicism, Aristotelianism, Pythagoreanism, and Platonism; and through it all, he argues that Christianity achieves the highest goal of all pagan philosophies and must be considered the most worthy of all philosophy.

Against accusations that charged Christians with atheism, immorality such as cannibalism and incest, and novelty, Justin Martyr defended the rationale behind Christian behavior. The historical context of 2 *Apology* offers the background of these topics since the execution of several Christians by Urbicus, an urban prefect between 146 and 160, preceded the document. "In spite of, or because of, Justin's petitions, Christianity enjoyed relative tranquility during the reign of Antoninus Pius," momentarily.[97] This was followed by an epidemic in Rome under M. Aurelius, which subsequently placed many Christians to persecution and even martyrdom, including Justin himself. "Another period of quiet followed, and we possess no traces of Christian apologetic literature until late in the reign of M. Aurelius, at a point after the revolt of Avidius Cassius."[98]

---

93. Fairweather, "The Greek Apologists of the Second Century," 141.
94. Döpp, *Dictionary of Early Christian Literature*, 357.
95. Döpp, *Dictionary of Early Christian Literature*, 358.
96. Edgar and Oliphint, *Christian Apologetics Past and Present*.
97. Grant, "Chronology of the Greek Apologists," 26.
98. Grant, "Chronology of the Greek Apologists," 26.

Brief Outline of Apologetics Argument

First Apology[99]

Justin Martyr addresses 1 *Apology* to the emperor Titus Aelius Adrianus Antoninus Pius Augustus Caesar, and to his son Verissimus the Philosopher, and to Lucius the Philosopher, the natural son of Caesar, and the adopted son of Pius, as well as to the sacred Senate, with the whole People of the Romans.[100] He begins by demanding justice for Christians, that they must be tried fairly and justice, rather than condemned just by bearing the name Christian.[101] Justin claims that the Christians are not atheists for they profess their faith in God and that idolatries are follies.[102] Christians live in light of God's judgment, serve God rationally, and demons make people go astray.[103] Justin explicates that Jesus taught moral life and civil obedience.[104] Justin continues by arguing that the resurrection is possible, and employs various analogies from culture.[105] Justin asserts that numerous prophecies point to Jesus Christ and are fulfilled in him, worship of false gods must be abandoned and that God and is to be contrasted with pagan mythology.[106] Furthermore, Justin argues that Moses precedes Plato and that he borrowed from Moses.[107] Justin finally discusses various aspects of Christian sacraments and concludes by addressing the emperor again.[108]

---

99. Roberts, et al., *The Ante-Nicene Fathers*. Hereafter after all citations will be given as 1 *Apo.*
100. 1 *Apo.* 1.
101. 1 *Apo.* 2–4.
102. 1 *Apo.* 5–11.
103. 1 *Apo.* 12–14.
104. 1 *Apo.* 15–17.
105. 1 *Apo.* 18–22.
106. 1 *Apo.* 23–34.
107. 1 *Apo.* 35–60.
108. 1 *Apo.* 61–68.

CONTEXTUALIZATION OF SECOND-CENTURY APOLOGISTS

Second Apology[109]

The second *Apology* is addressed to the Roman Senate.[110] Urbicus falsely and harshly condemns Christians to death and Crescens is unaware and ignorant of the Christians beliefs, and thus must be corrected.[111] Though the angels transgressed, the name Jesus drives them out.[112] Because of the seed of Christians, God still spares the world though eternal punishment must not be taken lightly.[113] Though Socrates partially knew Christ, Christ is not "merely an instrument of human reason."[114] Christians, in light of death, do not live in wickedness or pleasure.[115] Justin finally concludes by hoping that the world will see Christianity unique than any other philosophy, that the *Apology* be published, and that the hearers of his *Apology* be converted.[116]

Dialogue with Trypho the Jew[117]

Justin first introduces himself to Trypho and begins his dialogue by informing Trypho of his conversion experience, setting the limits of the debate.[118] Justin first explains that Christian faith does not promote a new God but stands as the advancement of the new covenant and explains why they do not follow ritual Mosaic laws.[119] Justin argues that Jesus is the only true Messiah who has already come and that Scripture is fulfilled in him.[120] Justin continues to explain who Jesus is via virgin birth, Scriptures about Christ, and Psalm 22.[121] He asserts that Jesus is the High Priest, Gentiles are God's new people, and that Jews and Gentiles are in the elect as he

109. Roberts, et al., *The Ante-Nicene Fathers*. Hereafter after all citations will be given as 2 *Apo.*
110. 2 *Apo.* 1.
111. 2 *Apo.* 2–4.
112. 2 *Apo.* 5–6.
113. 2 *Apo.* 7–9.
114. 2 *Apo.* 10.
115. 2 *Apo.* 12.
116. 2 *Apo.* 13–15.
117. Roberts, et al., *The Ante-Nicene Fathers*. Hereafter after all citations will be given as *Dia.*
118. *Dia.* 1–8
119. *Dia.* 9–30
120. *Dia.* 31–54.
121. *Dia.* 55–106.

concludes by discussing the free will of men and angels, urging Trypho to make a different verdict than his teachers.[122]

Cultural Connection in Justin Martyr

Cultural Point of Contact

Justin Martyr's apologetics writing is also full of cultural points of contact. In fact, he was "one of the first to apply the categories and to utilize philosophical terminology in Christian thought."[123] Justin's strategy is to contrast the primitive with the present state of philosophy, characterizing the philosophy familiar to his audience as the degenerate issue of an original revelation.[124] However, Justin Martyr does not present preceding philosophies with contempt, but rather as "containing undeniable truths and valuable insights, approving certain elements in the teachings of Plato and the Stoics."[125] Justin even denotes Socrates as a precursor of the work of Christ, establishing an undeniable cultural point of contact. "Justin appeals to current schematizations of the history of philosophy which teach that an original deposit of truth has been deformed and dismembered by the successors of those who first received the revelation."[126]

Justin Martyr's usage of cultural point of contact through the use of primitive philosophy is further exhibited by *Logos spermatikos*.[127] For Justin, divine Logos, in the human reason, is *spermatikos*: it gives rise to the germinal notions or seeds of man's knowledge of God and of the principles of conduct. Richard Norris finds this to be paralleled with the Stoic idea:

> Justin, then, in the passage which we have cited, is employing a Stoic idea to extend the meaning of the scriptural 'Word of God' but he employs this Stoic idea in a non-Stoic form. His use of the conception of the Logos reflects the transformation of the original Stoic notion through its incorporation into a Platonist system. The character of this transformation can be observed in the writings of such authors as Philo and Plutarch. The Logos is identified with

---

122. *Dia.* 107–142.
123. Falls, *Writings of Saint Justin Martyr*, 17.
124. Norris, *God and World in Early Christian Theology*, 48.
125. Norris, *God and World in Early Christian Theology*, 49.
126. Norris, *God and World in Early Christian Theology*, 49.
127. Norris, *God and World in Early Christian Theology*, 51.

the Platonist World Soul, and is understood to be an immaterial Mind rather than a physical Energy... To envisage or interpret the Word of God as Logos was immediately to insert the biblical idea into the world-picture of a Greek theological cosmology. And this procedure, in turn, had two correlative results. It brought about a Hellenization of the scriptural conception, while at the same time it compelled a modification of the philosophical notions which were being used to elucidate the status of the Word of God.[128]

In other words, according to Norris, Justin sees that the seed of logos can function as "personal contact between Christ and Christians," thus using the concept as a means to awaken pagans to true divine reality.[129]

Dialogue with Trypho also features Justin's use of point of contact. Justin's overall approach in defending the faith, as well as his fundamental element of "pro-Jewish" apologetic is his typological approach to hermeneutics. "Part of the reason for this was because he wanted to use Rabbinic traditions via Haggadic materials in order to find a theological point of contact with Trypho."[130] Justin draws parallels from the Old Testament figures, events, and themes, though at times literal and other times allegorical, to demonstrate the continuity of Christianity with Jewish heritage, but also its superiority; and they equally depict the way the second-century apologist employed the factors out of Trypho's culture and used them to establish a point of contact.[131]

All of these testify to Justin's plan to communicate the identity of Christ as the divine reason, "representing a crucial step in the assimilation of Christianity to the Hellenistic world."[132] While the orthodoxy of Justin's theology may be debatable, at least it is clear that "Justin used terminology that was familiar to the philosophy of his day, and it is the universal opinion of his readers that this was in the least an attempt to establish some sort of contact with his audience."[133] Justin, like Paul and other apologists, demonstrates that "appealing to a non-Christian source can be a legitimate

---

128. Norris, *God and World in Early Christian Theology*, 52–55.
129. Keith, "Justin Martyr and Religious Exclusivism," 67.
130. Berry, "How the Post-Apostolic Church Responded to Government," 58.
131. Berry, "How the Post-Apostolic Church Responded to Government," 58.
132. Norris, *God and World in Early Christian Theology*, 53.
133. Troxel, "'All Things to All People,'" 29.

point of contact, without affirming it as common ground (in a Van Tilean sense)."¹³⁴

Enculturated Communication in Justin Martyr

Leslie Barnard sees Justin Martyr playing the role Socrates played in philosophy. He writes,

> It was based on the magnificent defense which Socrates had made at his trial before the people of Athens in which he showed the essential rationality of his position. The Christian Apologists, therefore, set themselves the wider task of showing how Christianity was the embodiment of the noblest conceptions of Greek philosophy and was the truth *par excellence*.¹³⁵

Scholars generally agree that Justin's *Apologies* were addressed to the imperial court and "both the internal and external evidence appear to support the position" that they were indeed read that way.¹³⁶ "Ample evidence from Roman administrative history" suggests that imperial petitions were frequently presented in eloquence.¹³⁷ Justin Martyr seizes such opportunities to engage in enculturated communication.

Similarly, Justin engages the Jewish audience in his culturally contextualized apologetics in his *Dialogue with Trypho the Jew*. He "made use of the popular medium of his day: dialogue."¹³⁸ Justin's "dialogue for the purpose of monologue" would have been "well-known and comfortable to his readers."¹³⁹ Justin's approach towards the Jewish audience is clearly distinguished in that rather than using a literary form accustomed to the Greek audience, he establishes his case from the Scripture and fulfilled prophecies since both Justin and Trypho agree on their authority.¹⁴⁰

---

134. Troxel, "'All Things to All People,'" 41.
135. Barnard, *Justin Martyr: His Life and Thought*, 3.
136. Buck, "Justin Martyr's Apologies," 49.
137. Buck, "Justin Martyr's Apologies," 50.
138. Troxel, "'All Things to All People,'" 27.
139. Troxel, "'All Things to All People,'"27.
140. Werline, "The Transformation of Pauline Arguments in Justin Martyr's Dialogue with Trypho," 82.

CONTEXTUALIZATION OF SECOND-CENTURY APOLOGISTS

Response to Cultural Objections through Life in Christ

A Virtue of the Christian Life

In a world where the state, the philosophers, the Jews, and the heretics all objected to Christianity, Christians were "political Jonahs that must be thrown overboard if the ship of the state were to keep a steady course."[141] Recognizing that there are such prevalent impressions amongst the people of the state caused by rampantly circulated accusations against Christians, "Justin naturally appeals to the moral precepts delivered by Christ, and to the fact that the Christians lived in conformity to them."[142]

Justin, as "an intense moralist," presents Christianity as "morality *par excellence*."[143] By appealing to the virtues of Christians' moral life, Justin like other apologists repudiates slanderous accusations against the Christian faith; and Justin's theological foundation for such a claim follows the same pattern as that of other apologists. In *Apology* Justin explains:

> Truth, purity, generosity, humility with fearlessness, patience with courage, were their characteristic traits. They had broken down racial barriers and had risen above the fear of death. They might be slain—but they could not be injured since they believed death for Christ's sake to be only a deliverance.[144]

Moreover, the message of deliverance from death was not Justin's only power to overcome hostility; instead, "It was the teaching of the incarnate logos which had given men their new ideal, giving them hope, making them fearless and pure."[145] The Christian life in communion with God and the logos was the source of the moral elevation that Justin set forth. Justin correlates the ethical teaching and moral life of Christians to that of "honored philosophic teachers or school."[146] This is to demonstrate that the Christian doctrines, though originating in Christ, were in connection with universal humanity. Justin "even points out resemblances between the facts

---

141. Osborn, *Justin Martyr*, 1.
142. Kaye, *Some Account of the Writings and Opinions of Justin Martyr*, 114.
143. Barnard, *Justin Martyr*, 155.
144. Barnard, *Justin Martyr*, 155–56.
145. Barnard, *Justin Martyr*, 156.
146. Purves, *The Testimony of Justin Martyr to Early Christianity*, 75.

of Christ's life and the fables of mythology" in pursuit of using Christian life as an appeal for the Christian faith.[147]

Exposition of the Resurrection

The exposition of the resurrection is straightforward in Justin's 1 *Apology*: Justin presents the resurrection as proof of immortality.[148] Not only does the resurrection function as a pointer to eternal judgment, but it also works to demonstrate God's omnipotence.[149] Exposition of Christ's resurrection hence

> meets the objection against the resurrection of the body, which the heathen drew from the supposed impossibility of the fact, with the singular remark, that the formation of the human body from so small a quantity of a fluid secretion, would in itself appear equally impossible, and yet it is actually the case.[150]

ANALYSIS OF APOLOGETICS OF TATIAN

Cultural Context

Tatian is unique to the rest of the second-century Greek apologists in that he features a stark difference in his tone.[151] No matter how one rates the tone, as Eusebius says, Tatian was prolific.[152] Tatian's surviving works include *Address to the Greeks* and *Diatessaron*, in which Tatian synthesizes the gospel traditions. Grant explains in Tatian's *Address to the Greeks* Chapter 19, he speaks of an emperor who has endowed teachers of philosophy with salaries of 600 aurei a year, and there is only one emperor who had done that—Marcus Aurelius.[153] Grant suggests that "Tatian wrote not in the name

---

147. Purves, *The Testimony of Justin Martyr to Early Christianity*, 75.
148. 1 *Apo.* 18.
149. 1 *Apo.* 19.
150. Semisch, *Justin Martyr*, 181.
151. Nasrallah, "Mapping the World," 287.
152. Jackson, *The Apostolic Fathers and the Apologists of the Second Century*, 127.
153. Grant, "Chronology of the Greek Apologists," 28.

CONTEXTUALIZATION OF SECOND-CENTURY APOLOGISTS

of Christianity, but as an individual gnostic teacher; Roman authorities still could not understand the difference."[154]

Brief Outline of Apologetics Argument

Perhaps based on this sentiment, Tatian launches his polemic in his *Address to the Greeks*.[155] Against the Greek culture, Tatian argues that all "institutions" have derived from various Barbarian sources.[156] Philosophers also have numbers of errors and failures; but "God alone is to be feared," is the beginning, "the power of Logos," and "wills to restore all through his resurrection."[157] Free will has brought the corruption; and demons are responsible for trickery, depravity, and slavery of the soul.[158] Yet, God is unlike any other Greek gods, demons or gladiators; He is unparalleled to philosophers and philosophies.[159] Tatian points out that Christians are persecuted unjustly and discusses how he was converted, now persistently resisting demons.[160] He also explains that Christian philosophy is more ancient than the "system of Greeks," that Christian women are wise, that boasting in statues is foolishness.[161] Tatian not only introduces his testimony but also the testimonies of Chaldeans, Phoenicians, and Egyptians, all the while showing the superiority of Moses, urging the reader to examine Tatian's life in order to verify the truthfulness of his doctrine.[162]

Cultural Connection in Tatian

Enculturated Communication in Tatian

Typically, Tatian's *Address to the Greeks*' rather harsh discussion stands out amongst the other apological works in the second century due to the

---

154. Grant, "Chronology of the Greek Apologists," 28.

155. Roberts, et al., *The Ante-Nicene Fathers*. Hereafter after all citations will be given as *Add*.

156. *Add*. 1.

157. *Add*. 2–6.

158. *Add*. 7–19.

159. *Add*. 20–26.

160. *Add*. 27–30.

161. *Add*., 31–34.

162. *Add*., 35–41.

"violent polemic against the Greek culture."¹⁶³ Scholars recognize the areas of difficulties that arise from "haphazard structure" and "list of biblical 'problems.'"¹⁶⁴ Tatian's vivid descriptions and polemical discourse aimed at various aspects of Greek culture do generate questions about Tatian's aim.

However, a number of scholars have suggested alternative vantage points in interpreting Tatian's *Address*. Michael McGhee suggests that the *Address* is neither an "*Apology*" nor a "harangue"—which are the most common classifications. Instead, he contends that it is meant to be an ancient *protrepticus*, an oratorical exercise designed to attract students to philosophical instruction.¹⁶⁵ McGhee argues that the tone and digressive denigration of the *Address* disallows one to see it as an *Apology*.¹⁶⁶ Equally, reading the *Address* as a harangue is dissatisfactory as well.¹⁶⁷ McGhee thus claims that Tatian, through the *Address* as a *protrepticus*, urges the readers to "receive instruction in the 'barbarian philosophy' of Christianity," inviting them to respond to such teachings through action.¹⁶⁸ If such classification is granted, one can see that Tatian is employing the same strategy in Epicurus, (*To Menoeceus*), Isocrates (*To Nicocles*), Pseudo-Isocrates (*To Demonicus*), Pseudo-Justin (*To the Greeks*), Clement of Alexandria (*Protrepticus*), and numerous fragments.¹⁶⁹ Tatian presents himself as a teacher of a new philosophy called Christianity, through enculturated communication.

Alternatively, satirical conventions of the second sophistic can also explain Tatian's *Address*.¹⁷⁰ Laura Nasrallah argues that Tatian's *Address*'s genre remains elusive; yet it is a "piece of humor, a satire, a joke of sorts" that Tatian signals in various places, invoking the audience jokes and laughter again and again.¹⁷¹ She writes, "Irony, joking, and satire can reveal the core of a bitter truth. In Tatian's work, the joke is on the Greeks, since he mocks their famed philosophers and customs through quick, devastating

---

163. Barnard, "Heresy of Tatian-Once Again," 9.
164. Crawford, "The Problemata of Tatian," 575.
165. McGehee, "Why Tatian Never 'Apologized' to the Greeks," 143–58.
166. McGehee, "Why Tatian Never 'Apologized' to the Greeks," 145–46.
167. McGehee, "Why Tatian Never 'Apologized' to the Greeks," 147.
168. McGehee, "Why Tatian Never 'Apologized' to the Greeks," 151–52.
169. McGehee, "Why Tatian Never 'Apologized' to the Greeks," 144.
170. Nasrallah, "Mapping the World," 299.
171. Nasrallah, "Mapping the World," 300.

character sketches and illustrations."[172] In either case, Tatian uses enculturated communication to advance his case.

Allan Georgia too suggests an alternate reading. He asserts that Tatian in the *Address* "develops a cultural critique by placing himself in his Greek education and his 'barbarian' ethnicity within the scope of the text's argument," embodying a "cultural monster—a hybrid creature that reflected both the mainstream of Greek *paideutic* values and the barbarian cultures that were antithetical to them."[173] This is Tatian's rhetorical strategy, Georgia argues, that "situate him as a conscientious outsider within the sophistic Greek landscape," aiming to "upend the notion of Greek cultural purity "and "develop a critique of the prevailing opinions about παιδεία and Greek-ness with his entire being."[174] Tatian gains entrance to the culture through such rhetorical strategy, yet again demonstrating culturally contextualized apologetics through enculturated communication.

Cultural Solidarity in Tatian

Tatian's cultural contextualization does not stop at the method of his communication but continues through his cultural solidarity. Placing Tatian in the second century sophistic figures, Nasrallah contends that Tatian's cultural experiences "authorize" his arguments and "signal the fluidity of Greek identity and the seeming solidity of Greek παιδεία (instruction) in the Roman world."[175] Tatian's travels, personal experiences in the Greek world, participation in mysteries, and testing cults grants him greater authority to instruct, adding credibility.[176] Such is precisely the role of cultural solidarity in culturally contextualized apologetics; Tatian displays such an approach.

Response to Cultural Objections through Life in Christ

A Virtue of the Christian Life

Robert Grant argues that Tatian's claim that the more obvious features of the Greek culture were all borrowed from barbarians was a strategy for

172. Nasrallah, "Mapping the World," 300.
173. Georgia, "The Monster at the End of His Book," 191–219.
174. Georgia, "The Monster at the End of His Book," 192, 219.
175. Nasrallah, "Mapping the World," 286–87.
176. Nasrallah, "Mapping the World," 288.

Tatian to "employ a treatise or two 'on discoveries' of the sort well known to his contemporaries."[177] Considering that for many centuries Greek writers oscillated between claiming that everything good came from the Greeks or barbarians, Tatian "is saying that he is barbarian; but expresses Greek thoughts in Greek for Greeks."[178] Grant's verdict is clear:

> Tatian did not view Christianity as hostile to culture, but that as a representative of a minority group in the heterogeneous culture of the empire he adopted the views held by others, sometimes those of minorities, sometimes not."[179]

Exposition of the Resurrection

Tatian's chapter 6 discusses Christians' belief in the resurrection, Tatian exposits it to substantiate his argument that God the Logos is the necessary ground of all beings.[180] Contrary to the "fleshly" resurrection in Tatian as a resurrection of the Spirit and soul only, Helen Hunt argues that "the reason Tatian gives for a bodily resurrection is God's creation of matter."[181] Tatian connects his discussion from chapter 5 and aims to support the concept of Logos by asserting that "man's body is part of matter and part of creation, so it also takes part in the resurrection at the end of the world."[182]

ANALYSIS OF APOLOGETICS OF MELITO OF SARDIS

Melito of Sardis is known as another student of Justin Martyr who became a bishop of Sardis in Asia Minor.[183] Eusebius of Caesarea's *Ecclesiastical History* 4.26 has the longest fragment of his apologetics writing.[184] Melito's

---

177. Grant, *After the New Testament*, 11.
178. Grant, *After the New Testament*, 11.
179. Grant, *After the New Testament*, 12.
180. Hunt, *Christianity in the Second Century*, 35.
181. Hunt opposes Grant's view here by stating that "Tatian's protracted explanation at the end of Chapter 6 of how the body can be resurrected if it is destroyed and scattered proves that matter does play a part in his vision of the resurrection." Hunt considers Tatian's expectation of a 'bodily' resurrection to be a non-gnostic element in his system. Hunt, *Christianity in the Second Century*, 35.
182. Hunt, *Christianity in the Second Century*, 36.
183. Manis, "Melito of Sardis: Hermeneutic and Context," 388.
184. Straton, "Melito of Sardis, Preacher Extraordinary," 167.

reputation is largely attributed to his homily on the Passover entitled *Peri Pascha* in which he viciously dismisses the status of Jews as God's people.[185]

Cultural Context

Melito of Sardis's main apologetic concern illumines the cultural context. The bishop complains bitterly about new decrees which led to the expropriation of Christian property and even to death, also leading the bishop to cast doubt on the origin of the decrees, asserting Christians' loyalty to the empire.[186] Considering how Melito refers to Commodus as the successor to Aurelius, Grant concludes that "like Apollinaris, Melito writes in defense of Christians at a point after the revolt of Avidius Cassius, when measures are being taken to defend the internal security of the empire."[187] The year also was when the emperor, with his empress and son Commodus, visited Asia Minor, making a royal tour in order to strengthen the ties that still bound the eastern half of the empire together.[188]

Brief Outline of Apologetics Argument

For this reason, Melito begins to make a case before the emperor by appealing to his just nature.[189] According to Eusebius, Melito first reports the type of persecutor who takes advantage of Christians by being a 'shameless informer and lover of other people's property;" and if the emperor has ordered these actions against the Christians, then he must have believed it to be for a genuinely good reason, as no righteous emperor would allow such unjust events to be undertaken under his rule. Melito continues to argue that Christianity first arose among "the barbarians;" yet, not only did it flourish during the time of Augustus, but it also became "a good omen of good to the empire, for from that time the power of Romans became great and splendid." This, Melito claims, is evidenced by the fact that under Augustus the empire became glorious, while Nero and Domitian were exceptions to the favorable sentiment towards the flourishing of the empire

---

185. Cohick, "Melito of Sardis's Peri Pascha and Its 'Israel,'" 352.
186. Eusebius, *Ecc.* Book IV. 26.7–11 (Lake, LCL).
187. Grant, "Chronology of the Greek Apologists," 27.
188. Grant, "Chronology of the Greek Apologists," 27–28.
189. There is no chapter division or pagination in this fragment. Therefore, the following summary is from Eusebius's record.

due to Christians. Melito pleads with the emperor that since his grandfather Hadrian sent out letters to ensure that "no new measures" were taken against the Christians to many different regions, an emperor even greater and more philosophic than his grandfather should do the same.[190]

Cultural Connection in Melito

Enculturated Communication

Melito's *Apology* may only exist in fragments, but many have recognized its rhetorical cleverness. "Melito was also known in the ancient world for the brilliance and elegance of his style. It is not surprising that his homily indicates that he surely was a persuasive and popular preacher."[191] Melito's homily contains elaborate use of rhetorical features including "typology, analogy, parallelism, and elegant and profuse application of rhetorical devices." To note, Melito's homily, entitled *Peri Pascha*, clearly demonstrates Melito's rhetorical rigor, even though it is not an apologetics work per se. In regard to Melito's rhetorical ability, Richard White assesses:

> Prior to the discovery of that work, it was usual to assume that early preaching after the apostles was (as indicated by so-called Second Clement) rather poor— loosely organized, rustic and quite unpolished, probably mostly extempore, certainly innocent of the skills and conventions of rhetoric until such men as Hippolytus and Origen, two generations later than Melito. We had thought that, as one historian puts it, "the age of eloquence began in the third century." We know that second-century preaching was, at least when Melito did it, carefully and artistically prepared, with great skill in rhetorical concerns, and quite moving even when read now. Knowing that one of them was, we must question whether other second century preachers, at least in the east if not also in the west, were possessed of high rhetorical and homiletical skills much earlier than has been presumed.[192]

Likewise, Melito's enculturated communication becomes vaguely traceable when one examines Melito's *exordium*-like tone in his Apology. Melito uses the expressions that function as similar to *captio benevolentae*

---

190. Eusebius, *Ecc.* Book IV. 26.7–11
191. White, "Melito of Sardis: Earliest Christian Orator?" 8.
192. White, "Melito of Sardis: An Ancient Worthy Reappears," 16–17.

as he exalts the emperor with expressions such as "great reign of Augustus" that led to "greatness" and "splendor" of the empire. Furthermore, in Melito's plea for removal of the oppressive edict against Christians, he deems the emperor "more generous and wise" than those who persecute the believers.[193] These are expressions that resemble a common feature in Greco-Roman rhetoric.

Cultural Solidarity in Melito

Melito can also be seen as forging cultural solidarity with his audience, the emperor Marcus Aurelius. Richard White believes Melito's oratory may share similarities with other apologists, "but the furthest step in this direction (of a positive political standpoint) was taken by Melito."[194] Adolf Harnack affirms that Melito is building an argument that "the world-empire and the Christian religion are foster-sisters; they form a pair; they constitute a new stage of human history."[195] In other words, Melito is forging cultural solidarity between the emperor's world and the Christian religion. Melito's perception that Christianity is responsible for the empire's blessing and flourishing of the empire, operates based on cultural solidarity established between him and the emperor. "The inference is that in the Christianity which formed part of the world-empire he really recognizes a co-ordinate and sustaining inward force."[196] This exemplifies another aspect of culturally contextualized apologetics.

Response to Cultural Objections through Life in Christ

A Virtue of the Christian Life

Due to the brevity of the content in the fragment, most of the scholarly discussion interacts with Melito's *Peri Pascha*.[197] However, Melito's short

---

193. Eusebius, *Ecc.* Book IV. 26.7–11
194. Harnack, *The Mission and Expansion of Christianity*, 260–61.
195. Harnack, *The Mission and Expansion of Christianity*, 261.
196. Harnack, *The Mission and Expansion of Christianity*, 262.
197. Some of the published articles include Cohick, "Melito of Sardis's Peri Pascha and Its 'Israel'"; Straton, "Melito of Sardis, Preacher Extraordinary"; Manis, "Melito of Sardis"; Cohick, "Melito of Sardis's Peri Pascha and Its 'Israel'"; Wahlde, "The References to the Time and Place of the Crucifixion in the Peri Pascha of Melito of Sardis," 556–69;

apologetics writing is not without scholarly value as it pertains to how the apologetics argument is constructed. In the short, fragmented writing of Melito, indeed he does not seem to have sufficient space to develop an exposition of the resurrection. Yet, one is capable of extracting Melito's presentation of the virtue of the Christian life of his *Apology*. To be exact, I suggest that Melito's culturally contextualized apologetics is exemplified here as he parallels the flourishing of the empire with unhindered religious activities of the Christians.[198] In other words, Melito is building an argument that the empire flourished along with Christians, for "(Christianity) became an omen of good to the empire," and that during its peaceful co-existence, the empire "met no evil." Even though the resurrection and the virtue of Christian life are not made explicit here; nevertheless, a slight variation of the scheme is hinted.[199]

ANALYSIS OF APOLOGETICS OF EPISTLE TO DIOGNETUS

Cultural Context

The text known as the Epistle to Diognetus may not be referenced in any of the ancient texts; yet, it is known as one of the most beautiful Christian texts from the second century.[200] The letter is addressed to a particular person by the name of Diognetus. However, Henry Meecham finds that the letter seems to have been written in noticeably generalized style since it lacks "inclusion of any homely personal touches"; therefore, the intended recipient is debatable.[201] The letter urges the reader to reexamine the validity of prejudice against Christians and invites the reader to see the superiority of Christians. One of the reasons this letter is categorized as apologetics is due to the binding of the codex in which the manuscript was bound. "Marrou lists the twenty-two works that this 260-page manuscript contained; the first five were works attributed to Justin, of which the *Epistle to Diognetus* was

---

White, "Melito of Sardis"; Duncan, "The Covenant Idea in Melito of Sardis: An Introduction and Survey," 12–33.

    198. Eusebius, *Ecc.* Book IV. 26.7–11 (Lake, LCL).
    199. Melito extensively covers the resurrection in *Peri Pascha*.
    200. Foster, "The Epistle to Diognetus," 162.
    201. Meecham, *Light from Ancient Letters*, 8.

the fifth and bore the title in Greek, *Of Him to Diognetus*."[202] However, due to the anonymous nature of the letter, cultural context is largely shrouded in the unknown.[203]

Brief Outline of Apologetics Argument

Epistle to Diognetus begins with a salutation.[204] With an *exordium* that reads "most excellent Diognetus," the author recognizes that Diognetus is "exceedingly zealous."[205] The author invites Diognetus to investigate the matter further, as he argues for the futility of both paganism and Judaism.[206] The author continues by explaining that Christians have a unique identity, heavenly citizenship—"dwelling in their own fatherlands, but as if sojourners in them, sharing all things as citizens, and suffering all things as strangers."[207] He discusses God's sending of his Child to reveal the purpose and salvation.[208] The author extends an invitation to behold the mystery of this God, explaining the ministry of the Word; he encourages that Diognetus be open to this truth.[209]

Cultural Connection in Epistle to Diognetus

Enculturated Communication

One of the immediate features that appear in the letter is an element that frequently appears in Greco-Roman rhetoric, *exordium*. Alluding to Luke, Paul Foster suggests that the opening words of the letter may be caused by conscious modeling on the introduction of Luke or simply the similarities resulting from employing wider rhetorical conventions.[210]

---

202. Foster, "The Epistle to Diognetus," 164.
203. Haykin, *Rediscovering the Church Fathers*, 40.
204. Roberts, et al., *The Ante-Nicene Fathers*. Hereafter after all citations will be given as *Epi*.
205. *Epi*. 1.
206. *Epi*. 2–4.
207. *Epi*. 5–6.
208. *Epi*. 7–9.
209. *Epi*. 10–12.
210. Foster, "The Epistle to Diognetus," 163.

Response to Cultural Objections through Life in Christ

A Virtue of the Christian Life

Michael Haykin observes that the author of the *Epistle* extensively argues for the truthfulness of the Christian faith by virtuous lives of the Christians as evidence.[211] He cites two examples of evidence from *Epistle to Diognetus*: the Christian community and cultural opposition to the ethical norms, particularly those pertaining to women and children.[212] Christians distinguished themselves, as presented by *Epistle to Diognetus*, in their love towards one another and "in the way that believers were prepared to swim against the stream of their contemporaries' ethical values and even to die for their beliefs."[213]

Exposition of the Resurrection

Brandon Crowe believes that *Epistle to Diognetus* deserves an elevated status as an early apologetics writing due to the soteriological nature of its content.[214] He, along with Henry Meecham and Joseph Leinhard, argues that Christology of the letter is the most prominent feature.[215] Additionally, Crowe argues that "the centrality of Son's Incarnation as a paradigmatic, epoch-altering event entails more than simply a once-for-all assumption of flesh, but has significant soteriological implications." The idea that makes *Epistle to Diognetus*'s soteriologically unique is found in the author's assertion that the Son "counteracts the unrighteousness and lawlessness of humanity through His incarnate life."[216] Moreover, the letter demonstrates a mature theology as it clearly distinguishes the Creator-Father with the Son in the letter.[217] This distinction reveals the centrality of the Son as the apologetic appeal, for "He is the one who comes with justice and power to a world that is helpless and unrighteous."[218]

---

211. Haykin, *Rediscovering the Church Fathers*, 47.
212. Haykin, *Rediscovering the Church Fathers*, 78–80.
213. Haykin, *Rediscovering the Church Fathers*, 79.
214. Crowe, "Oh Sweet Exchange!," 96–109.
215. Crowe, "Oh Sweet Exchange!," 98.
216. Crowe, "Oh Sweet Exchange!," 109.
217. Lienhard, "Christology of the Epistle to Diognetus," 280–89.
218. Lienhard, "Christology of the Epistle to Diognetus," 289.

Contextualization of Second-Century Apologists

On top of this soteriology, the author points out the gift of the resurrection. He writes,

> Instead of hating us and rejecting us and remembering our wickedness against us, he showed how long-suffering he is. He bore with us, and in pity, he took our sins upon himself and gave his own Son as a ransom for us— the Holy for the wicked, the Sinless for sinners, the just for the unjust, the Incorruptible for the corruptible, the Immortal for the mortal.

Here, the author is showing that the corruptible being replaced by the incorruptible and mortal replaced by immortal. The future resurrection of believers is presented as the outcome of the author's soteriology.

SUMMARY AND ANALYSIS

Cultural Contextualization of the Apologists

As shown above, Paul's scheme of culturally contextualized apologetics appears as a pattern in the generation of apologists that come immediately after Paul. Though not air-tight or completely uniform, the scheme emerges as the argument and structure are considered. Robert Grant reaffirms that culturally contextualized apologetics responds to cultural objections. He explains that

> the writing of apologetic works did not take place in a historical vacuum. Each work had some specific historical occasions. Quadratus wrote when Hadrian visited Athens. Aristides and Justin probably replied to the attack made by the rhetorician Fronto. Apollinaris, Melito, Tatian, Athenagoras, and Miltiades reflect the relatively severe persecution of 176–180. This persecution, in turn, was due to the Roman need for internal security after the abortive revolt of Avidius Cassius . . . The apologists recognized the critical nature of their times. This much is proved by the occasions on which they wrote.[219]

Abraham Malherbe equally argues the point and substantiates it by shedding greater light on pagan perception of Christianity. He observes that the world of the post–New Testament considered both Judaism and Christianity as a form of philosophy.[220] Malherbe finds evidence in Aristotle,

219. Grant, "Chronology of the Greek Apologists," 30–33.
220. Malherbe, "Apologetic and Philosophy in the Second Century," 20.

as well as his successor, Theophrastus, who called the Jews "a philosophical race," possibly because of monotheism.[221] This apprehension was not any different from Christianity.[222] After all, Philosophy was seen "an intermediary between God and man, of which the end was not to construct a system, but to be assimilated to God."[223]

Though the Greeks were "quite generous in bestowing a title of philosopher," that "Christians were at times regarded as philosophers by no means implies that this was the usual view that outsiders had of them."[224] To illustrate, Pliny, Tacitus, and Suetonius do not regard Christianity as philosophy; Celsus "places the Christians on the same level as votaries of the popular imported cults"; and Lucían of Samosata's writings indicate that pagans generally perceived Christianity as "an Oriental mystery religion." The closest classification Christianity could be filed under was Cynicism; yet, "field philosophers who swarmed across the empire" were also classified in the same way.[225] Christianity was something that the pagan world did not know how to categorize: Christianity accepted their doctrine based on faith, yet pagans did not understand how this was possible and became a source of derision.[226] Christians were subject to abhorrence, ridicule, and hatred because Christians formed their beliefs through "un-demonstrated laws," "uncritical faith," and "unreasoned."[227]

For this reason, Greek apologists introduce themselves as "philosophers."[228] What is striking is that this contextualization of the Apologists takes place even while they do not self-categorize Christianity as a philosophy: An Apologist "nowhere expressly calls Christians

---

221. Malherbe explicates that consequently, the recognition of Aristobulus as philosopher prepared the way for Philo and the Christian Apologist to be labeled as the same. Teachings in the synagogue that bear resemblance of public philosophical institution, Josephus's designation on Jewish sect as "philosophy," and Jewish' emphasis on monotheism and morals all paved a way for the Greek perception of Judaism as purely philosophical doctrine.

222. Malherbe, "Apologetic and Philosophy in the Second Century," 22.
223. Malherbe, "Apologetic and Philosophy in the Second Century," 22.
224. Malherbe, "Apologetic and Philosophy in the Second Century," 22.
225. Malherbe, "Apologetic and Philosophy in the Second Century," 25–26.
226. Malherbe, "Apologetic and Philosophy in the Second Century," 25.
227. Malherbe, "Apologetic and Philosophy in the Second Century," 25–26.
228. Maràs, "The Issue of Rhetoric for Christian Apologists in the Second Century," 412.

philosophers or styles Christianity a philosophy."[229] Malherbe sums up the approaches of the Apologists: "It suited their polemic to call Christianity a philosophy and themselves philosophers. It made it possible to demand from the state the same treatment for themselves that was accorded to the philosophic schools."[230] It is against this backdrop that the apologists of the second century engage in cultural contextualization.

The Legacy of the Second-Century Apologetics in Culture

Second-century apologists' cultural contextualization resulted in various cultural influences. The Apologists appealed to the political authorities to treat Christians for just treatment; engaged in the polemic against the inconsistencies and vanity of pagan beliefs and practices; presented and defended virtuous Christian life; and provided theological concepts to justify the legitimacy of Christianity as a viable religion within the Roman Empire.[231]

Establishment of Public Ethics of the Christian Life

Uniformly, Greek apologists of the second century demonstrate the moral superiority of the Christian life. This is another pattern that is established in these apologists. Apologetics of the second century sought to provide an answer to that question through culturally contextualized apologetics. Apologists' coherent scheme included presenting Christian morality as a form of a good life. James Papandrea confirms this assessment as he writes, "To show that Christianity is a *virtue* (italics his), the apologists argued that Christian morality is a higher standard than that of Roman society, and is in fact the best way to achieve the good life."[232]

However, Christian apologists in the second century do not stop at just dismissing the charges or rejecting pagan practices. They consistently draw

---

229. Malherbe, "Apologetic and Philosophy in the Second Century," 27.

230. Malherbe does recognize that these apologists were philosophers to begin with, prior to their conversion; and they engaged in philosophy because the issue at hand was a philosophical problem. Different apologists had differing valuation of pagan philosophies; and they practiced in various forms. Malherbe, "Apologetic and Philosophy in the Second Century," 27.

231. Berry, "How the Post-Apostolic Church Responded to Government," 54.

232. Papandrea, *Reading the Early Church Fathers*, 35.

attention to the virtuous lives of Christians. Marcus Bockmuehl notices an important expression of ethics in the cultural context. He writes,

> Ever since the time of Homer, "the concept of virtue was a basic staple of Greek thought and literature. It was given a clearer definition in the ethics of Plato, who first outlined the classic four cardinal virtues of justice, temperance, courage, and wisdom. In various modified forms, this material soon found its way into a good deal of both Jewish and Christian ethical thought. By the time of the New Testament, lists of widely recognized virtues and vices were a common way of expressing in a nutshell how a good citizen of the Roman Empire ought to behave; Jews and Christians adapted these lists for the purposes of explaining their own ethics to outsiders in intelligible terms. Although pagan virtue and vice lists were never taken over uncritically, they were emended and adjusted to express in contemporary terms the meaning of God's commandments in Scripture.[233]

Moreover, culturally contextualized apologetics of the second century sought to establish public ethics in pursuit of a virtuous life. Making cases before public figures such as the emperor also symbolized their apologetics argument intended to reach a wider Roman public.[234] Discussion of morality in the Christian life incorporated topics such as Christian marriages, Christian welfare for the poor and oppressed, and humanitarian charity to all. For this reason, "Christianity emerges as the true humanism, eminently reasonable in doctrine and profoundly humanizing in practice."[235] Hence, these Christian practices were intelligible symbols to those in the Greco-Roman culture. Second-century Greek apologists also argued that Christians were loyal to the emperor, though clear qualifying conditions were attached to such claims.[236] Continuous appeal to restore justice also strengthens the idea that the Apologists sought to fortify public ethics in the cultural context.

---

233. Bockmuehl, "Public Ethics in a Pluralistic Society?," 4–5.
234. See Bockmuehl, "Public Ethics in a Pluralistic Society?"
235. Bockmuehl, "Public Ethics in a Pluralistic Society?," 8.
236. Rhee's chap. 4, "Christian Loyalty to the Empire" discusses this topic in length.

Contextualization of Second-Century Apologists

Propagation of Sexual Ethics as Virtue

As shown above, another repeated topic in the second-century Greek apologist is the sexual ethic of Christians. Helen Rhee diagnoses that "the general controlling paradigm behind the Christian ascetic attitude toward the world is that of a certain dualism, namely, dualism of this world and the other world, motivated by the eschatological impetus and Platonic dualism."[237] It is true that the ascetic attitude toward the world was not unique to the Christian faith. Middle Platonism, Stoics, and Cynics all embraced a form of chastity akin to that of nascent Christianity during this time.[238] However, Christian asceticism was fueled by the notion that death, even martyrdom, signified joyful exit from this world. The result was a greater degree of moral discipline and shunning away from pagan immorality and fornication.[239]

The second-century apologetics consistently—and thus as a scheme—construct an argument from sexual morality. Despite the differences, Tatian and all the other apologists that are treated in this book unanimously associate sexual immorality with idol worship. Kathy Gaca argues that Tatian's fervor to eliminate any sexual activity is driven by his understanding of "the Greek gods and their powers, the gods' origins and Stoic grounding in nature, and the human condition under the control of the immanent gods."[240] Sexual purity is presented "as distinctive Christian value and (they) categorically dissociated sexual sins from Christian practice."[241] The apologists' view of chastity and abstinence was eventually recognized as "exceptional in character" and "praised it as a virtue."[242]

---

237. Rhee, *Early Christian Literature*, 108.

238. Rhee, *Early Christian Literature*, 107.

239. There exists a deviation in apologists' culturally contextualized apologetics. Tatian's extreme perspective on asceticism claimed that that all must renounce all sexual activity in order to receive salvation. Though flawed, Tatian's "encratite ideas were also pivotal as a catalyst for more authoritative ecclesiastical sexual norms." Tatian's ideas functioned as a catalyst that led church fathers, including Irenaeus, to respond to this heretical advocacy of sexual encratism, leading the church fathers to better formulate alternative notions of Christian sexual morality. Culturally contextualized apologetics that draws from the Christian life contributed to development of a heightened sense of asceticism.

240. Gaca, "Driving Aphrodite from the World," 28–52.

241. Rhee, *Early Christian Literature*, 156.

242. Rhee, *Early Christian Literature*, 157.

When it comes to marriage, the matter of divorce functioned as an area of distinction between the Christian faith and the first-century Greco-Roman world as well. Furfey paints the backdrop to the culturally contextualized apologetics as he writes,

> Under the early Empire, divorce was invoked for the most frivolous reasons . . . In the meantime, morals had declined. Augustus was forced to legislate on adultery and chastity and the encouragement of marriage. He boasted that he restored the ancient traditions which were falling into disuse. It is hard to say just what this moral decline meant to the average Roman woman since our sources deal nearly exclusively with the aristocracy; but the satirists of the time have much to say about the immorality, irresponsibility, and cruelty of high-born Roman matrons.[243]

Against this cultural tide, Apologists of the second century persistently emphasized social order. Social order established through solid marriage and renewed dignity of women was another apologetics strategy employed as a scheme. The apologists explain that Christians marry for the sake of bringing up children.[244] "Procreation of children is the measure of Christian's indulgence in appetite.[245] Sexual relation outside of marriage is adultery and fornication. "Whereas the Apologists denounced both vulgar immorality and radical asceticism as threatening the traditional norms, they presented Christian sexual asceticism as in accordance with the preservation of the Greco-Roman social structure in which Christianity should take its root."[246]

CONCLUSION

Second-century Greek apologists and their works demonstrate the structure of argument much akin to the scheme found in Paul's speeches. Specifically, a cultural connection that takes place through the cultural point of contact and enculturated communication repeatedly appears in their apologetics. Responses to various cultural objections through the discussion of the virtue of the Christian life and the exposition of the resurrection equally are patterned in their content. These elements are consistently included in their

---

243. Furfey, "Social Action in the Early Church," 93.
244. Justin Martyr, 1 *Apo.* 29.
245. Aristides, *Apology* 33
246. Rhee, *Early Christian Literature*, 123.

apologetics. Such consistency parallels that of Paul's apologetics strategy outlined in chapter 4 of this book. Hence, Paul models a culturally contextualized apologetics to the generation of apologists immediately after him.

Chapter 6

Cultural Contextualization of Apologetics Preaching

WHAT DOES A CULTURALLY CONTEXTUALIZED APOLOGETICS look like in today's world? How will Paul's apologetics model function as such in practical application? I investigate answers to these questions in this concluding chapter, particularly with regard to preaching. Having considered that Paul's speeches are an important mode of culturally contextualized apologetics communication, one of the immediate applications is to the art of preaching. In the following, I suggest that Paul stands out as an apologetics preaching *exemplar*, offering a way forward to the traditional modes of apologetics preaching.

Albert Mohler decries that there is a dire need for apologetics preaching in today's world, and claims that preaching in its essence must be apologetical.[247] Despite such urgency, contemporary scholarship has largely overlooked this subject of apologetics preaching.[248] Effectiveness and faithfulness in apologetics preaching are critical needs of contemporary preaching.

---

247. Mohler, *He Is Not Silent*, 130.

248. Besides the works I will cite in the section below, many works appear in periodicals and not scholarly journals. The rare exceptions are Malherbe, "The Apologetic Theology of the Preaching of Peter," 205–23; Knupp, "The Apologetic Preaching of Paul Tillich," 395–407; Welsh, "Preaching as Apologetics," 239–52.

CONTEXTUALIZATION OF APOLOGETICS PREACHING

To be sure, the theology of preaching has generated many valuable works.[249] Numerous works have dealt with the practical nature of preaching.[250] More recently, preaching with a specific target or mode has received more treatment.[251] However, greater exploration of the topic of apologetics preaching is still needed.

In the following, I will briefly survey various approaches to carrying out apologetics preaching in contemporary samples. These approaches to apologetics preaching closely trace the traditional approaches of apologetics, namely the classical, evidential, presuppositional, and fideistic.[252] Upon exploring ways in which the apologetics preaching has been exhibited or theorized in the contemporary setting, I demonstrate that Paul not only fits the mode of apologetics preaching in the traditional sense but also offers a model of apologetics preaching beyond the traditional system. I now turn to the examination of apologetics preaching in the contemporary setting.

MODELS OF APOLOGETICS PREACHING

The following surveys various models of apologetics preaching that principally trace the four basic approaches of apologetics, namely classical, evidential, presuppositional, and fideistic. There are examples of real-life preachers who follow these theories and exemplify these models of apologetics preaching: to be specific, Richard Charles Buck's preaching project

---

249. Adam, *Speaking God's Words*; Barth, *Homiletics*; Buttrick, *Homiletic: Moves and Structures*; Carrick, *The Imperative of Preaching*; Craddock Jr., *Preaching*; Dargan, *A History of Preaching*,; Duke, *The Sermon as God's Word: Theologies for Preaching*; Edwards, *A History of Preaching*; Kaiser Jr., *Toward an Exegetical Theology: Biblical Exegesis for Preaching and Teaching*; Kuruvilla, *Privilege the Text!*; Litfin, *Paul's Theology of Preaching*.

250. Just to name a few: Mohler, *He Is Not Silent*; Stott, *Between Two Worlds: The Art of Preaching in the Twentieth Century*; Keller, *Preaching: Communicating Faith in an Age of Skepticism*; Chapell, *Christ-Centered Preaching*; Piper, *The Supremacy of God in Preaching*; Lloyd-Jones, *Preaching and Preachers*,; Robinson and Gibson, *Making a Difference in Preaching*.

251. Gibson, *Evangelistic Preaching*; Gresham, *Evangelistic Preaching*; Perry, *Evangelistic Preaching*; Walker, *Evangelistic Preaching*; Eswine, *Preaching to a Post-Everything World*; Jensen, *Thinking in Story: Preaching in a Post-Literate Age*; Allen, *The Sermon without End: A Conversational Approach to Preaching*; Stiller, *Preaching Parables to Postmoderns*.

252. Cowan distinguishes between the presuppositional approach and reformed epistemological. While this is helpful in many regards, the distinction is not so sharp in the practicality of preaching ministry. Thus, I outline four traditional apologetics system as outlined by Boa and Bowman cited in chap. 2. See Cowan, *Five Views on Apologetics*.

takes the classical and evidentialist approach; the analysis of Tim Keller's preaching reveals that he takes the presuppositional approach to preaching; Craig Loscalzo's convictions for apologetics preaching follows the fideistic approach.[253] I will discuss and illustrate these models of apologetics preaching in order.

Classical and Evidentialist Apologetics Preaching

Richard Charles Buck is a preacher at Emmanuel Baptist Church in Ontario, Canada. His Doctor of Ministry project at Trinity Evangelical Divinity School features a twelve-week preaching series entitled "Confident Christianity: Ready to Give an Answer." In this project, he constructs a macro-apologetics argument by first dealing with objections to the Christian faith, then moving on to build a positive case for the Christian faith.[254] Buck deals with issues such as relativism, the possibility of the Absolute Truth, a defense of Christian exclusivism, the reliability of the Scripture, the issue of intolerance and the issue of faith and science.[255]

Buck exhibits how preaching can be apologetics preaching: apologetics preaching can follow the pattern of classical apologetics strategy.[256] As in the classical approach, Buck's preaching aims to establish theism, subsequently constructing a case for the unique status of Christian faith. His preaching follows the pattern of the classical apologetical approach on a macro-level: moving from theism to Christian theism is his larger scheme of preaching. Moreover, his preaching, on a micro-level, provides evidence after evidence presenting rationality behind upholding Christian faith—which

---

253. Regrettably, due to the scarcity of the samples, I use Buck's DMin project as a real-life example of apologetics preaching project. Keller offers both a real-life example and a theory of preaching, while Loscalzo's work is limited to the theoretical aspect. Buck, "Apologetics Preaching Today in the Context of a Local Church"; Keller, *Preaching*; Craig A Loscalzo, *Apologetic Preaching: Proclaiming Christ to a Postmodern World*.

254. Buck, "Apologetics Preaching Today in the Context of a Local Church," 73.

255. Buck, "Apologetics Preaching Today in the Context of a Local Church," 77–111.

256. In this part, Buck is constructing a case for Christian theism through his sermons on a macro level. He preaches on the issue of suffering and pain, then Buck presents a form of teleological argument for God's existence, finally showing that unless one comes to grips with the concept of sin, the gospel is not good news at all. Buck professes that the only and genuine solution is the person and the work of Jesus Christ. This section is a sequential argument that not only further establishes the classical approach to apologetics, but also serves as the evidentialistic approach since it aims to demonstrate the truthfulness of the Christian faith through the resurrection and evidence.

Contextualization of Apologetics Preaching

is an important aspect of the evidentialistic apologetical approach. Hence, Buck's apologetics preaching corresponds to two of the major patterns of apologetical approaches.

Presuppositional Apologetics Preaching

Tim Keller, a former senior pastor of Redeemer Presbyterian Church New York City, is known for his preaching that engages the secular audience.[257] Close analysis of his preaching demonstrates that his apologetics preaching strives to dismantle the secular worldview while presenting the Christian worldview as the superior one; in other words, as the presuppositional approach to apologetics would, Keller preaches to convince the hearers of the "impossibility of the contrary."[258]

The concept of the 'impossibility of the contrary' is the heart of presuppositional apologetics.[259] Travis Allen Freeman explicates how Tim Keller employs presuppositional apologetics to bring about worldview deconstruction.[260] He argues that Keller's method of apologetics preaching involves a movement from (1) intelligibility, (2) credibility, (3) plausibility, and (4) intimacy; all aimed to destabilize the audience's worldview and to demonstrate how their set of beliefs cannot produce internal or logical consistencies.[261] Keller, in his apologetics preaching, aims to demonstrate how their set of beliefs cannot produce internal or logical consistencies.[262] Keller's final step is highlighting the superiority of Christianity as a worldview while illuminating that the competing worldviews cannot logically be upheld.[263]

Fideistic Approach

Among the rare pieces of literature that deal with apologetics preaching, Craig A. Loscalzo's *Apologetic Preaching: Proclaiming Christ to a Postmodern*

---

257. See Keller, *Center Church*.
258. Freeman, "Preaching to Provoke a Worldview Change,".
259. Bahnsen, *Van Til's Apologetic*.
260. Freeman, "Preaching to Provoke a Worldview Change," 115.
261. Freeman, "Preaching to Provoke a Worldview Change," 112–16.
262. Freeman, "Preaching to Provoke a Worldview Change," 117.
263. Keller, *Preaching*, 157–89.

World is one of the works that specifically interacts with the subject of apologetics preaching.[264] While somewhat basic and straightforward, he presents a vision for apologetics preaching in a strategy geared specifically to respond to such challenges of postmodernism.[265] Loscalzo first explains that apologetic preaching is preaching that proclaims mystery in an age of information: "Postmoderns are not only skeptical about religion but also skeptical about coming to conclusions through the use of deductive logic systems"; Loscalzo argues that preachers must describe "the mysteries of Christian faith in philosophical categories."[266] He thus emphasizes the aspect of mystery in the Christian faith as an apologetics strategy, akin to fideism. He next argues that preachers must employ narratives to connect to postmodern people.[267] Loscalzo also believes that the proclamation of Christian hope is a way to respond to a cultural climate of skepticism.[268] Loscalzo further contends that since postmoderns desire authenticity, preachers must "show the biblical account is a theological description of historical reality, rather than a scientific treatise."[269]

All of Loscalzo's proposal for apologetics preaching bears a striking resemblance to a fideistic approach to doing apologetics. Terminologies such as mystery, faith, story, and hope that transcend logical objections to Christian faith are one of the chief characteristics of the fideistic apologetics approach.[270] Loscalzo's apologetics preaching simply illustrates fideistic apologetics.

As shown above, the four traditional apologetics approaches function as a framework for apologetics preaching. Summing up, Classical apologetics preaching advances Christian theism based on the establishment of theism; evidentialistic apologetics preaching employs the resurrection and evidence; presuppositional apologetics preaching dismantles secular worldviews to advance the Christian worldview; and fideistic apologetics preaching emphasizes faith, hope, and personal story. Apologetics preaching in contemporary settings contours the four traditional structures of apologetics approaches.

---

264. Loscalzo, *Apologetic Preaching*.
265. Loscalzo's particular interest is apologetics preaching in the postmodern world.
266. Loscalzo, *Apologetic Preaching*, 33–34.
267. Loscalzo, *Apologetic Preaching*, 40.
268. Loscalzo, *Apologetic Preaching*, 54.
269. Loscalzo, *Apologetic Preaching*, 91.
270. Boa and Bowman, *Faith Has Its Reasons*.

ANALYSIS OF PAUL'S APOLOGETICS SPEECHES UNDER THE FOUR TRADITIONAL APOLOGETICS SYSTEM

Paul Employing Classical Apologetics?

Can contemporary approaches to Christian apologetics, including the classical approach, be applied to an understanding of Paul's approach? Can Paul's approach be characterized as possessing the same qualities of the classical approach to apologetics? Inquiry into this question requires comparing the elements found in Paul's apologetics speeches with that of the classical approach to apologetics.

Again, Classical apologetics is typically marked by a two-step method: it first establishes theism; then it moves to particularize Christian theism. In analyzing Paul's apologetics preaching, it becomes apparent that Apostle Paul also follows this two-step pattern of classical apologetics.[271] As shown in this book, in his apologetics speeches in Acts 14, and 17, Paul consistently exhibits this classical approach to apologetics. Paul repeatedly builds upon natural theology to introduce or reinforce theism, to ultimately establish Christian theism.[272] This is a classical approach to apologetics preaching; Paul engages in such an approach.

Paul Employing Evidentialistic Apologetics?

Evidentialistic apologetics' main strategy is to present the fact of the resurrection of Jesus as the central facet that defines all others.[273] Preaching that takes this logical approach—the use of the resurrection as proof—is evidentialistic apologetics preaching.[274] Paul also demonstrates the same strategy in all of his apologetics speeches, as shown in the earlier section of this book. To be more precise, the testimony of the resurrection fuels Paul's defense and vindication of Christian faith since this is a decisive event in history.[275]

---

271. Flemming, "Contextualizing the Gospel in Athens," 207.

272. Charles, "Engaging the (Neo) Pagan Mind," 47–62.

273. Boa and Bowman, *Faith Has Its Reasons*, 193–97.

274. Mărculeț, "Elements of Inculturation in Saint Paul's Speech from Areopagus," 46–47.

275. Shore, "Preaching for Mission," 87–102.

Paul Employing Presuppositional Apologetics?

Presuppositional apologetics presents a certain case against other worldviews by proving the impossibility of the contrary. C. Kavin Rowe in the important book, *World Upside Down: Reading Acts in the Greco-Roman Age*, persuasively argues that Paul's speeches work to undermine the entire religiosity or worldview of the Lystrans, Athenians, and everyone in between.[276] Rowe successfully shows that Paul destabilizes the pagan way of life, offering a brand new worldview called Christianity.[277] Presenting Christianity as the most superior worldview against pagan philosophies is precisely the approach the presuppositional apologetics preaching takes, and Paul engages in it.[278]

Paul Employing Fideistic Apologetics?

Fideistic apologetics preaching is a strategy of preaching that emphasizes the component of faith more so than rationality. While the approach does not deny the merit of rational investigation of Christian faith, fideistic apologetics stresses the importance of faith to make sense of the faith and emphasizes the element of mystery, hope, and story.

Paul's apologetics speeches constantly demand faith from the hearers.[279] Regardless of the audience, Paul's conclusion of the preaching is consistent: repent and believe.[280] The element of the mystery is also present in Paul's speeches: the interruptions in the speeches leaves the audience desiring for more.[281] Moreover, the story that narrates Paul's encounter with the Risen Lord becomes foundational when engaging with both Judaism

---

276. Rowe, *World Upside Down*, 21–22.

277. See chap. 2 of Rowe, *World Upside Down*.

278. This strategy becomes particularly evident in Paul's Areopagus speech. Paul's Areopagus apologetics preaching contains his polemic against the validity of pagan theology, especially with his discussion of locality of their gods. Paul's presentation of Christianity as a superior worldview challenges their stance.

279. Gray, "Implied Audiences in the Areopagus Narrative," 206. Pathrapankal, "From Areopagus to Corinth (Acts 17)," 72.

280. Given, "Not Either/Or but Both/And in Paul's Areopagus Speech," 368.

281. I have treated this subject in the earlier chapter, but for more on this, see Sandnes, "Paul and Socrates," 18–19.

and the Gentiles alike.[282] In this sense, Paul can also be seen as employing fideistic apologetics in his apologetics preaching.

Paul's Apologetics Preaching

As discussed above, Paul's apologetics speeches encapsulate all of the traditional apologetics approaches that appeal to rationality. It is fascinating to observe how Paul's apologetics speeches encompass major components from all of the traditional approaches of apologetics and their logical structures in his apologetics speeches. In this way, Paul models apologetics preaching *par excellence*.

CULTURALLY CONTEXTUALIZED APOLOGETICS APPLIED IN CONTEMPORARY SETTING

Having considered how Paul incorporates all four traditional approaches to apologetics, as well as having probed and pondered how Paul contextualized the defense of the gospel in light of the cultural milieu, one observes the clear benefits of applying Paul's culturally contextualized apologetics in contemporary apologetics preaching. The integration of Paul's model for cultural contextualization can continue to remain viable as its core components begin to structure contemporary apologetics preaching. In the following, I present an applied case of apologetics preaching, showcasing how Paul's model advances the contemporary apologetics preaching.

How would Paul defend the gospel and make a case for Christianity if he were ministering today? In the following, I offer various cases that reflect the applied model of Paul's culturally contextualized apologetics.

Enculturated Communication

Culturally contextualized apologetics makes full use of enculturated communication. In contemporary settings, the Internet and social media have completely revolutionized both transmission and consumption of information, and YouTube has "become the most prominent social media

---

282. Paul's speeches in Acts 24 and 26 illustrate this point as it contains a larger portion of Paul's testimony.

platform."²⁸³ YouTube is now more than a social media platform, it has become "the second largest search engine behind Google. With 3 billion searches per month, YouTube's search volume is larger than that of Bing, Yahoo, AOL and Ask.com combined."²⁸⁴ Hence, culturally contextualized apologetics preaching may well utilize the internet platform as an important means of communication.²⁸⁵

Cultural Point of Contact

Whether on a video blog in a YouTube video or from a wooden pulpit, culturally contextualized apologetics establishes a cultural point of contact. This may involve popularized sayings or simplified soundbites that reflect shared ideas of a public audience. "If it does not harm anybody, it will not hurt," "Whatever feels good is good," or "One man's meat is another man's poison" provide some examples. More specifically, cultural point of contact may come from various products of popular culture, such as in a book, music, television shows, or in a film. To illustrate, there is a line in the film *Star Wars Episode III: The Revenge of the Sith* where the evil lord Palpatine seduces young Anakin Skywalker, a leading character, by saying "Good is a point of view, Anakin. Only a Sith (an evil lord) deals in absolutes."²⁸⁶ A Billboard-Award-winning boyband BTS's message to the music listeners is clear: "love yourself."²⁸⁷ Regardless of the source of quote or sayings, culturally contextualized apologetics recognizes its place in culture. More importantly, it aims to uncover the underlying assumptions, presuppositions, and inner-working of the heart. Essentially, as aforementioned in

---

283. Irshad, et al., "Modeling Active Life Span of Youtube Videos Based on Changing Viewershiprate," 250.

284. Wagner, "Council Post: Are You Maximizing The Use Of Video In Your Content Marketing Strategy?"

285. Whether one would consider preaching given on a video blog platform as a legitimate preaching event is beyond the scope of the current discussion. Though this is merely a hypothetical scenario, I do speculate that preaching videos or video recordings of preaching given in other context uploaded on the Internet platform as a viable form of preaching may receive greater support. For instance, when a church must broadcast its services online due to a major impact of an epidemic behind closed doors, one may not dismiss the preaching given in the service as an illegitimate preaching because of lack of audience present.

286. Lucas, *Star Wars: Episode III*.

287. Leight, "Review: BTS."

CONTEXTUALIZATION OF APOLOGETICS PREACHING

chapter 2, the cultural point of contact serves to establish a connection and to pivot the logical flow.

Cultural Solidarity

In establishing a cultural connection, chapter 3 of the book demonstrated that the key component in engaging the audience is the credibility gained through an entrance into the culture of the hearers. There needs to be a dual aspect in building this solidarity: relatability is the first, and authority is the second. Relatability becomes more and more critical component in effective communication as increasing numbers of people seem to form their convictions based on either preconceived ideas or effects of emotions in the post-truth society.[288] Furthermore, cultural solidarity should allow the audience to render the speaker as a knowledgeable figure—even if not necessarily authoritative—of the Christian faith, and culturally contextualized apologists must function as a bridge between two worlds. In a real-life scenario, this may mean a youth pastor has an active interaction with a larger audience as a YouTuber. It may also translate to a pastor who engages with the skeptics as a philosopher. While the options are vast and not exhaustive, this does not mean that every apologist poses as an expert in every area familiar to the audience, but that there is an attempt to relate to the experience or emotions of the audience in some ways.

Cultural Objection Responded with the Virtue of Christian Life as an Appeal

One need not long before detecting a wide range of cultural objections. "God is a moral monster," "There is no absolute good or bad," or "Christianity is too restrictive on sex" are just a few sampling of a greater number of objections that exist against the Christian faith. Apologetics preaching identifies the cultural objection and presents a case that refutes the charges. Equally important, though, is the presentation of the virtue of the Christian life as an appeal and support for the case in culturally contextualized apologetics. For instance, culturally contextualized apologetics would draw attention to the fact that how the life of Christ fuels the love for the neighbors, moving beyond mere moral uprightness, let alone moral violence. Against the

---

288. I have discussed this issue in the introduction.

cultural notion that denies the existence of an absolute that separates good and evil, the position that renders exclusivity of Christian faith as outdated and untrue, the apologist would show how one cannot avoid being an exclusivist, an absurdity of life without absolute morality, and how Christian life lived in absolute exclusivity has the resource to be gentle with those who hold differing views and pursue goodness. Christian sexual ethics that exude beauty, satisfaction found in loving fidelity, and strengthened value of family contrasted with destructive outcomes of sexual immorality also serve to dismantle cultural opposition and to defend the Christian faith. Presentation of the gospel-driven life lived in the redemption from sexual sins, coupled with the power that enables one to live in deeper freedom, also exemplifies the applied cultural contextualization of apologetics.

Exposition of the Resurrection

Yet, not only does the commendation of the Christian faith stop at the refutation of cultural objections but it continues with the exposition of the resurrection. Culturally contextualized apologetics contains both the proclamation and the exposition of the resurrection. Because of the resurrection, the apologetics strategy shows that Christian God is not a moral monster, but in fact the only one who can truly vindicate the unjustly oppressed and successfully fulfill justice. The exposition of the resurrection also points to the fact that there is an event in history that proved the existence of the ultimate absolute, as well as an event that grants both the motivation and the power for people to demonstrate realness of good against evil in this world. The resurrection anticipates the day of his return, which will also be a day of matrimony—the marriage supper of the Lamb—shaping the way believers envision the role of spouses, sexual purity, and marriage practices.

PAUL'S CULTURALLY CONTEXTUALIZED APOLOGETICS: A WAY FORWARD

In conclusion, contemporary apologetics can both relate to and learn from the challenges that faced the defense of Christianity from the past. Everett Berry writes,

> Although one cannot look at the settings of these early second-century Christian thinkers and say that American evangelicals

are in the exact same cultural plight, there are undeniable points of commonality between the cultural incredulity of the second and twenty-first centuries. There were unwarranted accusations against the lifestyles of the early Christians, hostile attacks on central beliefs intrinsic to the coherence of the Christian faith, and even violent attempts to suppress the growth of converts to Christianity just as there are today around the world.[289]

As exemplified by Paul, contemporary preachers can enhance preaching communication by establishing a cultural connection. As discussed in length in this book, the cultural connection includes the cultural point of contact that finds common grounds with the audience, the enculturated communication that functions to optimize the hearing, and the cultural solidarity that not only forges associations with the audience but also gains an entrance into the hearer's world.

Moreover, contemporary preachers can better engage in apologetics preaching by being mindful of various cultural objections that may exist in the hearers. Removal of cultural objections opens up the hearts and minds of the audience to be better situated for cultural reception. Paul models a way to respond to cultural objections: presentation of the virtue of the Christian life. A vision of the Christian life preached through the Word, along with the absurdity of life apart from morality, can provide a way forward in Christian apologetics preaching.[290] Furthermore, apologetics preaching that exposits the fact and implication of the resurrection stays faithful to the biblical model of preaching.

Paul's apologetics preaching does not merely encompass the traditional system of apologetics but goes beyond to present how contemporary apologetics preaching can incorporate cultural components as Paul has shown. Therefore, Paul models culturally contextualized apologetics.

CULTURAL CONTEXTUALIZATION OF APOLOGETICS: PAST, PRESENT, AND FUTURE

I have argued that Paul offers a model of culturally contextualized apologetics. We have explored the past intending to gain insights for the present.

---

289. Berry, "How the Post-Apostolic Church Responded to Government," 53–67.

290. Craig begins his apologetics argument by asserting that life without the existence of God is ultimately absurd; one cannot sustain morality without practically assuming the existence of God. Craig, *Reasonable Faith*.

Cultural Contextualization of Apologetics

In the past, I demonstrated, that Paul exhibited a model of apologetics by both establishing cultural connections with the hearers and addressing the cultural issues that arise against the Christian faith. Furthermore, I noted specific elements involved in these apologetics. To begin, Paul's culturally contextualized apologetics engaged in defense of the gospel through cultural connection with the hearers. Cultural connection with the hearers employed a cultural point of contact, cultural solidarity, and enculturated communication. Next, Paul's model of culturally contextualized apologetics dealt with responses to cultural issues and objections. Paul's apologetics speeches contained his responses, and the second-century Greek apologists illustrated the same elements in the subsequent generation.

Now in the present, there are concerns over the effectiveness and relevance of rationalism-based apologetics. I highlighted the need to consider a new approach to apologetics communication. Given the fact that leading apologists are recognizing the same urgency to generate an approach to apologetics that deals with the cultural aspects, I argued that Paul offers a model of culturally contextualized apologetics.

As shown, Paul's model for culturally contextualized apologetics proved to offer a fresh approach to apologetics communications in the contemporary setting. Typically, apologetics preaching encompassed the traditional fourfold system of apologetics, namely classical, evidentialistic, presuppositional, and fideistic in its logical structure. Ordinarily, contemporary apologetics preaching thus far has demarcated its practice based on the traditional system. However, Paul illuminates a model of apologetics preaching communication to contemporary preachers by injecting the reflections resulting from cultural contextualization. I additionally substantiated that Paul's preaching fulfills the fourfold traditional model of apologetics preaching, evincing that his preaching is apologetics preaching *par excellence.* In an applied setting, Paul's model of cultural contextualization presents a scheme that can be used to both engender cultural receptivity and clear out cultural objection while witnessing the Christian message. In sum, Paul's model of culturally contextualized apologetics advances a fresh approach to apologetics communication, particularly in preaching, beyond the traditional fourfold system of apologetics.

With the exploration of the past and its application in the present, we must now gaze out to the future of Christian apologetics. Cultural contextualization of apologetics will continue to be a topic of great interest for those who strive to defend the gospel among those who do not find rationality appealing. Even when the cultural milieu of today fades away and shifts to yet another cultural ambiance, the efforts to contextualize apologetics endeavors will still prove to be an important task. To search wider for a model of engaging in cultural contextualization of apologetics, further work may focus on Latin apologists of the second and third centuries. A fascinating study awaits those who desire to compare and contrast the strategies employed by the Greek and Latin apologists, tracing any changes that appear over time.

When Christian apologetics commits to actively engaging in cultural contextualization, it will help heighten seekers' receptivity. Such apologetics communication will work to break down any barriers that may have been created due to cultural misconceptions. Through the forgery of greater cultural connection, the world will have a clearer and more accurate vision of the Christian faith. Hence, the cultural contextualization of Christian apologetics possesses timeless merit. It is now time that we enter into the world everywhere to communicate the life-changing news of the resurrection with culturally contextualized apologetics.

BIBLIOGRAPHY

Aarde, Andries G. van. "Reading the Areopagus Speech in Acts 17 from the Perspective of Sacral Manumission of Slaves in Ancient Greece." *Biblical Theology Bulletin* 47, no. 1 (February 1, 2017): 47–58.

Adam, Peter. *Speaking God's Words: A Practical Theology of Preaching.* Moore College Lectures 1993. Leicester, England: InterVarsity, 1996.

Adewuya, J. Ayodeji. "The Sacrificial-Missiological Function of Paul's Sufferings in the Context of 2 Corinthians." In *Paul as Missionary: Identity, Activity, Theology, and Practice.* Edited by Trevor J. Burke, Brian S. Rosner, 88–98. London: T&T Clark, 2011.

Aguirre, Roxanne Gaxiola. "Cultural Humility and Intercultural Engagement." *Brethren Life and Thought* 63, no. 2 (2018): 57–61.

Alexander, Loveday. "The Acts of the Apostles as an Apologetic Text." In *Apologetics in the Roman Empire: Pagans, Jews, and Christians.* Edited by Mark Edwards, Martin Goodman and Simon Price, in association with Christopher Rowland, 15–44. Oxford: Oxford University Press, 1999.

———. "Luke's Political Vision." *Interpretation* 66, no. 3 (July 2012): 283–93.

Allen, Ronald J. *The Sermon without End: A Conversational Approach to Preaching.* Nashville : Abingdon Press, 2015.

Aristides. *Apology.* Translated by J. Rendel Harris. Cambridge: The University Press, 1891.

Athenagoras. *Embassy for the Christians (and) The Resurrection of the Dead.* Translated by Joseph Hugh Crehan. London: Newman, 1958.

———. *Legatio and De Resurrectione.* Translated by William R. Schoedel. Oxford: Clarendon, 1972.

Bahnsen, Greg L. *Van Til's Apologetic: Readings and Analysis.* Phillipsburg, NJ: P&R, 1998.

Bailey, Raymond H. "Acts 17:16–34." *Review & Expositor* 87, no. 3 (1990): 481–85.

Barnard, Leslie William. *Athenagoras: A Study in Second Century Christian Apologetic.* Théologie Historique 18. Paris: Beauchesne, 1972.

———. "Heresy of Tatian-Once Again." *The Journal of Ecclesiastical History* 19, no. 1 (April 1968): 1–10.

———. *Justin Martyr: His Life and Thought.* Cambridge: University Press, 1966.

Barnett, Paul. *The Second Epistle to the Corinthians.* Grand Rapids: W. B. Eerdmans, 1997.

Barrett, C. K. *A Commentary on the First Epistle to the Corinthians.* Harper's New Testament Commentaries. New York: Harper & Row, 1968.

Barth, Karl. *Homiletics.* Louisville: Westminster/J. Knox Press, 1991.

Bibliography

Bauckham, Richard. *Jesus and the Eyewitnesses: The Gospels as Eyewitness Testimony*. Grand Rapids: W. B. Eerdmans, 2006.

———, ed. *The Christian World around the New Testament : Collected Essays II*. Wissenschaftliche Untersuchungen Zum Neuen Testament 386. Tübingen: Mohr Siebeck, 2017.

———. "Kerygmatic Summaries in the Speeches of Acts." In *History, Literature, and Society in the Book of Acts*. Edited by Ben Witherington, III, 185–217. Cambridge: Cambridge University Press, 1996.

Baum, Armin Daniel. "Paulinismen in Den Missionsreden Des Lukanischen Paulus: Zur Inhaltlichen Authentizität Der Oratio Recta in Der Apostelgeschichte." *Ephemerides Theologicae Lovanienses* 82, no. 4 (December 2006): 405–36.

Beker, J. Christiaan. "Suffering and Triumph in Paul's Letter to the Romans." *Horizons in Biblical Theology* 7, no. 2 (1985): 105–19.

Berry, C. Everett. "How the Post-Apostolic Church Responded to Government: Gleaning Public Do's and Don'ts from the Second-Century Apologists." *Criswell Theological Review* 5, no. 1 (2007): 53–67.

Bertschmann, Dorothea H. "What Does Not Kill Me Makes Me Stronger." In *Paul and the Giants of Philosophy*. Edited by Joseph R. Dodson and David E. Briones, 9–20. Downers Grove, IL: InterVarsity, 2019.

Bingham, Dwight Jeffrey. "'We Have the Prophets': Inspiration and the Prophets in Athenagoras of Athens." *Zeitschrift Für Antikes Christentum* 20, no. 2 (2016): 211–42.

Blenkinsopp, Joseph. *Sage, Priest, Prophet: Religious and Intellectual Leadership in Ancient Israel*. 1st ed. Library of Ancient Israel. Louisville: Westminster John Knox, 1995.

Bloomquist, L. Gregory. "Subverted by Joy: Suffering and Joy in Paul's Letter to the Philippians." *Interpretation* 61, no. 3 (2007): 270–82.

Boa, Kenneth, and Robert M Bowman. *Faith Has Its Reasons: An Integrative Approach to Defending Christianity : An Apologetics Handbook*. Colorado Springs, CO: NavPress, 2001.

Bock, Darrell L. *Acts*. Baker Exegetical Commentary on the New Testament. Grand Rapids: Baker Academic, 2007.

Bockmuehl, M. "Public Ethics in a Pluralistic Society? Lessons from the Early Church." *Crux* 28, no. 3 (1992): 2–9.

Braund, David. *Rome and the Friendly King: The Character of the Client Kingship*. London: Croom Helm, 1984.

Brenk, F. E., and F. Canali De Rossi. "The 'Notorious' Felix, Procurator of Judaea, and His Many Wives (Acts 23--24)." *Biblica* 82, no. 3 (2001): 410–17.

Breytenbach, Cilliers, ed. *Paul's Graeco-Roman Context*. Bibliotheca Ephemeridum Theologicarum Lovaniensium 237. Leuven: Peeters, 2015.

Brouwer, René. *The Stoic Sage: The Early Stoics on Wisdom, Sagehood and Socrates*. Cambridge: Cambridge University Press, 2014.

Bruce, F. F. *Commentary on the Book of the Acts; the English Text, with Introduction, Exposition, and Notes*. New International Biblical Commentary. Grand Rapids: Eerdmans, 1954.

———. *The Speeches in the Acts of the Apostles*. Tyndale New Testament Lecture 1942. London: Tyndale, 1942.

Buck, P. Lorraine. "Justin Martyr's Apologies: Their Number, Destination, and Form." *The Journal of Theological Studies* 54, no. 1 (April 2003): 45–59.

Bibliography

———. "Second-Century Greek Christian Apologies Addressed to Emperors: Their Form and Function." PhD diss, University of Ottawa, 1998.

Buck, Richard Charles. "Apologetics Preaching Today in the Context of a Local Church." DMin project, Trinity International University, 2013.

Bultmann, Robert. *Der Stil Der Paulinischen Predigt Und Die Kynisch-Stoische Diatribe*. Gottingen: Vandenhoeck & Ruprecht, 1964.

Buttrick, David. *Homiletic: Moves and Structures*. Philadelphia: Fortress, 1987.

Campbell-Jack, W. C., Gavin McGrath, and C. Stephen Evans, eds. *New Dictionary of Christian Apologetics*. Downers Grove, IL: InterVarsity, 2006.

Carhart, Ryan. "The Second Sophistic and the Cultural Idealization of Paul in Acts." In *Engaging Early Christian History: Reading Acts in the Second Century*, 187–207. eds. Rubén R. Dupertuis and Todd Penner. Durham, UK: Acumen, 2013.

Carnell, Edward John. *The Kingdom of Love and the Pride of Life*. Grand Rapids: W. B. Eerdmans, 1960.

Carrick, John, and Banner of Truth Trust. *The Imperative of Preaching: A Theology of Sacred Rhetoric*. Carlisle: Banner of Truth Trust, 2002.

Carriker, Andrew. *The Library of Eusebius of Caesarea*. Leiden: Brill, 2003.

Carrington, Philip. *Christian Apologetics of the Second Century in Their Relation to Modern Thought*. Jeannie Willis Memorial Fund. London: SPCK, 1921.

Case, Shirley Jackson. *The Social Origins of Christianity*. Chicago: The University of Chicago Press, 1923.

Cavarnos, Constantine. *The Seven Sages of Ancient Greece*. Belmont, MA: Institute for Byzantine and Modem Greek Studies, 1996.

Červenková, Denisa. "De Religione: How Christianity Became a Religion." *De Religione: Jak Se Křesťanství Stalo Náboženstvím*. 4, no. 1 (March 2014): 87–114.

Chalmers, Aaron. *Exploring the Religion of Ancient Israel: Priest, Prophet, Sage, and People*. Exploring Topics in Christianity Series. Downers Grove: IVP Academic, 2012.

Chance, J. Bradley. *Acts*. Smyth & Helwys Bible Commentary. Macon, GA: Smyth & Helwys, 2007.

Chapell, Bryan. *Christ-Centered Preaching: Redeeming the Expository Sermon*. Grand Rapids: Baker Books, 2003.

Charles, J. Daryl. "Engaging the (Neo) Pagan Mind: Paul's Encounter with Athenian Culture as a Model for Cultural Apologetics (Acts 17:16-34)." *Trinity Journal* 16, no. 1 (1995): 47–62.

Charles, Robert Henry, ed. *The Apocrypha and Pseudepigrapha of the Old Testament in English: With Introductions and Critical and Explanatory Notes to the Several Books*. Oxford: Clarendon, 1913.

Chatraw, Josh, and Mark D. Allen. *Apologetics at the Cross: An Introduction for Christian Witness*. Grand Rapids: Zondervan, 2018.

Ciampa, Roy E., and Brian S. Rosner. *The First Letter to the Corinthians*. Grand Rapids: Apollos, 2010.

Cicero. *The Republic*. Translated by Clinton W. Keyes. Loeb Classical Library. Cambridge, MA: Harvard University Press, 1928.

Clark, David K., and Norman L. Geisler. *Apologetics in the New Age: A Christian Critique of Pantheism*. Grand Rapids: Baker Book, 1990.

Clark, Elliot. "It's Time for a Holistic Apologetic." *The Gospel Coalition* (blog). Accessed December 14, 2019. https://www.thegospelcoalition.org/reviews/cultural-apologetics/.

Bibliography

Clark, Gordon H. *Religion, Reason, and Revelation*. Jefferson, MD: Trinity Foundation, 1986.

Cohick, Lynn H. "Melito of Sardis's Peri Pascha and Its 'Israel.'" *Harvard Theological Review* 91, no. 4 (October 1998): 351–72.

Colaclides, Peter. "Acts 17:28a and Bacchae 506." *Vigiliae Christianae* 27, no. 3 (September 1973): 161–64.

Colson, Charles W. "Post-Truth Society." *Christianity Today* 46, no. 3 (March 11, 2002): 112–112.

Conzelmann, Hans. "Address of Paul on the Areopagus." In *Studies in Luke-Acts: Essays Presented in Honor of Paul Schubert*. eds. Leander E. Keck, J. Louis Martyn. Nashville: Abingdon, 1966.

Cover, Michael Benjamin. "The Divine Comedy at Corinth: Paul, Menander and the Rhetoric of Resurrection." *New Testament Studies* 64, no. 4 (October 2018): 532–50.

Cowan, Steven B. *Five Views on Apologetics*. Grand Rapids: Zondervan, 2000.

Craddock, Fred B., Jr. *Preaching*. Nashville: Abingdon, 1985.

Craig, William Lane. *Apologetics: An Introduction*. Chicago: Moody, 1984.

———. *Reasonable Faith: Christian Truth and Apologetics*. 3rd ed. Wheaton, IL: Crossway, 2008.

Crawford, Matthew R. "The Problemata of Tatian: Recovering the Fragments of a Second-Century Christian Intellectual." *The Journal of Theological Studies* 67, no. 2 (October 2016): 542–75.

Crisp, Roger. "Virtue Ethics." In *Routledge Encyclopedia of Philosophy*, edited by Edward Craig, 9:622–26. London: Routledge, 1998.

Cross, Frank Leslie. *The Early Christian Fathers*. London: G. Duckworth, 1960.

Crowe, Brandon D. "Oh Sweet Exchange! The Soteriological Significance of the Incarnation in the Epistle to Diognetus." *Zeitschrift Für Die Neutestamentliche Wissenschaft Und Die Kunde Der Älteren Kirche* 102, no. 1 (2011): 96–109.

Croy, N. Clayton. "Hellenistic Philosophies and the Preaching of the Resurrection (Acts 17:18, 32)." *Novum Testamentum* 39, no. 1 (January 1997): 21–39.

Dahle, Lars. "Acts 17:16-34: An Apologetic Model Then and Now?" *Tyndale Bulletin* 53, no. 2 (2002): 313–16.

Dale C. Allison Jr.. "Acts 9:1-9, 22:6-11, 26:12-18: Paul and Ezekiel." *Journal of Biblical Literature* 135, no. 4 (2016): 807–26.

Dargan, Edwin C. *A History of Preaching*. Burt Franklin: Research and Source Works Series 177. New York: Franklin, 1968.

Deissmann, Adolf. *Light from the Ancient East; the New Testament Illustrated by Recently Discovered Texts of the Graeco-Roman World*. Translated by Lionel R.M Strachan. New York: George H. Doran Co., 1927.

Dembski, William A. *Intelligent Design: The Bridge between Science & Theology*. Downers Grove, IL: InterVarsity, 1999.

Dembski, William A., and Michael Ruse. *Debating Design: From Darwin to DNA*. New York: Cambridge University Press, 2004.

DeSilva, D. A. "Paul and the Stoa: A Comparison." *Journal of the Evangelical Theological Society* 38, no. 4 (1995): 549–64.

Di Mauro, Dennis R. "Witnessing Lessons from the Areopagus." *Word & World* 37, no. 2 (2017): 186–95.

Dibelius, Martin. *From Tradition to Gospel*. Library of Theological Translations. Cambridge: James Clarke, 1971.

BIBLIOGRAPHY

———. *Studies in the Acts of the Apostles*. New York: Charles Scribner's Sons, 1956.

Dionne, Christian. "La Figure Narrative de Dieu Dans Le Discours à Lystre (Ac 14,15-17)." *Science et Esprit* 57, no. 2 (May 2005): 101–24.

Dodd, C. H. *The Apostolic Preaching and Its Developments: Three Lectures with an Appendix on Eschatology and History*. Grand Rapids: Baker, 1980.

Dodson, Joseph R., and David E. Briones. *Paul and the Giants of Philosophy: Reading the Apostle in Greco-Roman Context*. Downers Grove, IL: IVP Academic, 2019.

Döpp, Siegmar. *Dictionary of Early Christian Literature*. New York: Crossroad, 2000.

Downing, F. Gerald. "Common Ground with Paganism in Luke and in Josephus." *New Testament Studies* 28, no. 4 (October 1982): 546–59.

Duff, Paul Brooks. "Apostolic Suffering and the Language of Processions in 2 Corinthians 4:7-10." *Biblical Theology Bulletin* 21, no. 4 (1991): 158–65.

Duke, Robert W. *The Sermon as God's Word: Theologies for Preaching*. Abingdon Preacher's Library. Nashville: Abingdon, 1980.

Dulles, Avery. *A History of Apologetics*. London: New York: Hutchinson; Corpus, 1971.

Duncan, J. Ligon. "The Covenant Idea in Melito of Sardis: An Introduction and Survey." *Presbyterion* 28, no. 1 (2002): 12–33.

Dupertuis, Ruben R. "Bold Speech, Opposition, and Philosophical Imagery in the Acts of the Apostles." In *Engaging Early Christian History: Reading Acts in the Second Century*, edited by Ruben R. Dupertuis and Todd Penner, 153–68. Durham, UK: Acumen, 2013.

Eddy, Paul R., and Gregory A. Boyd. *The Jesus Legend: A Case for the Historical Reliability of the Synoptic Jesus Tradition*. Grand Rapids: Baker Academic, 2007.

Edgar, William, and K. Scott Oliphint. *Christian Apologetics Past and Present: A Primary Source Reader*. Wheaton, IL: Crossway, 2009.

Edmonds, Menander. *The Fragments of Attic Comedy*. Leiden: Brill Archive, 1959.

Edwards, M. J., Martin Goodman, S. R. F. Price, and Christopher Rowland, eds. *Apologetics in the Roman Empire: Pagans, Jews, and Christians*. Oxford: Oxford University Press, 1999.

Edwards, O. C. *A History of Preaching*. Vol 1. Nashville: Abingdon, 2004.

———. *A History of Preaching*. Vol 2. Nashville: Abingdon, 2004.

Engberg-Pedersen, Troels. *Paul and the Stoics*. Louisville: Westminster John Knox, 2000.

Eswine, Zack. *Preaching to a Post-Everything World: Crafting Biblical Sermons That Connect with Our Culture*. Grand Rapids: Baker, 2008.

Evans, Craig A. *Ancient Texts for New Testament Studies: A Guide to the Background Literature*. Grand Rapids: Baker Academic, 2012.

Eve, Eric. *Behind the Gospels: Understanding the Oral Tradition*. Minneapolis: Fortress, 2013.

Faber, Riemer A. "'Evil Beasts, Lazy Gluttons': A Neglected Theme in the Epistle to Titus." *The Westminster Theological Journal* 67, no. 1 (2005): 135–45.

Fairweather, William. "The Greek Apologists of the Second Century." *The Biblical World* 26, no. 2 (1905): 132–43.

Falls, Thomas B. *Writings of Saint Justin Martyr*. The Fathers of the Church, a New Translation vol. 6. Washington, DC: Catholic University of America Press, 1965.

Fee, Gordon D. *Paul's Letter to the Philippians*. Grand Rapids: W. B. Eerdmans, 1995.

Fee, Gordon D. *The First Epistle to the Corinthians*. New International Commentary. Grand Rapids: W. B. Eerdmans, 1987.

Bibliography

Ferguson, John, and Clement of Clement of Alexandria. *Stromateis, Books 1-3*. Washington, DC: Catholic University of America Press, 1992.

Fitzgerald, John T. *Cracks in an Earthen Vessel: An Examination of the Catalogues of Hardships in the Corinthian Correspondence*. Atlanta: Scholars, 1988.

Flemming, D. "Contextualizing the Gospel in Athens: Paul's Aeropagus Address as a Paradigm for Missionary Communication." *Missionology* 30 (2002): 199-214.

Forbes, David James. "A Christian Apologetic to a Buddhist Christ." MA thesis., Liberty University, 2010.

Forell, George W. *The Proclamation of the Gospel in a Pluralistic World; Essays on Christianity and Culture*. Philadelphia: Fortress, 1973.

Foster, Paul. "The Epistle to Diognetus." *The Expository Times* 118, no. 4 (January 2007): 162–68.

Frame, John M. *Apologetics to the Glory of God: An Introduction*. Phillipsburg, NJ: P&R, 1994.

Francis, Thomas William. "Training Church Members to Integrate Apologetics with Evangelism at First Baptist Church of Walton, Kentucky." DMin project, The Southern Baptist Theological Seminary, 2012.

Fredrickson, David E. "Paul, Hardships, and Suffering." In *Paul in the Greco-Roman World*. Edited by J. Paul Sampley, 172-97. Harrisburg, PA: Trinity Press International, 2003.

Freeman, Travis Allen. "Preaching to Provoke a Worldview Change: Tim Keller's Use of Presuppositional Apologetics in Preaching." PhD diss, The Southern Baptist Theological Seminary, 2012.

Furfey, Paul Hanly. "Social Action in the Early Church, 30-180 AD: The Dignity of the Human Person." *Theological Studies* 3, no. 1 (February 1942): 89–108.

Gaca, Kathy L. "Driving Aphrodite from the World: Tatian's Encratite Principles of Sexual Renunciation." *The Journal of Theological Studies* 53, no. 1 (April 2002): 28–52.

Gager, John G. *Kingdom and Community: The Social World of Early Christianity*. Prentice-Hall Studies in Religion Series. Englewood Cliffs, NJ: Prentice-Hall, 1975.

Gammie, John Glenn. "The Sage in Hellenistic Royal Courts." In *Sage in Israel and the Ancient Near East*. Edited by John G. Gammie and Leo G. Perdue, 147–53. Winona Lake, IN: Eisenbrauns, 1990.

Gangel, Kenneth O. "Paul's Areopagus Speech." *Bibliotheca Sacra* 127, no. 508 (October 1970): 308–12.

Garland, David E. *1 Corinthians*. Baker Exegetical Commentary on the New Testament. Grand Rapids: Baker Academic, 2003.

———. *2 Corinthians*. Nashville: Broadman & Holman, 1999.

Garroway, Joshua D. "'Apostolic Irresistibility' and the Interrupted Speeches in Acts." *Catholic Biblical Quarterly* 74, no. 4 (October 2012): 738.

Gärtner, Bertil E. *The Areopagus Speech and Natural Revelation*. Acta Seminarii Neotestamentici Upsaliensis 21. Uppsala: C. W. K. Gleerup, 1955.

Geisler, Norman L. *Christian Apologetics*. Grand Rapids: Baker, 1976.

Geisler, Norman L., and Patrick Zukeran. *The Apologetics of Jesus: A Caring Approach to Dealing with Doubters*. Grand Rapids: Baker, 2009.

Gendy, Atef Mehanny. "Style, Content and Culture: Distinctive Characteristics in the Missionary Speeches in Acts." *Svensk Missionstidskrift* 99, no. 3 (2011): 247–65.

Georgia, Allan T. "The Monster at the End of His Book: Monstrosity as Theological Strategy and Cultural Critique in Tatian's Against the Greeks." *Journal of Early Christian Studies* 26, no. 2 (2018): 191–219.

BIBLIOGRAPHY

Gibson, Scott M. *Evangelistic Preaching*. South Hamilton, MA: Center for Preaching, Gordon-Conwell Theological Seminary, 2004.

Given, Mark D. "Not Either/Or but Both/And in Paul's Areopagus Speech." *Biblical Interpretation* 3, no. 3 (October 1995): 356–72.

Glad, Clarence E. "Paul and Adaptability." In *Paul in the Greco-Roman World*, 17–36. Harrisburg, PA: Trinity Press International, 2003.

Glancy, Jennifer A. "Boasting of Beatings (2 Corinthians 11:23-25)." *Journal of Biblical Literature* 123, no. 1 (2004): 99–135.

Gould, Paul M. *Cultural Apologetics: Renewing the Christian Voice, Conscience, and Imagination in a Disenchanted World*. Grand Rapids: Zondervan Academic, 2019.

Grant, Robert M. *After the New Testament*. Philadelphia: Fortress, 1967.

———. "Chronology of the Greek Apologists." *Vigiliae Christianae* 9, no. 1 (January 1955): 25–33.

———. *Greek Apologists of the Second Century*. Philadelphia: Westminster, 1988.

Gray, Patrick. "Athenian Curiosity (Acts 17:21)." *Novum Testamentum* 47, no. 2 (2005): 109–16.

———. "Implied Audiences in the Areopagus Narrative." *Tyndale Bulletin* 55, no. 2 (2004): 205–18.

Gray-Fow, Michael J. G. "Why Festus, Not Felix? Paul's Caesarem Appello." *Journal of the Evangelical Theological Society* 59, no. 3 (September 2016): 473–85.

Green, Gene L. *The Letters to the Thessalonians*. Leicester, England: Apollos, 2002.

Gresham, Charles. *Evangelistic Preaching*. Joplin, MO: College Press, 1991.

Groothuis, Douglas R. *Christian Apologetics: A Comprehensive Case for Biblical Faith*. Downers Grove: IVP Academic, 2011.

Guthrie, Donald. *The Pastoral Epistles: An Introduction and Commentary*. Tyndale New Testament Commentaries. Grand Rapids: W. B. Eerdmans, 1957.

Guthrie, George H. *2 Corinthians*. Grand Rapids: Baker Academic, 2015.

Hackett, Horatio B. *Commentary on Acts*. Grand Rapids: Kregel, 1992.

Haenchen, Ernst. *The Acts of the Apostles; a Commentary*. Philadelphia: Westminster, 1971.

Hafemann, Scott J. *2 Corinthians*. The NIV Application Commentary. Grand Rapids: Zondervan, 2000.

Hamm, Dennis. "Paul's Blindness and Its Healing: Clues to Symbolic Intent (Acts 9; 22 and 26)." *Biblica* 71, no. 1 (1990): 63–72.

Harnack, Adolf von. *The Mission and Expansion of Christianity in the First Three Centuries*. London: Williams and Norgate, 1908.

Harris, Helen B. *The Newly Recovered Apology of Aristides: Its Doctrine and Ethics*. 2nd ed. London: Hodder and Stoughton, 1893.

Harris, James Rendel. *The Apology of Aristides on Behalf of the Christians: From a Syriac Ms. Preserved on Mount Sinai*. Piscataway, NJ: Gorgias, 2004.

Haykin, Michael A. G. *Rediscovering the Church Fathers: Who They Were and How They Shaped the Church*. Wheaton, IL: Crossway, 2011.

Helm, Paul. *Faith and Understanding*. Reason & Religion. Edinburgh: Edinburgh University Press, 1997.

Hemer, Colin J. "The Speeches of Acts: Pt 1: The Ephesian Elders at Miletus; Pt 2: The Areopagus Address." *Tyndale Bulletin* 40, no. 2 (November 1989): 239–59.

Hendriksen, William. *Exposition of I and II Thessalonians and Exposition of the Pastoral Epistles*. New Testament Commentary. Grand Rapids: Baker, 1979.

Bibliography

Hiebert, Paul G., and Eloise Hiebert Meneses. *Incarnational Ministry : Planting Churches in Band, Tribal, Peasant, and Urban Societies*. Grand Rapids: Baker, 1995.

Hodge, Charles. *An Exposition of the First Epistle to the Corinthians*. New York: R. Carter, 1857.

Hodgson, Robert. "Paul the Apostle and First Century Tribulation Lists." *Zeitschrift Für Die Neutestamentliche Wissenschaft Und Die Kunde Der Älteren Kirche* 74, no. 1–2 (1983): 59–80.

Hogan, Derek. "Paul's Defense: A Comparison of the Forensic Speeches in Acts, Callirhoe, and Leucippe and Clitophon." *Perspectives in Religious Studies* 29, no. 1 (2002): 73–87.

Holladay, Carl R. *Acts: A Commentary*. The New Testament Library. Louisville: Westminster John Knox, 2016.

Holtz, Traugott. "Paul and the Oral Gospel Tradition." In *Jesus and the Oral Gospel Tradition*, Edited by Henry Wansbrough, 380–92. Sheffield, England: JSOT, 1991.

Hubbard, Moyer V. *Christianity in the Greco-Roman World: A Narrative Introduction*. Grand Rapids: Baker Academic, 2010.

Hughes, Frank W. "Paul and Traditions of Greco-Roman Rhetoric." In *Paul and Ancient Rhetoric: Theory and Practice in the Hellenistic Context*, 86–95. Cambridge: Cambridge University Press, 2016.

Hunt, Emily J. *Christianity in the Second Century : The Case of Tatian*. London: Routledge, 2003.

Jackson, George Anson. *The Apostolic Fathers and the Apologists of the Second Century*. New York: Appleton and Company, 1879.

Jameson, Beverley. "God, Post-Truth." *Theology* 121, no. 3 (May 2018): 180–87.

Jensen, Richard A. *Thinking in Story : Preaching in a Post-Literate Age*. Lima, OH: C.S.S., 1993.

Jeremias, Joachim. *Unknown Sayings of Jesus*. London: S.P.C.K., 1964.

Jipp, Joshua W. "Paul in Athens: The Popular Religious Context of Acts 17." *Themelios* 40, no. 3 (December 2015): 524–26.

———. "Paul's Areopagus Speech of Acts 17:16-34 as Both Critique and Propaganda." *Journal of Biblical Literature* 131, no. 3 (2012): 567–88.

Johnson, Luke Timothy, and Daniel J. Harrington. *The Acts of the Apostles*. Sacra Pagina Series vol. 5. Collegeville, MN: Liturgical, 1992.

Johnson, Phillip E. *Darwin on Trial*. 2nd ed. Downers Grove, IL: InterVarsity, 1993.

Jones, Todd. "Moving from Cross-Cultural to Intercultural Collaboration in Missions." *Lutheran Mission Matters* 27, no. 1 (May 2019): 100–106.

Joo, Man Sung. "The Use of Apologetics in Evangelism: A Model for University Teaching Ministry." DMin project, Regent University, 2001.

Kaiser, Walter C. Jr. *Toward an Exegetical Theology: Biblical Exegesis for Preaching and Teaching*. Grand Rapids: Baker, 1981.

Kautsky, Karl. *Foundations of Christianity*. New York: S.A. Russell, 1953.

Kaye, John. *Some Account of the Writings and Opinions of Justin Martyr*. 3rd ed. London: F&J Rivington, 1853.

Keener, Craig S. *1-2 Corinthians*. New Cambridge Bible Commentary. Cambridge: Cambridge University Press, 2005.

Keener, Craig S. *Acts: An Exegetical Commentary*. Grand Rapids: Baker Academic, 2012.

Keener, Craig S., and InterVarsity Press. *The IVP Bible Background Commentary: New Testament*. 2nd ed. Downers Grove, IL: InterVarsity, 2014.

Bibliography

Keith, Graham A. "Justin Martyr and Religious Exclusivism." *Tyndale Bulletin* 43, no. 1 (May 1992): 57–80.

Kelhoffer, James A. "Suffering as Defense of Paul's Apostolic Authority in Galatians and 2 Corinthians 11." *Svensk Exegetisk Årsbok* 74 (2009): 127–43.

Keller, Timothy. *Center Church: Doing Balanced, Gospel-Centered Ministry in Your City*. Grand Rapids: Zondervan, 2012.

———. *Preaching: Communicating Faith in an Age of Skepticism*. New York: Viking, 2015.

Kennedy, George A. *The Art of Rhetoric in the Roman World, 300 B.C.-A.D. 300*. Princeton, NJ: Princeton University Press, 1972.

Keown, Mark J. "Congregational Evangelism in Paul: The Paul of Acts." *Colloquium* 42, no. 2 (November 2010): 231–51.

Kerferd, G. B. *The Sophistic Movement*. Cambridge: Cambridge University Press, 1981.

Kerferd, George B. "The Sage in Hellenistic Philosophical Literature (399 BCE-199 CE)." In *Sage in Israel and the Ancient Near East*, eds. John G. Gammie and Leo G. Perdue. Winona Lake, IN: Eisenbrauns, 1990.

Kesmez, Selim. "A Wholistic Model of Apologetics for Equipping the Youth." MA thesis, Andrews University, 2016.

Kilgallen, John J. "Paul before Agrippa (Acts 26:2-23): Some Considerations." *Biblica* 69, no. 2 (1988): 170–95.

Klauck, Hans-Josef. "With Paul in Paphos and Lystra: Magic and Paganism in the Acts of the Apostles." *Neotestamentica* 28, no. 1 (1994): 93–108.

Knight, George W. *The Pastoral Epistles: A Commentary on the Greek Text*. Grand Rapids; Carlisle, England: W.B. Eerdmans; Paternoster, 1992.

Knupp, Ralph E. "The Apologetic Preaching of Paul Tillich." *Encounter* 42, no. 4 (1981): 395–407.

Kochenash, Michael. "Better Call Paul 'Saul': Literary Models and a Lukan Innovation." *Journal of Biblical Literature* 138, no. 2 (2019): 433–49.

Koontz, Adam C. "Apostolic Suffering in 2 Corinthians." *Logia* 24, no. 2 (2015): 39–42.

Kretzschmar, Aaron. "Effective Apologetics Education for Lutheran Youth in a Postmodern Age." DMin project, Oral Roberts University, 2011.

Kruse, Colin G. *Paul's Letter to the Romans*. Grand Rapids: W. B. Eerdmans, 2012.

Kuhn, Karl Allen. *The Kingdom According to Luke and Acts: A Social, Literary, and Theological Introduction*. Grand Rapids: Baker Academic, 2015.

Kuruvilla, Abraham. *Privilege the Text! A Theological Hermeneutic for Preaching*. Chicago: Moody, 2013.

Lambrecht, Jan. "Paul and Suffering." In *God and Human Suffering*, eds. Jan Lambrecht and Raymond F. Collins. Louvain: Peeters, 1990.

Lau, Doris Man Yee. "Intentional Instruction in Christian Basics and Apologetics: Giving Christian Students More Confidence in Their Faith." DMin project, Biola University, 2015.

Lausberg, Heinrich, Matthew T. Bliss, David E. Orton, and R. Dean Anderson. *Handbook of Literary Rhetoric: A Foundation for Literary Study*. Leiden: Brill, 1998.

Lea, Thomas D., and Hayne P. Griffin. *1, 2 Timothy, Titus*. The New American Commentary. Nashville: Broadman, 1992.

Lenski, Gerhard. *Power and Privilege: A Theory of Social Stratification*. New York: McGraw-Hill, 1966.

Lenski, R. C. H. *The Interpretation of the Acts of the Apostles*. Minneapolis: Augsburg, 1961.

Bibliography

Lentz, John Clayton. *Luke's Portrait of Paul*. Monograph Series | Society for New Testament Studies 77. Cambridge: Cambridge University Press, 1993.

Lienhard, Joseph T. "Christology of the Epistle to Diognetus." *Vigiliae Christianae* 24, no. 4 (December 1970): 280–89.

Lieu, Judith. *Christian Identity in the Jewish and Graeco-Roman World*. Oxford: Oxford University Press, 2004.

Lightfoot, J. B., and Ben Witherington. *The Acts of the Apostles: a Newly Discovered Commentary*. Downers Grove, IL: IVP Academic, 2014.

Litfin, A. Duane. *Paul's Theology of Preaching: The Apostle's Challenge to the Art of Persuasion in Ancient Corinth*. Rev. and exp. ed. Downers Grove, IL: InterVarsity, 2015.

Lloyd-Jones, David Martyn. *Preaching and Preachers*. Ministry Resources Library. Grand Rapids: Zondervan, 1972.

Long, William Rudolf. "The Trial of Paul in the Book of Acts : Historical, Literary, and Theological Consideration." PhD diss., Brown University, 1982.

Longenecker, Richard N. *The Epistle to the Romans: A Commentary on the Greek Text*. Grand Rapids: W. B. Eerdmans, 2016.

Loscalzo, Craig A. *Apologetic Preaching: Proclaiming Christ to a Postmodern World*. Downers Grove, IL: InterVarsity, 2000.

Lotter, George A, and G G. (Glendon Glenford) Thompson. "Acts 17:16-34 as Paradigm in Responding to Postmodernity." *In Die Skriflig* 39, no. 4 (December 2005): 695–714.

Lüdemann, Gerd. *Early Christianity According to the Traditions in Acts: A Commentary*. Minneapolis: Fortress, 1989.

MacMullen, R. *Christianizing the Roman Empire (A.D. 100--400)*. New Haven, CT: Yale University Press, 1984.

Malherbe, Abraham Johannes. "Apologetic and Philosophy in the Second Century." *Restoration Quarterly* 7, no. 1–2 (1963): 19–32.

———. "The Apologetic Theology of the Preaching of Peter." *Restoration Quarterly* 13, no. 4 (1970): 205–23.

———. *Light from the Gentiles: Hellenistic Philosophy and Early Christianity: Collected Essays, 1959-2012*. Leiden: Brill, 2014.

Malina, Bruce J., and John J. Pilch. *Social-Science Commentary on the Book of Acts*. Social-Science Commentary. Minneapolis: Fortress, 2008.

Manis, Andrew M. "Melito of Sardis: Hermeneutic and Context." *The Greek Orthodox Theological Review* 32, no. 4 (1987): 387–401.

Manus, Chris U. "Apostolic Suffering (2 Cor 6:4-10): The Sign of Christian Existence and Identity." *The Asia Journal of Theology* 1, no. 1 (April 1987): 41–54.

Maràs, A. G. "The Issue of Rhetoric for Christian Apologists in the Second Century." *Augustinianum* 50, no. 2 (2010): 409–21.

Mărculeţ, Ştefan. "Elements of Inculturation in Saint Paul's Speech from Areopagus." *Revista Teologica* 23, no. 3 (July 2013): 28–48.

Marguerat, Daniel. *Paul in Acts and Paul in His Letters*. Tübingen: Mohr Siebeck, 2013.

Markos, Louis. *Apologetics for the Twenty-First Century*. Wheaton, IL: Crossway, 2010.

Marshall, I. Howard. *The Acts of the Apostles: An Introduction and Commentary*. Grand Rapids: W.B. Eerdmans, 1980.

Marshall, I. Howard, and Philip Towner. *A Critical and Exegetical Commentary on the Pastoral Epistles*. The International Critical Commentary. Edinburgh: T&T Clark, 1999.

Bibliography

Martin, Ralph P. *2 Corinthians*. Waco, TX: Word Books, 1986.

Martin, Richard P. "The Seven Sages as Performers of Wisdom." In *Cultural Poetics in Archaic Greece: Cult, Performance, Politics*. Edited by Carol Dougherty and Leslie Kurke, 108-28. New York: Oxford University Press, 1993.

Maxwell, Kathy Reiko. "The Role of the Audience in Ancient Narrative: Acts as a Case Study." *Restoration Quarterly* 48, no. 3 (2006): 171–80.

McDowell, Sean. *Apologetics for a New Generation*. Eugene, OR: Harvest House, 2009.

McDuffie, Adam. "Searching for Truth in a Post-Truth World: The Southern Baptist Schism as Case Study in the Power of Narrative for the Construction of Truth." *Baptist History and Heritage* 52, no. 2 (2017): 74–86.

McGehee, Michael. "Why Tatian Never 'Apologized' To The Greeks." *Journal of Early Christian Studies* 1, no. 2 (1993): 143–58.

McGrath, Alister E. *Mere Apologetics : How to Help Seekers and Skeptics Find Faith*. Grand Rapids: Baker, 2012.

Meecham, Henry George. *Light from Ancient Letters: Private Correspondence in the Non-Literary Papyri of Oxyrhynchus of the First Four Centuries, and Its Bearing on New Testament Language and Thought*. London: G. Allen & Unwin, 1923.

Meeks, Wayne A. *The First Urban Christians: The Social World of the Apostle Paul*. New Haven, CT: Yale University Press, 1983.

———. *The First Urban Christians: The Social World of the Apostle Paul*. New Haven, CT: Yale University Press, 1983.

Meeks, Wayne A., L. Michael White, and O. Larry Yarbrough. *The Social World of the First Christians: Essays in Honor of Wayne A. Meeks*. Minneapolis: Fortress, 1995.

Miller, William M. "Preaching in a Postmodern Setting: An Analysis of the Apologetic Preaching of Mark Driscoll." PhD diss., New Orleans Baptist Theological Seminary, 2011.

Mohler, R. Albert. *He Is Not Silent: Preaching in a Postmodern World*. Chicago: Moody, 2008.

Morris, Leon. *The Apostolic Preaching of the Cross*. Grand Rapids: W. B. Eerdmans, 1955.

Mounce, William D. *Pastoral Epistles*. Word Biblical Commentary. Nashville: Thomas Nelson, 2000.

Murray, John. *The Epistle to the Romans; the English Text with Introduction, Exposition, and Notes*. Grand Rapids: W. B. Eerdmans, 1959.

Nasrallah, Laura Salah. "Mapping the World: Justin, Tatian, Lucian, and the Second Sophistic." *Harvard Theological Review* 98, no. 3 (July 2005): 283–314.

Naylor, Peter. *A Study Commentary on 1 Corinthians*. EP Study Commentary. Webster, NY: Evangelical, 2004.

Neyrey, Jerome H. "The Forensic Defense Speech and Paul's Trial Speeches in Acts 22-26: Form and Function." In *Luke-Acts: New Perspectives from the Society of Biblical Literature Seminar*, 210–24. New York 1984.

———. "Luke's Social Location of Paul: Cultural Anthropology and the Status of Paul in Acts." In *History, Literature, and Society in the Book of Acts*. Edited by B. Witherington, 251–79. Cambridge: Cambridge University Press, 1996.

———. *The Social World of Luke-Acts: Models for Interpretation*. Peabody, MA: Hendrickson, 1991.

Norris, Richard A. Jr. *God and World in Early Christian Theology*. New York: Seabury, 1965.

Bibliography

O'Brien, Peter Thomas. *The Epistle to the Philippians: A Commentary on the Greek Text*. Grand Rapids: W. B. Eerdmans, 1991.

O'Ceallaigh, G. C. "'Marcianus' Aristides, on the Worship of God." *Harvard Theological Review* 51, no. 4 (October 1958): 227–54.

Origen, and Joseph T. Lienhard. *Homilies on Luke: Fragments on Luke*. Washington, DC: Catholic University of America Press, 1996.

Osborn, Eric Francis. *Justin Martyr*. Beiträge Zur Historischen Theologie ; 47. Tübingen: Mohr (Siebeck), 1973.

"Oxford Word of the Year 2016: Oxford Languages." Definitions, Meanings, Synonyms, and Grammar by Oxford Dictionary on Lexico.com. Accessed December 5, 2018. https://en.oxforddictionaries.com/word-of-the-year/word-of-the-year-2016.

Padilla, Osvaldo. *Acts of the Apostles : Interpretation, History, and Theology*. Downers Grove, IL: InterVarsity, 2016.

Papandrea, James Leonard. *Reading the Early Church Fathers: From the Didache to Nicaea*. New York: Paulist, 2012.

Parsons, Mikeal C. *Acts*. Paideia: Commentaries on the New Testament. Grand Rapids: Baker Academic, 2008.

Pathrapankal, Joseph. "From Areopagus to Corinth (Acts 17:22-31; I Cor 2:1-5): A Study on the Transition from the Power of Knowledge to the Power of the Spirit." *Mission Studies* 23, no. 1 (2006): 61–80.

Penner, Myron B. *The End of Apologetics: Christian Witness in a Postmodern Context*. Grand Rapids: Baker Academic, 2013.

Perdue, Leo G. *Scribes, Sages, and Seers: The Sage in the Eastern Mediterranean World*. Göttingen: Vandenhoeck & Ruprecht, 2008.

Perry, Lloyd Merle. *Evangelistic Preaching*. Chicago: Moody, 1979.

Pervo, Richard I., and Harold W. Attridge. *Acts: A Commentary*. Hermeneia--a Critical and Historical Commentary on the Bible. Minneapolis: Fortress, 2009.

Peterson, David. *The Acts of the Apostles*. Nottingham: Apollos, 2009.

Pilch, John J. "Sickness and Healing in Luke-Acts." In *The Social World of Luke-Acts: Model for Interpretation*. Edited by Jerome H. Neyrey, 181–209. Peabody, MA: Hendrickson, 1991.

Piper, John. *The Supremacy of God in Preaching*. Grand Rapids: Baker, 1990.

Plantinga, Alvin. *Warranted Christian Belief*. New York: Oxford University Press, 2000.

Plantinga, Alvin., and Nicholas. Wolterstorff. *Faith and Rationality: Reason and Belief in God*. Notre Dame, IN: University of Notre Dame Press, 1983.

Polhill, John B. *Acts*. The New American Commentary. Nashville: Broadman, 1992.

———. *Paul and His Letters*. Nashville: Broadman & Holman, 1999.

Polybus. *The Histories*. Translated by W. R. Paton. Loeb Classical Library. Cambridge, MA: Harvard University Press, 2010.

Porter, Stanley E. "The Language That Paul Did Not Speak." In *Paul's World*. Edited by Stanley E. Porter, 131–49. Leiden: Brill, 2008.

———. *Paul in Acts*. Peabody, MA: Hendrickson, 2001.

———. *The Paul of Acts: Essays in Literary Criticism, Rhetoric, and Theology*. Wissenschaftliche Untersuchungen Zum Neuen Testament ; 115. Tübingen: Mohr Siebeck, 1999.

———. *Paul and Ancient Rhetoric: Theory and Practice in the Hellenistic Context*. New York: Cambridge University Press, 2016.

BIBLIOGRAPHY

Porter, Stanley E., and Brian R. Dyer, eds. "Ancient Literate Culture and Popular Rhetorical Knowledge." In *Paul and Ancient Rhetoric: Theory and Practice in the Hellenistic Context*. Cambridge: Cambridge University Press, 2016.

Price, Randall. *The Stones Cry Out*. Eugene, OR: Harvest House, 1997.

Proudfoot, Merrill. "Imitation or Realistic Participation: A Study of Paul's Concept of 'Suffering with Christ.'" *Interpretation* 17, no. 2 (1963): 140–60.

Purves, George Tybout. *The Testimony of Justin Martyr to Early Christianity*. Stone Lectures, 1888. New York: A.D.F. Randolph, 1889.

Rackham, R. B. *The Acts of the Apostles: An Exposition*. London: Methuen, 1951.

Rahbar, Muhammad Daūd. "Christian Apologetic to Muslims." *International Review of Mission* 54, no. 215 (July 1965): 353–59.

Rapske, Brian. *The Book of Acts and Paul in Roman Custody*. Grand Rapids: W. B. Eerdmans, 1994.

Reiner, Erica. "The Etiological Myth of the 'Seven Sages.'" *Orientalia* 30, no. 1 (1961): 1–11.

Rhee, Helen. *Early Christian Literature: Christ and Culture in the Second and Third Centuries*. Routledge Early Church Monographs. London: Routledge, 2005.

Richardson, Cyril Charles. *Early Christian Fathers*. Philadelphia: Westminster, 1953.

Roberts, Alexander, James Donaldson, and A. Cleveland Coxe, eds. *The Ante-Nicene Fathers: Translations of the Writings of the Fathers down to A.D. 325*. Translated by Marcus Dods and George Reith. Vol. 1. Grand Rapids: W. B. Eerdmans, 1950.

———, eds. *The Ante-Nicene Fathers: Translations of the Writings of the Fathers down to A.D. 325*. Translated by B.P. Pratten. Vol. 2. Grand Rapids: W. B. Eerdmans Pub. Co., 1950.

Robinson, Haddon W., and Scott M. Gibson. *Making a Difference in Preaching: Haddon Robinson on Biblical Preaching*. Grand Rapids: Baker, 1999.

Root, Andrew. "A Screen-Based World: Finding the Real in the Hyper-Real." *Word & World* 32, no. 3 (Sum 2012): p 237-244.

———. "Faith Formation in a Secular Age." *Word & World* 37, no. 2 (2017): 128–41.

Roseman, Jeremy. "A Christian Apologetic to the Doctrine of Grace in Shin Buddhism." MA thesis, Liberty University, 2010.

Roubekas, Nickolas P. "Unexpected Encounters: Aristides the Philosopher, Friedrich Max Müller, and the Origins of Religion." *NTT: Journal for Theology and Study of Religion* 73, no. 1 (2019): 1–16.

Rowe, C. Kavin. "The Grammar of Life: The Areopagus Speech and Pagan Tradition." *New Testament Studies* 57, no. 1 (January 2011): 31–50.

———. *World Upside Down: Reading Acts in the Graeco-Roman Age*. Oxford: Oxford University Press, 2009.

Rutherford, William C. "Citizenship among Jews and Christians: Civic Discourse in the Apology of Aristides." In *Studia Patristica*. ed. Markus Vinzent and Willemien Otten. Leuven, Belgium: Peeters, 2013.

———. "Reinscribing the Jews: The Story of Aristides' Apology 2.2–4 and 14.1b–15.2." *Harvard Theological Review* 106, no. 1 (January 2013): 61–91.

Sampley, J. Paul. "Paul and Frank Speeches." In *Paul in the Greco-Roman World: A Handbook*. Edited by J. Paul Sampley, 293–318. Harrisburg, PA: Trinity Press International, 2003.

Sandnes, Karl Olav. "Paul and Socrates: The Aim of Paul's Areopagus Speech." *Journal for the Study of the New Testament* 15, no. 50 (April 1993): 13–26.

Schirrmacher, Christine. "Muslim Apologetics and the Agra Debates of 1854: A Nineteenth Century Turning Point." *Bulletin of the Henry Martyn Institute of Islamic Studies* 13, no. 1–2 (Ja-Je 1994): 74–84.
Schnabel, Eckhard J. *Acts*. Zondervan Exegetical Commentary on the New Testament. Grand Rapids: Zondervan, 2012.
———. "Contextualising Paul in Athens: The Proclamation of the Gospel before Pagan Audiences in the Graeco-Roman World." *Religion & Theology* 12, no. 2 (2005): 172–90.
———. *Paul the Missionary: Realities, Strategies and Methods*. Downers Grove, IL: IVP Academic, 2008.
Schreiner, Thomas R. *Paul, Apostle of God's Glory in Christ: A Pauline Theology*. Downers Grove, IL: InterVarsity, 2001.
———. *Romans*. Grand Rapids: Baker, 1998.
Schweizer, Eduard. "Concerning the Speeches in Acts." In *Studies in Luke-Acts: Essays Presented in Honor of Paul Schubert*, eds. Leander E. Keck, J. Louis Martyn. Nashville: Abingdon, 1966.
Seifrid, Mark A. *The Second Letter to the Corinthians*. Grand Rapids: Apollos, 2014.
Semisch, Karl Gottlob. *Justin Martyr*. Edinburgh: T. Clark, 1843.
Sennett, James F., and Douglas R. Groothuis. *In Defense of Natural Theology: A Post-Humean Assessment*. Downers Grove, IL: InterVarsity, 2005.
Sherwin-White, A. N. *Roman Society and Roman Law in the New Testament*. Oxford: Clarendon, 1963.
Shields, Bruce E. "The Areopagus Sermon and Roman 1:18ff: A Study in Creation Theology." *Restoration Quarterly* 20, no. 1 (1977): 23–40.
Shore, Mary Hinkle. "Preaching for Mission: Ancient Speeches and Postmodern Sermons: Acts 7:2-53; 13:16-41; 14:15-17." In *Mission in Acts: Ancient Narratives in Contemporary Context*. Edited by Robert Gallagher and Paul Hertig, 87–102. Maryknoll, NY: Orbis Books, 2004.
Silva, Moisés. *Philippians*. Grand Rapids: Baker Academic, 2005.
Sire, James W. *Apologetics beyond Reason: Why Seeing Really Is Believing*. Downers Grove, IL: IVP Academic, 2014.
Smith, Christian. *Moral, Believing Animals: Human Personhood and Culture*. Oxford: Oxford University Press, 2003.
Smith, Daniel Lynwood. "Interrupted Speech in Luke-Acts." *Journal of Biblical Literature* 134, no. 1 (2015): 177–91.
Smith, James K. A. *Desiring the Kingdom: Worship, Worldview, and Cultural Formation*. Cultural Liturgies. Grand Rapids: Baker Academic, 2009.
———. *You Are What You Love: The Spiritual Power of Habit*. Grand Rapids: Brazos, 2016.
Soards, Marion L. *The Speeches in Acts: Their Content, Context, and Concerns*. Louisville: Westminster/John Knox, 1994.
Stamatopoulou, Zoe. "Hesiodic Poetry and Wisdom in Plutarch's Symposium of the Seven Sages." *American Journal of Philology* 135, no. 4 (2014): 533–58.
Stiller, Brian. *Preaching Parables to Postmoderns*. Minneapolis: Fortress, 2005.
Stott, John R. W. *Between Two Worlds: The Art of Preaching in the Twentieth Century*. Grand Rapids: W. B. Eerdmans, 1982.
Strait, Drew J. "The Wisdom of Solomon, Ruler Cults, and Paul's Polemic against Idols in the Areopagus Speech." *Journal of Biblical Literature* 136, no. 3 (2017): 609–32.

Bibliography

Strandenaes, Thor. "The Missionary Speeches in the Acts of the Apostles and Their Missiological Implications." *Svensk Missionstidskrift* 99, no. 3 (2011): 341–54.

Straton, Hillyer Hawthorne. "Melito of Sardis, Preacher Extraordinary." *Anglican Theological Review* 29, no. 3 (July 1947): 167–70.

Tabb, Brian J. *Suffering in Ancient Worldview: Luke, Seneca and 4 Maccabees in Dialogue.* Library of New Testament Studies 569. London: T&T Clark, 2017.

Tajra, H. W. *The Trial of St. Paul: A Juridical Exegesis of the Second Half of the Acts of the Apostles.* Wissenschaftliche Untersuchungen Zum Neuen Testament 2, Reihe 35. Tübingen: J.C.B. Mohr, 1989.

Talbert, Charles H. *Perspectives on Luke-Acts.* Danville, VA: Association of Baptist Professors of Religion, 1978.

———. *Reading Acts: A Literary and Theological Commentary on the Acts of the Apostles.* Reading the New Testament Series. New York: Crossroad, 1997.

———. *Reading Luke-Acts in Its Mediterranean Milieu.* Supplements to Novum Testamentum. Leiden: Brill, 2003.

Tannehill, Robert C. *The Narrative Unity of Luke-Acts: A Literary Interpretation.* Foundations and Facets. Philadelphia: Fortress, 1986.

Theissen, Gerd. *The Social Setting of Pauline Christianity: Essays on Corinth.* Philadelphia: Fortress, 1982.

Thiselton, Anthony C. *The First Epistle to the Corinthians: A Commentary on the Greek Text.* The New International Greek Testament Commentary. Grand Rapids: W. B. Eerdmans, 2000.

———. "The Logical Role of the Liar Paradox in Titus 1:12,13: A Dissent from the Commentaries in the Light of Philosophical and Logical Analysis." *Biblical Interpretation* 2, no. 2 (July 1994): 207–23.

Thom, Johan C. "Paul and Popular Philosophy." In *Paul's Graeco-Roman Context.* Edited by Cilliers Breytenach, 47–74. Bibliotheca Ephemeridum Theologicarum Lovaniensium. Bristol, UK: Leuven, 2015.

Thomas, Derek. *Acts.* Reformed Expository Commentary. Phillipsburg, NJ: P&R, 2011.

Tilak, Pradeep. "A Christian Worldview Apologetic Engagement with Advaita Vedanta Hinduism." PhD diss., The Southern Baptist Theological Seminary, 2013.

Tino, James. "Paul's Greatest Missionary Sermon: A Lesson in Contextualization from Acts 17." *Lutheran Mission Matters* 25, no. 1 (May 2017): 165–75.

Todd, Jeremy Neil. "Teaching Worldview Apologetics to Increase Evangelistic Confidence at Piperton Baptist Church, Collierville, Tennessee." DEdMin project, The Southern Baptist Theological Seminary, 2014.

Toren, Bernard Van Den. *Christian Apologetics as Cross-Cultural Dialogue.* London: T&T Clark, 2011.

Troeltsch, Ernst, and Olive Wyon. *The Social Teaching of the Christian Churches.* Halley Stewart Publications. New York: The Macmillan, 1931.

Troxel, A Craig. "'All Things to All People': Justin Martyr's Apologetical Method." *Fides et Historia* 27, no. 2 (1995): 23–43.

Uusimäki, Elisa. "The Rise of the Sage in Greek and Jewish Antiquity." *Journal for the Study of Judaism in the Persian, Hellenistic and Roman Period* 49, no. 1 (2018): 1–29.

Van Til, Cornelius. *The Defense of the Faith.* Philadelphia: P&R, 1955.

Von Wahlde, Urban C. "The References to the Time and Place of the Crucifixion in the Peri Pascha of Melito of Sardis." *The Journal of Theological Studies* 60, no. 2 (October 2009): 556–69.

Bibliography

Walker, Alan. *Evangelistic Preaching*. Grand Rapids: Asbury, 1988.

Welsh, Clement W. "Preaching as Apologetics." *Anglican Theological Review* 62, no. 3 (July 1980): 239–52.

Werline, Rodney Alan. "The Transformation of Pauline Arguments in Justin Martyr's Dialogue with Trypho." *Harvard Theological Review* 92, no. 1 (January 1999): 79–93.

White, Richard C. "Melito of Sardis: An Ancient Worthy Reappears." *Lexington Theological Quarterly* 14, no. 1 (January 1979): 6–18.

———. "Melito of Sardis: Earliest Christian Orator?" *Lexington Theological Quarterly* 2, no. 3 (July 1967): 82–91.

Wieland, George M. "Roman Crete and the Letter to Titus." *New Testament Studies* 55, no. 3 (July 2009): 338–54.

Wilken, Robert Louis. *The Christians as the Romans Saw Them*. New Haven, CT: Yale University Press, 1984.

Williams, David John. *Acts*. New International Biblical Commentary. Peabody, MA: Hendrickson, 1990.

Willimon, William H. *Acts*. Interpretation, a Bible Commentary for Teaching and Preaching. Atlanta: John Knox, 1988.

Winter, Bruce W. "Introducing the Athenians to God: Paul's Failed Apologetic in Acts 17?" *Themelios* 31, no. 1 (October 2005): 38–59.

———. "Official Proceedings and the Forensic Speeches in Acts 24-26." In *Book of Acts in Its First Century Setting*, 305–36. Grand Rapids: W. B. Eerdmans, 1993.

———. "On Introducing Gods to Athens: An Alternative Reading of Acts 17:18-20." *Tyndale Bulletin* 47, no. 1 (May 1996): 71–90.

Winter, Bruce W., and Andrew D. Clarke, eds. *The Book of Acts in Its Ancient Literary Setting*. Vol. 1. The Book of Acts in Its First Century Setting. Grand Rapids: W. B. Eerdmans, 1993.

Witherington, Ben. *Conflict and Community in Corinth: A Socio-Rhetorical Commentary on 1 and 2 Corinthians*. Grand Rapids: W. B. Eerdmans, 1995.

———. *The Acts of the Apostles: A Socio-Rhetorical Commentary*. Grand Rapids; Carlisle, UK: W.B. Eerdmans Publishing; Paternoster Press, 1998.

Witherington, Ben III. *Jesus the Sage: The Pilgrimage of Wisdom*. Minneapolis: Fortress Press, 1994.

Wittkowsky, Vadim. "'Pagane' Zitate Im Neuen Testament." *Novum Testamentum* 51, no. 2 (April 2009): 107–26.

Wolff, Robert Lee. "The Apology of Aristides: A Re-Examination." *Harvard Theological Review* 30, no. 4 (October 1937): 233–47.

Worthington, Ian. *Aspects of Performance in Greco-Roman Oratory and Rhetoric: A Theatre of Justice*. Edited by Sophia Papaioannou, Andreas Serafim, and Beatrice da Vela. Boston: Brill, 2017.

Wright, N. T. *Paul and the Faithfulness of God*. Minneapolis: Fortress, 2013.

Young, Frances M. *Biblical Exegesis and the Formation of Christian Culture*. Cambridge: Cambridge University Press, 1997.

Zweck, Dean W. "The Exordium of the Areopagus Speech, Acts 17:22,23." *New Testament Studies* 35, no. 1 (January 1989): 94–103.

Zwiep, A. W. *Christ, the Spirit and the Community of God: Essays on the Acts of the Apostles*. Wissenschaftliche Untersuchungen Zum Neuen Testament. 2. Reihe 293. Tübingen: Mohr Siebeck, 2010.